M000073029

A Night to Remember

THE HAGGADAH OF CONTEMPORARY VOICES

by **Mishael Zion** and **Noam Zion**

Illustrations: Michel Kichka

Design: Dvora Lipshitz

Editing: Ehud Zion Waldoks

Printed in Jerusalem, Israel, 5767/2007   © Zion Holiday Publications Inc. / Halaila Hazeh Ltd.   www.haggadahsrus.com   zionsacs@netvision.net.il

מִדּוֹר לְדוֹר

From Generation to Generation

Philip Wachs and Juliet I. Spitzer
for their beloved daughters
Michal Fannie, Aleeza Kathy and Gabriella Abbe

David Lowenfeld and Sally Mendelsohn
for their wonderful children
Jonah, Lea and Elie

Eunice and Ernie Benchell
as a gift of love for their grandchildren
Benjamin, Alex, Eli, Cassie, Joseph, Emma, and Naomi

Henry and Bella Muller
as a legacy for their grandchildren
Elisha & Laura, Sara & Alan, Seffy; Tali, Liat, Matan; Jacob, Rachel, Rebecca, Izzy, and Avi

Marc Alan Silverstein,
"in memory of my Cousins Netta and Lee Frame and Lillian Eisenberg,
at whose home I first began learning why this night was different from all other nights."

לְזֵכֶר
Dedicated by the editors to the memory of our friend

Marla Ann Bennett

A smiling presence, she celebrated her last Seder at our home.

Marla was murdered in the terrorist attack on the Hebrew University cafeteria,

22 Av 5762, July 31, 2002.

May her memory be a blessing.

בְּרוּכִים הַבָּאִים לַסֵּדֶר
Welcome to Our Seder

Tonight is "A Night to Remember!"
Tonight is the Jewish people's birthday
and the rebirth of personal freedom for each individual.
Tonight is a journey of rediscovery: to relive slavery and
poverty, and then to experience liberation
and taste abundance.

Eating together
we become a community of caring for each other's needs.

Reading, discussing and arguing
we become a community of learners.

Asking questions and telling stories
we become a community of memory.

Playing and acting
we become a community of imagination.

Praying together
we become a community of hope, willing to take a stand.

Singing together
we become a community of joy and appreciation.

Join in, take part, feel free to ask, to add (and to skip)...
No matter your background, no matter your age,
no matter your knowledge,
make this Seder your own.

Feel Free!

The Order of the Seder הַסֵּדֶר

INTRODUCTION

Searching for Hametz	בְּדִיקַת חָמֵץ	2
Burning Hametz	בְּעוּר חָמֵץ	4
The Seder Plate	קַעֲרַת הַסֵּדֶר	5
Blessing Candles and Children	הַדְלָקַת נֵרוֹת וּבִרְכַּת הַיְלָדִים	6
Signposts for the Seder	סִימָנֵי הַסֵּדֶר	8

FIRST CUP: KIDDUSH

Kadesh	Sanctifying Time	קַדֵּשׁ	10
Urkhatz, Karpas	Washing Hands, Dipping Vegetables	וּרְחַץ, כַּרְפַּס	12
Yakhatz	Breaking Matza	יַחַץ	14

SECOND CUP: STORYTELLING

	Maggid	Telling	מַגִּיד	16
Ha Lakhma Anya	The Story of Matza	הָא לַחְמָא עַנְיָא	20
Ma Nishtana	Questioning	מַה נִּשְׁתַּנָּה	24
Avadim Hayeenu	"We were Slaves"	עֲבָדִים הָיִינוּ	28
More Storytelling and Newspaper	כָּל הַמַּרְבֶּה	32
The Longest Seder	Rabbis of Bnei Brak	מַעֲשֶׂה בְּרַבִּי אֱלִיעֶזֶר	36
Four Children	אַרְבָּעָה בָנִים	40
"Our Ancestors were Slaves to Idolatry"	מִתְּחִלָּה	56
V'hi Sheh-Amda	The Promise	וְהִיא שֶׁעָמְדָה	62
Arami	The Symposium	אֲרַמִּי אֹבֵד אָבִי	64
Ten Plagues	עֶשֶׂר הַמַּכּוֹת	78
Dayeinu	דַּיֵּנוּ	82
Pesach, Matza, Maror	Explaining Symbols	פֶּסַח, מַצָּה, וּמָרוֹר	86
In Every Generation	Identifying Personally	בְּכָל דּוֹר וָדוֹר	90
Hallelujah	Singing Praise (Psalms 113-114)	הַלְלוּיָהּ	92
The Second Cup	Toasting our Redemption	כּוֹס שְׁנִיָּה	96

THIRD CUP: FAMILY MEAL

Rakhtza, Motzi, Matza	Washing Hands and Eating Matza	רַחְצָה, מוֹצִיא, מַצָּה	98
Maror, Korekh	Eating Maror, Haroset and Hillel's Sandwich	מָרוֹר, כּוֹרֵךְ	100
Shulkhan Oreikh	Eating Dinner	שֻׁלְחָן עוֹרֵךְ	102
	Afikoman	צָפוּן	104
Birkat HaMazon	Thanking God	בָּרֵךְ	106
Third Cup	Toasting the Creator of our Food	כּוֹס שְׁלִישִׁית	110

FOURTH CUP: CONCLUDING THE HALLEL

	Pouring Elijah's Cup	כּוֹס אֵלִיָּהוּ	112
	"Pour Out Your Wrath and Your Love"	שְׁפֹךְ חֲמָתְךָ	114
Festival Hallel	Singing Praise (Psalms 115-118,136)	הַלֵּל, וְהַלֵּל הַגָּדוֹל	118
Fourth Cup	Toasting the God of Praise	כּוֹס רְבִיעִית	122
Sefirat HaOmer	Counting the Omer	סְפִירַת הָעוֹמֶר	122

CONCLUDING POEMS AND FOLKSONGS

	Pesach Poems	וַיְהִי בַּחֲצִי הַלַּיְלָה, אַדִּיר בִּמְלוּכָה, אַדִּיר הוּא	124
	"Who Knows One?"	אֶחָד מִי יוֹדֵעַ	127
Khad Gadya	Just One Little Kid	חַד גַּדְיָא	132
Nirtza	"Next Year in Jerusalem"	נִרְצָה: לְשָׁנָה הַבָּאָה בִּירוּשָׁלַיִם	136
Pesach Children's Story	"Way Down in Egypt Land"		143
	Permissions, References, Acknowledgements		148

The User's Guide for *A Night to Remember* – "A *very* Different Night"

Contemporary Sidedishes As the Haggadah is being read, spice up the evening with "add-ons" to be read aloud or to yourself. Some trigger discussion, some suggest activities, and others share a poem, a story or an insight. Browse and taste as you wish.

The Main Dish The full traditional Haggadah text appears on the white background (rightside) opposite the contemporary sidedishes, on a color background.

Illustrations, Photographs

Quotes, Poems and Songs

Haggadah: Hebrew Text and Translation

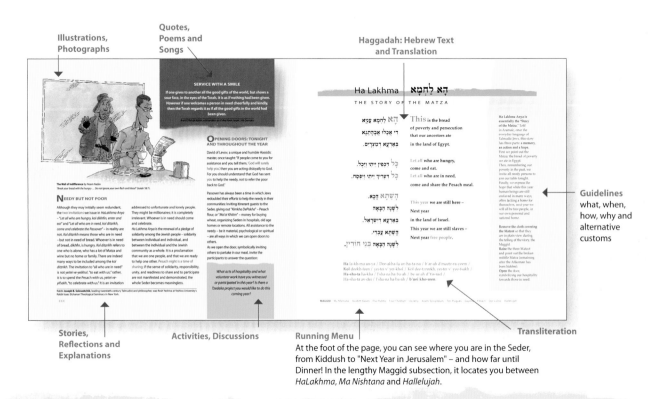

Guidelines what, when, how, why and alternative customs

Stories, Reflections and Explanations

Activities, Discussions

Running Menu

Transliteration

Running Menu
At the foot of the page, you can see where you are in the Seder, from Kiddush to "Next Year in Jerusalem" – and how far until Dinner! In the lengthy Maggid subsection, it locates you between *HaLakhma, Ma Nishtana* and *Hallelujah*.

A PASSOVER SEDER WITHOUT OUR GRANDPARENTS

So many Seders take place around a great gap – the grandparent who isn't here anymore. Many families reminisce with longing about the wonderful Seders that their grandparents used to prepare and lead. "Ever since grandpa or grandma, *zaide* and *bobie*, passed away, we haven't been able to fill their place." Grandpa insisted we read the entire Haggadah and out of respect we lingered a little longer around the table. Grandma's recipes were our tie to tradition. They made us feel that they had heard the story of the Exodus from Moses himself – even if their Seder was long and sometimes boring.

Tonight we miss them and we feel apprehensive – how will we fill the gap they left?

Yet we have to admit – there is also a certain feeling of release: Now we can add variety to the Haggadah and create something new, our own Seder. If we're lucky and we invest in preparing our own memorable night, some day we might become the "grandparent" and our traditions might be carried on by our children and our children's children.

Shai Zarhi, kibbutz educator

A Menu of Treats
"Top Twenty" Sidedishes

Children's Activities:

Search for Hametz   p. 3

Exodus Skit   p. 16

Frog Song   p. 81

Exodus Children's Story   p. 143

Stories

Four Cups of Milk   p. 23

Seder in the Syrian Prison   p. 37

Elijah's Curse   p. 113

Mikhel   p. 116

Women as Liberators

We Women are still Slaves   p. 31

Women's Resistance   p. 71, 73

Pharaoh's Daughter's Dilemma   p. 75

Miriam's Cup   p. 97

Social Conscience: *Tikkun Olam*

Being Poor   p. 15

Synagogue becomes a Hotel   p. 22

Modern Slavery   p. 31

Dream Freedom   p. 39

Discussions

Who are you calling "Wicked"?   p. 45

The Generation Gap   p. 58

Slavery & Freedom quotations   p. 73

Pour out your Wrath/Love?   p. 114-117

BY TOMORROW – TODAY WILL BE A STORY

"When a day passes, it is no longer there. What remains of it? Nothing more than a story. If stories weren't told or books weren't written, humans would live like the beasts, only for the day."

Reb Zebulun said, "Today we live, but **by tomorrow today will be a story**. The whole world, all human life, is one long story."

Children are as puzzled by passing time as grownups. What happens to a day once it is gone? Where are all our yesterdays with their joys and sorrows? Literature helps us remember the past with its many moods. To the storyteller yesterday is still here as are the years and the decades gone by.

In stories time does not vanish. Neither do people and animals. For the writer and his readers, all creatures go on living forever. What happened long ago is still present.

I.B. Singer, Nobel laureate, *Zlateh the Goat*

SEDER GENERAL WARNING:
Too many additions may be harmful to your Seder

While the Seder is a night of changes and innovations, it is also a night of tradition and ritual. Adding too many new readings, activities or ideas may tire or alienate the participants. It's best to feast on a few new sidedishes – and leave others for next year. Adapt your "Seder Plan" to the changing needs and interests of the participants around the table each year.

Searching for Hametz בְּדִיקַת חָמֵץ

THE NIGHT BEFORE THE SEDER

Before the search recite this blessing:

בָּרוּךְ אַתָּה יי אֱלֹהֵינוּ
מֶלֶךְ הָעוֹלָם,
אֲשֶׁר קִדְּשָׁנוּ בְּמִצְוֹתָיו,
וְצִוָּנוּ עַל בִּעוּר חָמֵץ.

Blessed are You, Adonai our God, Ruler of the Universe, who sanctified us by commanding us to remove all hametz.

Ba-rukh ata Adonai / Elo-hei-nu me-lekh ha-olam / asher kee-d'sha-nu b'meetz-vo-tav / v'tzee-va-nu **al bee-ur hametz**.

After the search recite this formula in Aramaic, for disowning any hametz still undiscovered in the home:

כָּל חֲמִירָא וַחֲמִיעָא
דְּאִכָּא בִרְשׁוּתִי,
דְּלָא חֲמִתֵּה וּדְלָא בְעַרְתֵּה,
לִבְטִיל וְלֶהֱוֵי הֶפְקֵר
כְּעַפְרָא דְאַרְעָא.

All hametz in my possession, whether I have seen it or not and whether I have removed it or not, shall be nullified and ownerless as the dust of the earth.

The Search for Hametz is the ceremonial culmination of several weeks of transforming the house into a sanctified setting for Pesach. The physical efforts help create a psychological readiness for the Seder.

"Hametz" refers to grain products that may have leavened, fermented and risen like yeast.

Jews usually clean all the rooms where food might have been eaten or stored. Many collect hametz products (like spaghetti or whiskey) in a sealed cabinet, mark it as hametz, and sell its contents to a non-Jew for the duration of the holiday. Generally a local rabbi will serve as an agent for the ritual "sale."

After dark, on the night before the Seder, conduct a search for hametz into all the corners of the house. The search is conducted in the dark, with a candle or a flashlight for spotting the hametz, and a feather or a spoon for collecting it. All hametz found is burned the next morning.

When Seder night falls on Saturday evening, the search is conducted on Thursday night and the bonfire on Friday morning. Hallah is put aside in a special "hametz zone" in the house to be eaten by approximately 10 a.m. on Shabbat morning. The leftovers may be removed by means of a flush of the toilet.

Six bags of Hametz have been hidden in this illustration.
Good luck ferreting them out!

HIDE AND GO SEEK

A medieval custom perfectly suited to a children's game involves hiding ten pieces of bread throughout the house before the candlelight search for hametz begins. Originally this was done to guarantee that even after the scrupulous cleaning, the ritual search on the last night before Seder would still uncover some hametz. Today it provides an occasion for a game in which ten pieces of bread secured in closed plastic bags are carefully concealed. To enhance the fun for the children, a word, clue or question may be attached to each bag (the words can form a secret message or a Pesach song; the clues hint at the next hiding place; the ten questions constitute a quiz about basic Pesach facts).

Remember that besides finding the pre-hidden bags of hametz, one must genuinely check the typical "hang-outs" of forgotten hametz (like the car's glove compartment, coat pockets, etc.).

INSPECTION AND INTROSPECTION

"The human soul is the light, the candle of Adonai, for searching the hidden, innermost self" (Proverbs 20:27).

The Search for Hametz is not simply a search for leavened bread, but rather an opportunity for us to examine ourselves. On the night before Pesach, when each of us is at home within our own walls, where there is no one else around, and we are not troubled by daily affairs, it is then that we can sit alone and confront all of our outstanding obligations to God, saying to our soul:

"Let us awaken and arise... let us examine our ways and turn away from all our sins. Let us cleanse and purify ourselves and remove our evil ways from God's sight. Let us become allies, my soul, and stand guard together. We will abjure slumber from our eyes day and night. We will not rest, rather we will be as gatekeepers lest we return to our evil ways. May God be with us as God was with our mothers and fathers..."

Rabbi **Moshe Alsheikh**, Safed Kabbalist, 16th C.

Burning the Hametz בִּעוּר חָמֵץ

כָּל חֲמִידָא וַחֲמִיעָא דְּאִכָּא בִרְשׁוּתִי,

דַּחֲזִיתֵהּ וּדְלָא חֲזִיתֵהּ,

דַּחֲמִתֵהּ וּדְלָא חֲמִתֵהּ,

דִּבְעַרְתֵּהּ וּדְלָא בְעַרְתֵּהּ,

לִבְטִיל וְלֶהֱוֵי הֶפְקֵר כְּעַפְרָא דְאַרְעָא.

All hametz in my possession,

whether I have seen it or not and

whether I have removed it or not,

shall be nullified and ownerless as

the dust of the earth.

Meditation
After nullifying the physical hametz, the Sephardic custom is to recite this prayer for purification from spiritual hametz and the power of the evil *Yetser* [selfish inclination]:

May it be your will, Adonai our God and God of our ancestors, that just as we burned the hametz out of our homes today,
so You will help us to burn out the evil inclination from our hearts.
Please God, remove from our hearts the bad part of our ego, and purify us lovingly, empowering the good sides of our ego.
Let our souls shine and be empowered with your light, and be connected to You in the highest holiness, which shall be with us always.

Rabbi **Yosef Hayim**, the "Ben Ish Hai", Baghdad, 19th C.

The Burning of the Hametz marks the symbolic division between hametz and matza, winter and spring, the evil inclination and the desire for purity.

Before approximately 10 a.m. on the day of the Seder, we stop eating hametz and gather the leftovers for a ritual bonfire outside.

After the hametz has been burned (or rendered inedible in some other way), repeat the Aramaic formula disowning any undiscovered hametz on the premises. From now on no hametz may be eaten.

4

קָעֲרַת הַסֵּדֶר

PREPARING THE SEDER PLATE

OPTIONAL ADD-ONS
FOR YOUR SEDER PLATE

The Seder plate has from time to time included some unusual additions:

One Brick: Jewish Union soldiers in the Civil War, fighting a war against slavery themselves, prepared their Seder in the wilderness of West Virginia. Lacking haroset, symbolizing mortar, they literally placed a brick on the Seder Plate.

Some Brick: The Jews in Gibraltar prepare their haroset using granules shaved off a real brick! One medieval rabbi condemned this custom as the height of idiocy.

Prepare haroset recipes from around the globe and label them. Ask your guests to taste each one and identify the ingredients (see Korekh, pg. 101).

Vegetarians often replace the roasted bone with something else that represents God's outstretched arm. Try a sugar cane.

Sweets: Add candies to the Seder Plate for the children, to arouse their curiosity.

Three Matzot
covered in a cloth, under or next to the Seder Plate. This is the food of poor slaves, but also the food of our liberation from Egypt. The three matzot symbolize the entire Jewish community with its three groups: Cohen, Levi and Israel.

Beitza
roasted, hardboiled egg symbolizing the second sacrifice offered on holidays (often dipped in salt water)

Zeroa
any bone, roasted symbolizing the sacrificial Pesach lamb and God's outstretched arm which liberated us from Egypt (not to be eaten)

Maror
bitter herbs symbolizing the bitterness of slavery (often romaine lettuce)

Karpas
greens for dipping in salt water or any tangy sauce (often celery, parsley or potato)

Haroset
sweet or tangy condiment symbolizing the mortar of slavery (often including apples, wine and cinnamon)

Hazeret
more bitter herbs (often horseraddish, *khrein*)

The Seder Plate combines the various symbols of tonight's story and ritual.

Some families make one central Seder Plate, while others make many, ensuring that every participant can see the symbols as tonight's story unfolds.

Candle Lighting　הַדְלָקַת נֵרוֹת

בָּרוּךְ אַתָּה יי אֱלֹהֵינוּ מֶלֶךְ הָעוֹלָם, אֲשֶׁר קִדְּשָׁנוּ בְּמִצְוֹתָיו, וְצִוָּנוּ לְהַדְלִיק נֵר שֶׁל (שַׁבָּת וְשֶׁל) יוֹם טוֹב.

Blessed are You, Adonai our God, Ruler of the Universe, who sanctified us by commanding us to light the [Shabbat and] **holiday** candles.

בָּרוּךְ אַתָּה יי אֱלֹהֵינוּ מֶלֶךְ הָעוֹלָם, שֶׁהֶחֱיָנוּ וְקִיְּמָנוּ וְהִגִּיעָנוּ לַזְּמַן הַזֶּה.

Blessed are You, Adonai our God, Ruler of the Universe, who has kept us alive and brought us to **this happy moment** in our lives.

Ba-rukh ata Adonai / Elo-hei-nu me-lekh ha-olam /
asher kee-d'sha-nu b'meetz-vo-tav / v'tzee-va-nu l'ha-d'leek ner shel / [Shabbat v'shel] Yom Tov.

Ba-rukh ata Adonai / Elo-hei-nu me-lekh ha-olam /
she-he-khee-ya-nu / v'kee-ma-nu / v'hee-gee-anu / la-z'man ha-ze.

Light at least two candles before the Seder. Some families light one candle for each family member, while others prepare two candles for each woman over bat mitzvah age. Many add the blessing *Shehekhiyanu* when lighting the candles, while others recite it later with Kiddush. A silent personal prayer is often said after the blessing. See contemporary prayer on page 7.

Blessing our Children　בִּרְכַּת הַיְלָדִים

For male children:
May God make you like Ephraim and Menashe.
(Genesis 48:20 from Jacob's blessing for his grandchildren)

יְשִׂמְךָ אֱלֹהִים כְּאֶפְרַיִם וְכִמְנַשֶּׁה.

For female children:
May God make you like Sarah and Rebecca, Rachel and Leah.
(See Ruth 4:11, the women's blessing for Ruth, a Jew by choice)

יְשִׂמֵךְ אֱלֹהִים כְּשָׂרָה רִבְקָה רָחֵל וְלֵאָה.

For all:
May God bless you and keep you.

May God's face shine upon you and favor you.

May God's face turn to you and grant you Shalom.
(Numbers 6:24-26, the priestly benediction)

יְבָרֶכְךָ יי וְיִשְׁמְרֶךָ.
יָאֵר יי פָּנָיו אֵלֶיךָ וִיחֻנֶּךָּ.
יִשָּׂא יי פָּנָיו אֵלֶיךָ וְיָשֵׂם לְךָ שָׁלוֹם.

The blessing of the children is recited. Parents and grandparents may place their hands on the head of each child (of whatever age) and bless them in their own words and / or using the priests' benediction of peace.

A WOMAN'S PRAYER TO REPAIR THE WORLD

O GOD, creator of Heaven and Earth, creator of humankind and of all living things, grant me the power to feel as others feel, the power to listen and to hear, to behold and truly see, to touch and be touched.

KEEP fresh within me the memory of my own suffering and the suffering of *Clal Yisrael* (the whole community), not in order to stimulate eternal paranoia, but rather that I may better understand the suffering of strangers.

MAY that understanding lead me to do everything in my power to alleviate and to prevent such suffering. Guide me in the ways of *Tikkun Olam*, of mending the world. Enable me to be like Yourself – to feed the hungry, clothe the naked, tend the sick, and comfort the bereaved.

AS I delight in a loving marriage of true minds, may I never forget the thousands of women battered and beaten by their spouses.

AS I rejoice in the bliss of my children and grandchildren, may I never forget the pleading eyes and swollen bellies of starving infants deprived of physical and emotional nourishment.

MAY there always be a place at my table for those who are homeless or hungry.

MAY my woman's capacities for concern, compassion, and caring never be dulled by complacency or personal contentment.

MAY my feelings always lead me to act.

Alice Shalvi, professor of Shakespeare, founder of the Israeli women's lobby and of a progressive religious girls' school in Jerusalem.

Everyone must know that within them burns a candle and no one's candle is identical with the candle of another. It is our obligation to work hard to reveal the light of our candle, and make of it a great torch to enlighten the whole world.

Rabbi **Abraham Isaac HaCohen Kook**

A SOUL ON THE RISE

The Seer of Lublin interpreted the priestly blessing, *Veyi-shmer-ekha*, as derived from the Hebrew root *shemarim*, yeast:

"May God create yeast in your soul, causing you to ferment and mature, to rise and elevate, to your highest possibilities, to reach your highest self."

Karl Gabor, Swedish *A Different Night* Haggadah

Signposts for the Seder   סִימָנֵי הַסֵּדֶר

All sing:

קַדֵּשׁ	*Kadesh*	First Cup and Kiddush
וּרְחַץ	*Urkhatz*	First handwashing
כַּרְפַּס	*Karpas*	First dipping: vegetables and dips
יַחַץ	*Yakhatz*	Breaking the middle matza
מַגִּיד	*Maggid*	Exodus Storytelling
רַחְצָה	*Rakhtza*	Second handwashing
מוֹצִיא	*Motzi*	First blessing over the matza
מַצָּה	*Matza*	Second blessing over the matza
מָרוֹר	*Maror*	Second dipping: maror in haroset
כּוֹרֵךְ	*Korekh*	Hillel sandwich
שֻׁלְחָן עוֹרֵךְ	*Shulkhan Orekh*	Festive meal
צָפוּן	*Tzafun*	Afikoman (dessert)
בָּרֵךְ	*Barekh*	Birkat HaMazon (blessing after eating) and Third Cup
הַלֵּל	*Hallel*	Psalms of Praise and Fourth Cup
נִרְצָה	*Nirtza*	Concluding poem, songs and "Next Year in Jerusalem"

We review briefly the order of the Seder by singing the medieval poem by Rabbenu Shmuel of Falaise (France) that summarizes the Signposts of the Seder ("*Kadesh Urkhatz*").

Now is a good time to preview this year's Seder's "coming attractions," announce the menu, thank those who prepared, and introduce the participants. Invite people to add their own questions, comments and songs.

FROM SACRIFICE TO SYMPOSIUM

The term "Seder Pesach" once meant the Order of the Passover Sacrifice in the Temple. But after the Temple's destruction in 70 CE, the Rabbis remodeled the Seder after the Greco-Roman symposium (*sym* – together, *posium* – drinking wine). At these Hellenistic banquets, guests would recline on divans while servants poured them wine, washed their hands and served appetizers and dips before the meal. The guests would then take part in a philosophical debate, after which the meal was served. An ancient how-to manual for conducting such a symposium says:

> "A symposium is a communion of serious and mirthful entertainment, discourse and actions. It leads to deeper insight into those points that were debated at table, for the remembrance of those pleasures which arise from meat and drink is short-lived, but the subjects of philosophical queries and discussions remain always fresh after they have been imparted." (Plutarch, *Quaestiones*, Greece, 2nd C)

Thus the Rabbis prescribed such a banquet for Passover: much wine (four cups); appetizers (karpas); reclining on pillows; having our hands ceremonially washed by others; a royal feast; and most importantly – a philosophical discussion on the story of the Exodus and the issues of freedom versus slavery. The Rabbis wanted Pesach to be an experience of freedom and affluence – thus they chose to borrow the dining habits of their aristocratic contemporaries.

However, there is a fundamental difference: The Greco-Roman feast was for the rich only, it exploited slaves, it restricted asking questions and exchanging opinions to the ruling class, men only. But at the Pesach Seder all people, including the spouses and the youngest children, are invited to eat like royalty, to ask questions and to express opinions. Alongside the wine of the rich, there is the bread of poverty. The needy must be invited to share our meal. Stylish banquets may easily turn corrupt, but the Seder encourages us to savor our liberty, without exploiting or excluding others.

4 CUPS, 4 PROMISES AND 4 MOTHERS

The Talmud connects the Four Cups of wine drunk at the Seder to God's Four Promises to Israel: "Tell the children of Israel: I am Adonai! I will take them out... I will rescue them... I will redeem them... and I will marry them taking them as my people and I will be their God" (Exodus 6:6-7, Jerusalem Talmud Pesachim 10:1).

However, two 16th C. mystic rabbis identify the Four Cups with the Four Matriarchs of Israel. The Maharal of Prague (famous for the legend of Golem) and Rav Isaiah Horowitz of Tsfat explain:

(1) The Cup of Kiddush stands for Sarah who was the mother of a community of converts, believers by choice.
(2) The Cup of Maggid is for Rebecca who knew how to mother both Esav and Jacob, two opposed natures.
(3) The Cup of the Blessing after Eating represents Rachel whose son Joseph provided the whole family of Jacob with bread in a time of great famine.
(4) The Cup of Hallel (Praise) is for Leah the first woman to praise God (Genesis 29:35).

S A N C T I F Y I N G   T I M E

בְּשַׁבָּת:

וַיְהִי עֶרֶב וַיְהִי בֹקֶר יוֹם הַשִּׁשִּׁי. וַיְכֻלּוּ הַשָּׁמַיִם וְהָאָרֶץ וְכָל צְבָאָם.
וַיְכַל אֱלֹהִים בַּיּוֹם הַשְּׁבִיעִי מְלַאכְתּוֹ אֲשֶׁר עָשָׂה
וַיִּשְׁבֹּת בַּיּוֹם הַשְּׁבִיעִי מִכָּל מְלַאכְתּוֹ אֲשֶׁר עָשָׂה.
וַיְבָרֶךְ אֱלֹהִים אֶת יוֹם הַשְּׁבִיעִי וַיְקַדֵּשׁ אֹתוֹ
כִּי בוֹ שָׁבַת מִכָּל מְלַאכְתּוֹ אֲשֶׁר בָּרָא אֱלֹהִים לַעֲשׂוֹת.

בָּרוּךְ אַתָּה יי אֱלֹהֵינוּ מֶלֶךְ הָעוֹלָם בּוֹרֵא פְּרִי הַגָּפֶן.

בָּרוּךְ אַתָּה יי אֱלֹהֵינוּ מֶלֶךְ הָעוֹלָם,
אֲשֶׁר בָּחַר בָּנוּ מִכָּל עָם וְרוֹמְמָנוּ מִכָּל לָשׁוֹן וְקִדְּשָׁנוּ בְּמִצְוֹתָיו.
וַתִּתֶּן לָנוּ יי אֱלֹהֵינוּ בְּאַהֲבָה (שַׁבָּתוֹת לִמְנוּחָה וּ) מוֹעֲדִים לְשִׂמְחָה,
חַגִּים וּזְמַנִּים לְשָׂשׂוֹן, אֶת יוֹם (הַשַּׁבָּת הַזֶּה וְאֶת יוֹם) חַג הַמַּצּוֹת הַזֶּה,
זְמַן חֵרוּתֵנוּ (בְּאַהֲבָה), מִקְרָא קֹדֶשׁ, זֵכֶר לִיצִיאַת מִצְרָיִם.
כִּי בָנוּ בָחַרְתָּ וְאוֹתָנוּ קִדַּשְׁתָּ מִכָּל הָעַמִּים, (וְשַׁבָּת) וּמוֹעֲדֵי קָדְשֶׁךָ
(בְּאַהֲבָה וּבְרָצוֹן) בְּשִׂמְחָה וּבְשָׂשׂוֹן הִנְחַלְתָּנוּ.
בָּרוּךְ אַתָּה יי, מְקַדֵּשׁ (הַשַּׁבָּת וְ) יִשְׂרָאֵל וְהַזְּמַנִּים.

הַבְדָּלָה:

בָּרוּךְ אַתָּה יי אֱלֹהֵינוּ מֶלֶךְ הָעוֹלָם, בּוֹרֵא מְאוֹרֵי הָאֵשׁ.
בָּרוּךְ אַתָּה יי אֱלֹהֵינוּ מֶלֶךְ הָעוֹלָם הַמַּבְדִּיל בֵּין קֹדֶשׁ לְחֹל, בֵּין אוֹר לְחֹשֶׁךְ, בֵּין
יִשְׂרָאֵל לָעַמִּים, בֵּין יוֹם הַשְּׁבִיעִי לְשֵׁשֶׁת יְמֵי הַמַּעֲשֶׂה. בֵּין קְדֻשַּׁת שַׁבָּת לִקְדֻשַּׁת יוֹם
טוֹב הִבְדַּלְתָּ, וְאֶת יוֹם הַשְּׁבִיעִי מִשֵּׁשֶׁת יְמֵי הַמַּעֲשֶׂה קִדַּשְׁתָּ. הִבְדַּלְתָּ וְקִדַּשְׁתָּ אֶת
עַמְּךָ יִשְׂרָאֵל בִּקְדֻשָּׁתֶךָ, בָּרוּךְ אַתָּה יי הַמַּבְדִּיל בֵּין קֹדֶשׁ לְקֹדֶשׁ.

בָּרוּךְ אַתָּה יי אֱלֹהֵינוּ מֶלֶךְ הָעוֹלָם,
שֶׁהֶחֱיָנוּ וְקִיְּמָנוּ וְהִגִּיעָנוּ לַזְּמַן הַזֶּה.

The Kiddush sanctifies not the wine, but the holiday. On Pesach we dedicate ourselves to – "Remember the Day of your Exodus from Egypt" (Exodus 13:3).

Don't pour for yourself is the tradition tonight. At our banquet of liberation, let others fill your glass and you offer to pour for them.

When Seder falls on Friday night, we add the texts in shaded font and in parentheses in the body of the Kiddush to commemorate the Creation of the World as well.

Stand to recite the Kiddush, then recline to the left to drink the wine.

When Passover night falls on Saturday night we add a special Havdalah.

On Shabbat:

> There was evening and there was morning, and the sixth day was over.
> The sky and the earth and all their contents were completed.
> On the seventh day God completed all the work. God ceased on Shabbat
> from all activity. God blessed the seventh day and declared it holy,
> because on that day God ceased from all the work of creation. (Genesis 2:1-3)

Blessed are You, Adonai our God, Ruler of the Universe,

who creates the fruit of the vine.

Blessed are You, Adonai our God, Ruler of the Universe,

who has chosen us from among the nations and the languages,

sanctifying us by your mitzvot.

Lovingly, You have given us [Shabbat for rest and] **festivals for**

happiness, including today - [the Shabbat and] the Holiday of

the Matzot, **the season of our liberation, a sacred day to gather**

together and to commemorate the Exodus from Egypt.

For You have chosen us and sanctified us among the nations.

You have granted us [lovingly the Shabbat and] **joyfully the holidays.**

Blessed are You, Adonai, who sanctifies [the Shabbat and] **the people**

of Israel and the festivals.

Ba-rukh ata Adonai /
/ Elo-hei-nu me-lekh ha-olam /
/ bo-rei pree ha-gafen.

Barukh ata Adonai / Eloheinu Melekh
ha-olam / asher ba-khar-banu mi-kol am
/ v'rom'manu mi-kol lashon / v' ki-d'shanu
b'mitz-votav / va-ti-tein lanu Adonai
Eloheinu b'ahava / (Shabbatot li-m'nu-kha
oo) / moadim l'simkha, khagim uzmanim
l'sason, et yom (HaShabbat hazeh v'et yom)
/ Hag HaMatzot hazeh / z'man khei-ru-teinu
/ (b'ahava) mikra kodesh
/ zekher li-tzi-at Mitzraim.
Ki vanu vakhar-ta / v'otanu ki-dashta mi-kol
ha-amim / (v'Shabbat) u-moadei kodshekha
/ (b'ahava uv'ratzon) / b'simkha uv'sason
hin-khal-tanu.
Barukh ata Adonai / mika-desh (HaShabbat
v') haz'ma-nim.

Havdalah: When Seder falls on Saturday night:

> Blessed are You, Adonai our God, Ruler of the Universe, who creates the lights of fire.
> Blessed are You, Adonai our God, Ruler of the Universe, who differentiates between the holy and the secular,
> between light and darkness, between Israel and the other nations, between the seventh day and the six days
> of creation, between the sanctity of Shabbat and the sanctity of Yom Tov (the festivals).
> You sanctified the people of Israel with your holiness.
> Blessed are You, Adonai, who **differentiates** between the holiness of Shabbat and the holiness of Yom Tov.

Blessed are You, Adonai our God, Ruler of the Universe,

who has kept us alive and brought us to this happy moment in our lives.

Ba-rukh ata Adonai / Elo-hei-nu me-lekh ha-olam /
/ she-he-khee-ya-nu / v'kee-ma-nu / v'hee-gee-anu / laz-man ha-ze.

Urkhatz וּרְחַץ

THE FIRST HANDWASHING

The ritual handwashing prepares us for eating finger foods, Karpas, the hors d'oeuvres of the Pesach banquet. Following the priestly tradition of washing hands before eating bread and even vegetables, the ritual handwashing is performed now in order to sanctify the eating of the Karpas. However, no blessing is said for this handwashing.

Ask for two volunteers:
one to carry a pitcher of water and to pour water over each guest's hands, and one to carry a basin and a towel. Having our hands washed by someone else is part of the Seder night experience of liberty and nobility.

Karpas כַּרְפַּס

THE FIRST DIPPING: SPRING GREENS

בָּרוּךְ אַתָּה יי אֱלֹהֵינוּ מֶלֶךְ הָעוֹלָם,
בּוֹרֵא פְּרִי הָאֲדָמָה.

Blessed are You, Adonai our God, **Ruler of the Universe,**

who creates the fruit of the earth.

Ba-rukh ata Adonai / Elo-hei-nu me-lekh ha-olam / bo-rei pree ha-ada-ma.

Distribute Karpas (a vegetable, often spring greens), dip in salt water (or a tangy sauce), and recite the blessing.

Originating from the Greek "karpos," meaning "fruit of the soil," this tradition borrows from the Greco-Roman symposium which always began with washing and dipping "karpos" accompanied by discussion.

While some medieval rabbis strictly forbid eating more than an olive's size of vegetable for Karpas, you may wish to revive the ancient custom of eating extensive appetizers – each with its own dip.

Continue dipping and tasting various fresh vegetables and other appetizers during the Seder until sufficiently full to persevere during the extensive storytelling (Maggid), but not so full as to ruin one's appetite for the matza eaten later.

A SEDER FOR DREAMERS WITH NOTHING TO DIP

In 1974, at the age of 26, I participated in my first Seder with a group of Jewish activists in the Soviet Union. Though we knew little about that night's rituals, identifying with the seminal story of freedom's triumph was not particularly difficult for us – especially with KGB agents waiting in a car downstairs.

[The mitzvah to publicly sacrifice the paschal lamb which was considered a god by Egyptians] challenged each Jew to decide whether to smear the blood of the false Egyptian god on his doorpost. By publicly declaring our desire to emigrate to Israel, each of us refuseniks had chosen to challenge the Soviet god and stand up against tyranny. The same yearning for freedom that once drove our people felt as if it was literally pulsing through our veins.

Some years later, I led my own Seder for the first time. In truth, my memory of the text of the Haggadah was by then rather sketchy, and the Seder itself had none of the traditional trappings. There was [no celery to dip in salt water] and no unleavened bread to eat, no bitter herbs to taste, no Haggadah to read and I was the only Jew present. In fact, I was the only person in the room. But my outside "guests" didn't seem to mind. I retold the story of Pesach through the small window of my punishment cell to two fellow inmates and they too could immediately identify with its universal message.

The reason was simple. This isolated group of dissidents in the Soviet Union had already experienced the power of freedom to transform an individual and understood its power to transform a society. They needed no reminders. The idea that a nation of slaves could win its freedom and defeat the most powerful empire in the world was to us not an ancient legend, but an eternal truth...

Such thinking was extremely rare outside the Gulag. Western policymakers had largely forgotten the power of freedom. To them, sentiments about the triumph of liberty may have been inspiring but they were hardly practical. Like a Pesach tale that was nice to read but which no "serious" person would believe, most paid homage to the values of a free society but dismissed as hopelessly naive the notion of an imploding evil empire...

But history would show that the so-called "realists" were completely divorced from reality. Their failure to appreciate the awesome power of freedom blinded them to the inevitable collapse of the Soviet superpower. They were the ones exposed as hopelessly out of touch, and the so-called dreamers proved astute pragmatists.

Nathan Sharansky, Soviet refusenik, prisoner of Siberia, and former Israeli Cabinet Minister

Yakhatz　　יַחַץ

BREAKING THE MATZA

ENTERING THE BROKEN WORLD

The Pesach story begins in a broken world, amidst slavery and oppression. The sound of the breaking of the matza sends us into that fractured existence, only to become whole again when we find the broken half, the afikoman, at the end of the Seder. This brokenness is not just a physical or political situation.

In Hebrew, Egypt is called *Mitzrayim*, reminding us of the word *tzar*, narrow. Thus, in Hassidic thought, *Mitzrayim* symbolizes the inner straits that trap our souls. Yet even here we can find a unique value, as the Hassidic saying teaches us: "There is nothing more whole – than a broken heart."

Or as Leonard Cohen wrote:

"There's a crack in everything /
That's where the light comes in."

Some families pass out a whole matza to every Seder participant, inviting them to take a moment to ponder this entrance into a broken world, before they each break the matza themselves.

Break the middle matza, place the larger portion, the afikoman, in a napkin to be hidden.
The afikoman game begins now! For instructions and variations of the game, see page 105.

Of the three **matzas**, the top matza is for the usual blessing over bread (*ha-motzi lekhem*).

The bottom matza is for the Hillel sandwich (*korekh*) made with matza, maror, and haroset.

The middle matza has a dual purpose: The smaller portion will be eaten with the top matza when we begin the meal. The bigger portion will become the afikoman, to be eaten as the last taste of the Seder.

WHAT IF TOMORROW THERE IS NO BREAD?

Every year, on Seder night, when I break the matza in half and hide the afikoman, I am overcome with emotion as I recall my first day in Israel.

I arrived in Kibbutz Kedma together with other children, all of us new immigrants who had arrived in Israel without our parents after World War II. We were hungry, penniless and exhausted from our wandering and constant hunger.

On the table in the dining room, there were all kinds of delicious foods. There were plenty of vegetables, cheeses and bread, and we could take as much as we wanted. I couldn't believe my eyes.

I couldn't believe that at the next meal, we would also have as much bread to eat as we wanted.

There were many days in Europe when I could think of nothing else except bread – of which there was never enough. There were many nights when I went to bed hungry. I would remain awake for hours, with my stomach growling from hunger, dreaming of bread. But now in Israel there was so much food.

What did I do in those first days in the kibbutz, when we sat down at the table, loaded down with so many good foods? I was filled with fear that maybe there wouldn't be any bread the next day.

So I would break each slice of bread I received in half; I would eat half, and the other half I would hide in my pocket. I could not forget the days in which I was never sure if there would be bread tomorrow.

Retold by **Bina Talitman**, *Reliving Exodus*

HA(L)VES AND HAVE NOTS

Locate yourself in the Statistics on the Distribution of Wealth (2000):

If we could reduce the world's population to a village of precisely 100 people, with all existing human ratios remaining the same, the demographics would look something like this:

> 80 live in substandard housing / 24 don't have any electricity / 50 malnourished and 1 dying of starvation and 1 with HIV / 1 with a college education and 7 with Internet access / 5 control 32% of the entire world's wealth, all are US citizens /

If you have never experienced war, imprisonment, torture or famine You are probably happier than 500 million people in this world.

If you are able to go to church, mosque or synagogue without fear of harassment – you are happier than 3 billion people in this world.

If there is food in your refrigerator, if you have shoes, a bed and a roof above your head, you are better off than 75% of people in this world.

If you read this text, you do not belong to those 2 billion people who cannot read.

This is your World! And you are able to make changes! Hasten to do good works!

BEING POOR

Being Poor is …
having your heat shut off in the winter because your parents can't pay the bill

Being Poor is …
having two blankets for seven people in the family

Being Poor is …
wishing you could eat in a restaurant

Being Poor is …
wearing shoes that someone else threw out

Being Poor is …
lying when someone asks you what your father does for a living

Being Poor is …
pretending that you don't care that you got no gift for your birthday

Being Poor is …
waiting all day in a clinic to see a doctor you don't know

Being Poor is …
a welfare worker asking your mother too many questions and making her cry

Being Poor is …
not being afraid of the dentist because you've never seen one

Being Poor is …
always feeling a little mad because you never have what you need

Based on **Janet Rosenberg**, *Being Poor is…*

> Go around the table, adding your own continuation to the sentence "BEING POOR IS…."

Maggid מַגִּיד

TELLING THE STORY

בְּבְהִילוּ יָצָאנוּ מִמִּצְרָיִם.   **In haste we left Egypt!**

(based on Deuteronomy 16:3)

The heart of the Seder is *Maggid* from the term *Haggadah* meaning to tell a story. We retell the Exodus in words but also in drama.

Some families wrap a matza in a napkin, place it on their shoulders, and recite: *"The people took their dough before it was leavened, the kneading bowls wrapped in their cloaks upon their shoulders"* (Exodus 12:34).

Consider the importance of family memories and storytelling.

Many families act out the Exodus itself, dressing their children, or a dramatically inclined adult, in travelers clothing, with Matza-rations on their shoulder or in a backpack. The "travelers" then go outside, knock at the door, enter and tell their story.
Here is a semi-traditional script that may be used:

Children:	Knock, knock!
Adults:	Where are you coming from?
Children:	From the land of Egypt, where we were slaves.
Adults:	Where are you going now?
Children:	To Jerusalem.
Adults:	What is on your shoulder?
Children:	That is the dough we brought from Egypt when we rushed out. We had no time to let it rise into bread.
Adults:	Tell us about the harsh labor you did in Egypt!
Children:	Yes we will, and about the plagues by which God rescued us…

Prague Haggadah, 1526

IN HASTE WE LEFT COMMUNIST RUSSIA

The story of my liberation is the story of my teeth and the ballet "Swan Lake."
In August 1991 I prepared to make aliyah from the Soviet Union: we sold the apartment, I left my job, I was issued a visa for Israel, and I had bought tickets for November. And then, suddenly… I was about to leave the house one morning for a final root canal appointment at the dentist. But when I turned on the television and saw that all the channels were broadcasting the same performance of "Swan Lake," I realized right away that dramatic political events must be happening. The Soviet Union always broadcast "Swan Lake" to cover up when important things were happening. It quickly became clear that a coup was taking place, and that the Communist regime was about to end.

But I was worried – all the borders would probably be closed, and I was afraid I'd be stuck in the Soviet Union. I went to the Jewish Agency representatives and they told me that they had chartered a second plane to Israel that very day! I called home and said, "We're leaving for the airport in two hours, start packing!"
We managed to take documents and clothing, but I was forced to leave most of my books behind.

The root canal I should have finished that day left me with a gaping hole in my tooth that caused me great pain, but there wasn't time… I knew what I didn't finish in the crumbling Soviet Union, I would take care of in my own home, in the State of Israel.

Yigal Asnis, *Alei Tzameret Haggadah*

A TURTLE'S MEMORY

"Remember the days of old; consider the years of many generations." (Deuteronomy 32:7)
Every year, hundreds of giant green sea turtles swim hundreds of miles from their natural habitat on the Brazilian coast to tiny Ascension Island in the Atlantic Ocean in order to mate.
For years, researcher and pioneer conservation biologist Archie Carr tried to understand how the turtles found their way to the island from so great a distance, when even airplanes had trouble locating it. Carr's conclusions were fascinating: he claimed that the turtles navigate using genetic memory. Millions of years ago, when a strip of land bisected the Atlantic, the journey from Brazil to the closest stretch of the eastern shore was only a short swim.
That land was submerged millions of years ago. But the turtles, driven by their genetic memory, still search and find the last remaining remnant of the world that disappeared into the ocean - Ascension Island. Every year they return to perpetuate the species and the memory.

MARGE PIERCY

MAGGID

The courage to let go of the door, the handle.
The courage to shed the familiar walls whose very
 stains and leaks are comfortable as the little moles
 of the upper arm; stains that recall a feast,
a child's naughtiness, a loud battering storm
 that slapped the roof hard, pouring through.

The courage to abandon the graves dug into the hill,
 the small bones of children and the brittle bones
 of the old whose marrow hunger had stolen;
the courage to desert the tree planted and only
 begun to bear; the riverside where promises were
 shaped; the street where their empty pots were broken.

The courage to leave the place whose language you learned
as early as your own, whose customs however dangerous or demeaning, bind you like a halter
you have learned to pull inside, to move your load;
the land fertile with the blood spilled on it;
the roads mapped and annotated for survival.

The courage to walk out of the pain that is known
into the pain that cannot be imagined,
mapless, walking into the wilderness, going

barefoot with a canteen into the desert;
stuffed in the stinking hold of a rotting ship
sailing off the map into dragons' mouths,

Cathay, India, Siberia, goldeneh medina,
leaving bodies by the way like abandoned treasure.
So they walked out of Egypt. So they bribed their way
out of Russia under loads of straw; so they steamed
out of the bloody smoking charnelhouse of Europe
on overloaded freighters forbidden all ports -

out of pain into death or freedom or a different
painful dignity, into squalor and politics.
We Jews are all born of wanderers, with shoes
under our pillows and a memory of blood that is ours
 raining down. We honor only those Jews who changed
tonight, those who chose the desert over bondage,

who walked into the strange and became strangers
and gave birth to children who could look down
on them standing on their shoulders for having
been slaves. We honor those who let go of everything but freedom, who ran, who revolted, who fought,
who became other by saving themselves.

REFUGEES GIVE REFUGE: A RHODE ISLAND MITZVAH

When we retell the story of our flight from Egypt, we come to appreciate all those who have been refugees and fugitives. The oldest standing synagogue in North America was built in 1763 in Newport, Rhode Island, by Spanish-Portuguese immigrants, descendants of persecuted Marrano Jews. They had come to America so they could, for the first time in generations, openly practice their Judaism in their new home. In the center of the synagogue, under the Bima, they built a special hiding place, as a lesson learned from their many years of persecution and their undercover Jewish practice. For a 100 years the congregants retold their story and passed on the secret of the underground shelter.

Thankfully, Jews have never had to use this hideout. But there were other people who came to the synagogue in search of a hiding place on their way to freedom from oppression: In the years preceding the Civil War and the emancipation of slaves in the United States (1863), many slaves were smuggled from the South to the North, on their way to safety in Canada. The Jewish community put their synagogue and its underground hiding place at the disposal of the refugee slaves, fugitives from injustice, on their way to freedom. In this way they gave a renewed interpretation to the *mitzvah*:

> "If a slave has taken refuge with you from his persecutors, do not hand the slave over to the master. Let the fugitive slave live among you wherever he likes and in whatever town he chooses. Do not oppress the slave." (Deuteronomy 23:15-16)

No Future Without a Past

"A self-made man is as likely as a self-laid egg."
Mark Twain

The parent is a story-teller who narrates a world the children never knew. Parents transmit a knowledge of reality outside the child's experience. The father and mother must provide frames of reference rooted in the memories and the history of the covenantal community of Israel.

A primary source for evil according to Jewish tradition is the loss of memory. Those who do not build upon their memory and who are frightened and ashamed of their past may manifest hostility towards others because their sense of worth and dignity is derived only by manipulation and control of others. The poor people who prevail through difficult struggles to attain wealth, and then block out the memory of their past, become harsh taskmasters. "Self-made men" can be sensitive to others only when they are unashamed to talk about their former destitution. If they cannot bear the thought of their former poverty, they will act with cruelty to those who remind them of their former degradation.

In recalling Egypt, the Jews are exhorted to remember that they were once slaves. Rather than deny it, they are to incorporate that slavery into their consciousness. Thus, "love the stranger because you too were outcasts in Egypt." Have regard for the poor because you too were once servants; care for the oppressed because you too were persecuted. Be cautious with power because you have suffered the perversions of another's might.

The role of parents is to develop in the identity of the child a sense of history, a temporal consciousness, an empathy for a whole world of experience that was not theirs. Whether these memories are relevant and meaningful, and how the child will live by them, are different issues. The mother's and father's task is not to decide how the children will use their memories. Their obligation is to see to it that the child does not enter into the future without a past.

Rabbi **David Hartman**, Jerusalem philosopher

You Cannot Navigate Without a Point of Origin

I don't think you can be fully a member of the Jewish people and, creatively, a member of humanity, without knowing who you yourself are. The only way you achieve a deep sense of self is to know your own beginnings. That's why Torah is important to the Jews. Torah is a Jew's sense of self, the beginning of it, the foundation stones of it. Then you can pick and choose, quarrel with it, discard this, accept that; but at least know where the shoreline is before you begin to row away from it! If you are rowing and there is no shoreline at all, then you're navigating blind, and to navigate blind is to live in dread.

Rabbi **Chaim Potok**, American novelist and scholar

Zion Ozeri, Rehovot, 1981.

Ha Lakhma   הָא לַחְמָא

THE STORY OF THE MATZA

הָא לַחְמָא עַנְיָא
די אֲכַלוּ אֲבָהָתַנָא
בְּאַרְעָא דְמִצְרָיִם.

This is the bread
of poverty and persecution
that our ancestors ate
in the land of Egypt.

כָּל דִּכְפִין יֵיתֵי וְיֵכֹל,
כָּל דִּצְרִיךְ יֵיתֵי וְיִפְסַח.

Let all who are hungry,
come and eat.
Let all who are in need,
come and share the Pesach meal.

הָשַׁתָּא הָכָא,
לְשָׁנָה הַבָּאָה
בְּאַרְעָא דְיִשְׂרָאֵל.
הָשַׁתָּא עַבְדֵי,
לְשָׁנָה הַבָּאָה בְּנֵי חוֹרִין.

This year we are still here –
Next year
in the land of Israel.
This year we are still slaves –
Next year free people.

Ha Lakhma Anya is essentially the "Story of the Matza." Told in Aramaic, once the everyday language of Talmudic Jews, this story has three parts: **a memory, an action and a hope.** First we point out the Matza, the bread of poverty we ate in Egypt. Then, remembering our poverty in the past, we invite all needy persons to join our table tonight. Finally, we express the hope that while this year human beings are still enslaved in many ways, often lacking a home for themselves, next year we will all be free people, in our own personal and national home.

Remove the cloth covering the Matzot so that they are in plain view during the telling of the story, the Maggid.
Raise the three Matzot and point out the broken middle Matza (remaining after the Afikoman has been hidden).
Open the door, symbolizing our hospitality towards those in need.

Ha la-kh-ma an-ya / Dee-akha-lu av-ha-ta-na / b'ar-ah d'meetz-ra-yeem /
Kol deekh-feen / yei-tei v' yei-khol / Kol dee-tzreekh, yei-tei v' yee-fsakh /
Ha-sha-ta ha-kha / l'sha-na ha-ba-ah / be-ar-ah d'Yis-rael /
Ha-sha-ta av-dei / l'sha-na ha-ba-ah / **b'nei kho-reen.**

SERVICE WITH A SMILE

If one gives to another all the good gifts of the world, but shows a sour face, in the eyes of the Torah, it is as if nothing had been given. However if one welcomes a person in need cheerfully and kindly, then the Torah regards it as if all the good gifts in the world had been given.

Avot D'Rabbi Natan, elaboration on Pirkei Avot, Israel, 5th Century

The Wall of Indifference by Noam Nadav

"Break your bread with the hungry … Do not ignore your own flesh and blood" (Isaiah 58:7).

NEEDY BUT NOT POOR

Although they may initially seem redundant, the two invitations we issue in *HaLakhma Anya* – *"Let all who are hungry, kol dikhfin, enter and eat"* and *"Let all who are in need, kol ditzrikh, come and celebrate the Passover"* – in reality are not. *Kol ditzrikh* means those who are in need – but not in need of bread. Whoever is in need of bread, *dikhfin*, is hungry. *Kol ditzrikh* refers to one who is alone, who has a lot of Matza and wine but no home or family. There are indeed many ways to be included among the *kol ditzrikh*. The invitation to "all who are in need" is not *yeitei ve-yeikhol*, "to eat with us;" rather, it is to spend the Pesach with us, *yeitei ve-yifsakh*, "to celebrate with us." It is an invitation addressed to unfortunate and lonely people. They might be millionaires; it is completely irrelevant. Whoever is in need should come and celebrate.

Ha Lakhma Anya is the renewal of a pledge of solidarity among the Jewish people – solidarity between individual and individual, and between the individual and the Jewish community as a whole. It is a proclamation that we are one people, and that we are ready to help one other. Pesach night is a time of sharing; if the sense of solidarity, responsibility, unity, and readiness to share and to participate are not manifested and demonstrated, the whole Seder becomes meaningless.

Rabbi **Joseph B. Soloveitchik**, leading twentieth-century Talmudist and philosopher, was Rosh Yeshiva at Yeshiva University's Rabbi Isaac Elchanan Theological Seminary in New York.

OPENING DOORS: TONIGHT AND THROUGHOUT THE YEAR

David of Levov, a unique and humble Hassidic master, once taught: "If people come to you for assistance and you tell them, 'God will surely help you,' then you are acting disloyally to God. For you should understand that God has sent you to help the needy, not to refer the poor back to God."

Passover has always been a time in which Jews redoubled their efforts to help the needy in their communities: Inviting itinerant guests to the Seder, giving out "*Kimkha DePiskha*" – Pesach flour, or "*Ma'ot Khitim*" – money for buying wheat, organizing Seders in hospitals, old age homes or remote locations. All assistance to the needy – be it material, psychological or spiritual – are all ways in which we can open doors to others.

As we open the door, symbolically inviting others to partake in our meal, invite the participants to answer the question:

What acts of hospitality and what volunteer work have you witnessed or participated in this year? Is there a Tzedaka project you would like to do this coming year?

THE JEWISH MAYFLOWER

Three hundred years ago a ship called the Mayflower set sail to the New World. This was a great event in the history of England. Yet I wonder if there is one Englishman who knows at what time the ship set sail? Do the English know how many people embarked on this voyage? What quality of bread did they eat?

Yet more than three thousand three hundred years ago, before the Mayflower set sail, the Jews left Egypt. Every Jew in the world, even in America or Soviet Russia knows on exactly what date they left - the fifteenth of the month of Nisan; everyone knows what kind of bread the Jews ate - Matza. Even today the Jews worldwide eat Matza on the 15th of Nisan. They retell the story of the Exodus and all the troubles Jews have endured since being exiled, saying:

"This year, slaves. Next year, free!
This year here. Next year in Jerusalem, in Zion, in Eretz Yisrael!"
That is the nature of the Jews.

David Ben-Gurion, first prime minister of the State of Israel, from a speech in 1947 before the U.N. Commission on the Partition of Palestine.

Yahatz: The Partition Plan by Michel Kichka

SYNAGOGUE BECOMES FIVE STAR HOTEL

In Toronto's notoriously cold winters, the city's many homeless people must search for an open door, a shelter that will take them in from the cold. In 1995, despite objections from neighbors and members, the city's Holy Blossom Temple opened its doors as a homeless shelter. Some threatened to cancel their membership or refused to bring their children to the Hebrew school if those people were allowed in the Temple. Now however that attitude has changed completely. Over 500 people, aged 6 to 95, sign up annually to volunteer.

From early November until a week before Pesach, the homeless come for Thursday dinner and Friday breakfast. School children conduct clothing drives. Bnei Mitzvah families decorate their table center pieces with baskets of socks

and toiletries later given to the needy. Security guards maintain order as homeless line up.

A strict policy prevents admission of trouble makers and thieves who often plague the homeless themselves in other shelters and on the street. Alcohol, drugs and weapons may not be brought into the building.

The homeless are always called and treated as guests of the Temple. Most come to spend the evening and not just for a delicious meal. They enjoy the warm welcome and the respect shown as well as the companionship. Socializing teams provide books and magazines and join the guests in card or board games. Every other week there is an art show.

On an extremely cold night, a very disheveled street person arrived at the program. Speaking with great difficulty, hardly coherent, he asked for food. After he had eaten, he shuffled over to the piano. While the volunteers were still deciding how, without causing offense, they could ask him not to touch the piano, he sat down and played most beautifully works by Bach and Vivaldi. The whole room became hushed. After playing non-stop for about 30 minutes the man got up and, without saying a word, went back out into the cold night.

Guests of "Out of the Cold" show their appreciation in many small ways. But perhaps what gives the volunteers the biggest pleasure is to hear a guest say: "I am not coming back here anymore. I have got myself a good job."

Walter Seaton, chairperson of "Out of the Cold," Holy Blossom Temple, Toronto

PRIMO LEVI
PASSOVER

Tell me: how is this night different
From all other nights?
How, tell me, is this Passover
Different from other Passovers?

Light the lamp, open the door wide
So the pilgrim can come in, Gentile or Jew;
Under the rags perhaps the prophet is concealed.
Let him enter and sit down with us;
Let him listen, drink, sing and celebrate Passover;
Let him consume the bread of affliction,
The Pascal Lamb, sweet mortar and bitter herbs.

This is the night of differences
In which you lean your elbow on the table,
Since the forbidden becomes prescribed,
Evil is translated into good.

We spent the night recounting
Far-off events full of wonder,
And because of all the wine
The mountains will skip like rams.

Tonight they exchange questions:
The wise, the godless, the simple-minded and the child.
And time reverses its course,
Today flowing back into yesterday,
Like a river enclosed at its mouth.
Each of us has been a slave in Egypt,
Soaked straw and clay with sweat,
And crossed the sea dry-footed.

You too, stranger.
This year in fear and shame,
Next year in virtue and justice.

Primo Levi, Auschwitz survivor and novelist, Italy

> "We have moved into an era where we are called upon to raise certain basic questions about the whole society. We are still called upon to give aid to the beggar who finds himself in misery and agony on life's highway. But one day, we must ask the question of whether an edifice which produces beggars must not be restructured and refurbished."
>
> **Martin Luther King**, Jr., 1966

An End to Famine
Israeli stamp by A. Calderon, 1963

FOUR CUPS OF MILK: A FOLKTALE

Once, before Pesach, a man entered the home of Rabbi Yossi Ber, and asked him a question: "Tell me Rabbi, can I fulfill the commandment of the four cups with milk instead of wine?"
The rabbi asked him, "Are you - God forbid - ill?"
The man answered him, "No, thank God, I am quite healthy, but I cannot afford to buy wine this year."
Rabbi Yossi turned to his wife, and said, "Give this man twenty-five rubles."
The man said, "Honored Rabbi, I came to you to ask a question, not to beg for Tzedaka!"
The rabbi calmed him, saying, "This money is given to you as a loan, until God helps you."
The man took the money, thanked the rabbi and praised him.
After the man left, the rabbi's wife asked him: "Why did you tell me to give him twenty-five rubles? After all, wine costs only two or three rubles."
The rabbi answered, "I understood from the man's question that he does not have enough to prepare anything for the holiday. If he had had enough money for fish and meat, he would not have asked if it is permissible to use milk instead of wine. Milk cannot be drunk at the same meal with meat. That is why I gave him money to buy everything he needs for the holiday."

Ma Nishtana מַה נִּשְׁתַּנָּה

THE FOUR QUESTIONS

מַה נִּשְׁתַּנָּה הַלַּיְלָה הַזֶּה מִכָּל הַלֵּילוֹת?

Why is this night different from all other nights?

שֶׁבְּכָל הַלֵּילוֹת אָנוּ אוֹכְלִין חָמֵץ וּמַצָּה,
הַלַּיְלָה הַזֶּה - כֻּלּוֹ מַצָּה.

On all other nights, we eat either leavened bread or Matza, but on this night we eat only Matza.

שֶׁבְּכָל הַלֵּילוֹת אָנוּ אוֹכְלִין שְׁאָר יְרָקוֹת,
הַלַּיְלָה הַזֶּה - מָרוֹר.

On all other nights, we eat other kinds of vegetables, but on this night we eat Maror (bitter herbs).

שֶׁבְּכָל הַלֵּילוֹת אֵין אָנוּ מַטְבִּילִין אֲפִלוּ פַּעַם אֶחָת,
הַלַּיְלָה הַזֶּה - שְׁתֵּי פְעָמִים.

On all other nights, we need not dip our vegetables even once, but on this night we dip twice.

שֶׁבְּכָל הַלֵּילוֹת אָנוּ אוֹכְלִין בֵּין יוֹשְׁבִין וּבֵין מְסֻבִּין,
הַלַּיְלָה הַזֶּה - כֻּלָּנוּ מְסֻבִּין.

On all other nights, we eat either sitting upright or reclining, but on this night we all recline.

Ma nish-ta-na ha-lai-la ha-zeh / mee-kol ha-lei-lot?
Sheh-b'khol ha-lei-lot / anu okh-leen / kha-metz u-matza / Ha-lai-la ha-zeh / ku-lo matza.
Sheh-b'khol ha-lei-lot / anu okh-leen sh'ar y'ra-kot / Ha-lai-la ha-zeh / maror.
Sheh-b'khol ha-lei-lot / ein anu mat-bee-leen / afee-lu pa-am akhat / Ha-lai-la ha-zeh / shtei-p'ameem.
Sheh-b'khol ha-lei-lot / anu okh-leen / bein yo-shveen u-vein m'su-been / Ha-lai-la ha-zeh / ku-la-nu m'su-been.

Pour the second cup of wine for everyone and let the younger children sing "*Ma Nishtana*."

Before continuing with the story, we make sure the children around the table are interested and involved. For example, some families serve nuts and candies to arouse the children's curiosity and to reward their participation.

THE STUPIDITY OF HAVING AN ANSWER

A novel does not assert anything; a novel searches and poses questions. I invent stories, confront one with another, and by this means I ask questions. The stupidity of people comes from having an answer for everything. The wisdom of the novel comes from having a question for everything...

The novelist teaches the reader to comprehend the world as a question. There is wisdom and tolerance in that attitude. In a world built on sacrosanct certainties, the novel is dead. The totalitarian world is a world of answers rather than questions. There, the novel has no place. In any case, it seems to me that all over the world people nowadays prefer to judge rather than to understand, to answer rather than ask, so that the voice of the novel can hardly be heard over the noisy foolishness of human certainties.

Milan Kundera, novelist and anti-Communist activist, Czech Rep.

BEWARE! I WILL BE FORCED TO THROW CANDIES AT YOU

At the beginning of Seder night, Jerusalem's Professor Reuven Feuerstein, world renowned special needs educator, always warns the children around the table:
"Tonight is Seder night. This is an important occasion and we have much to read, so we cannot be bothered with all sorts of questions. If you ask any questions, I will be forced to punish you: I will throw lots and lots of candies at you. Understood?"
Unsurprisingly, the children spend the rest of the night asking many questions, stopping only to collect the candies thrown at them by the old professor...

This is but one of the many strategies for eliciting questions on Seder night: Prize-bearing quizzes and riddles, or just giving a candy to anyone who asks a question - regardless of the answer! Candies and nuts (like American Cracker Jacks) were used in Talmudic times as an advertising gambit by storekeepers to attract children to enter their stores (Mishna, Baba Metzia 4:12). In the Talmud, these tasty "come-ons" or prizes are mandated to keep the kids awake and involved in the Seder (Talmud Pesachim 109a). As Maimonides explains in his 12th century guidelines for Seder night:
"One should make changes on this night, so that one's children will notice it and ask, "What makes this night different from other nights?" And what changes may be made? Distributing snacks or nuts to the children [in short, serving dessert at the beginning of the meal], clearing the table before anyone has eaten, or by snatching the Matza away from the others, and other games like that." (Maimonides, Laws of Hametz and Matza, Chapter 7:3)

What tricks and games can you use this year for eliciting questions and participation?

> There is frequently more to be learned from the unexpected questions of a child than the discourses of men.
>
> **John Locke**, *Something Concerning Education*

QUESTIONS ARE A PARADOX

The key to Jewish exegesis is to assume that nothing is obvious. Questions are the great cultural paradox. They both destabilize and secure social norms. Nikita Khruschev, onetime leader of the Soviet Union, once explained why he hated Jews. He said, "They always ask why!" Questions tend to democratize. Ease with questions conveys a fundamental trust in the goodwill and the good sense of others. Autocrats hate questions. We train children at the Passover Seder to ask why, because tyrants are undone and liberty is won with a good question. It is for this reason that God loves it when we ask why.

Consequently we celebrate challenging the Torah to make sense, and above all to be a defensible expression of Divine goodness... When we ask good questions the Torah is given anew on Sinai at that very moment.

Rabbi **Steven Greenberg**, *Wrestling with God and Men*

Tribute to **Dr. Seuss**

NO QUESTIONS, NO CLASS

A story is told of Rabbi Joseph Dov Soloveitchik, the legendary teacher at Yeshiva University - a great philosopher and a great Talmudist - who demanded that his students prepare rigorously for each class. Often he began his class by asking if any of the hundreds of students crowding his lecture hall had any questions on the assigned text. Many of the students had reviewed the material and yet they feared to ask, lest the questions reveal their ignorance to their teacher. Once, when not one of the hundreds of students dared ask a question, Rav Soloveitchik demonstratively slammed his Talmud closed and walked out saying: "No questions? No class." Learning begins with questions. Learning requires the courage to expose your ignorance, so the teacher or parent can address the real issues.

ELIEZER SEGAL

UNCLE ELI'S HAGGADAH

Why is it only, on Passover night
we never know how, to do anything right?
We don't eat our meals, in the regular ways,
the ways that we do, on all other days.

> `Cause on all other nights we may eat
> all kinds of wonderful good bready treats,
> like big purple pizza that tastes like a pickle,
> crumbly crackers and pink pumpernickel,
> sassafras sandwich and tiger on rye,
> fifty felafels in pita, fresh-fried,
> and toasted whole-wheat bread with liver and ducks,
> and crumpets and dumplings, and bagels and lox,
> Yes - on all other nights we eat all kinds of bread,
> but tonight of all nights we munch matzah instead.

And on all other nights we devour
vegetables, green things, and bushes and flowers,
lettuce that's leafy and candy-striped spinach,
fresh silly celery (have more when you're finished!)
daisies and roses and inside-out grass
and artichoke hearts that are simply first class!
Sixty asparagus tips served in glasses
with anchovy sauce and some sticky molasses -
But on Passover night you would never consider
eating an herb that wasn't all bitter.

> And on all other nights you would probably flip
> if anyone asked you how often you dip.
> On some days I only dip one Bup-Bup egg
> in a teaspoon of vinegar mixed with nutmeg,
> but sometimes we take more than ten thousand tails
> of the Yakkity-birds that are hunted in Wales,
> and dip them in vats full of Mumbegum juice.
> Then we feed them to Harold, our six-legged moose.
> Or we don't dip at all! We don't ask your advice.
> So why on this night do we have to dip twice?

And on all other nights we can sit as we please,
on our heads, on our elbows, our backs or our knees,
or hang by our toes from the tail of a Glump,
or on top of a camel with one or two humps,
with our foot on the table, our nose on the floor,
with one ear in the window and one out the door,
doing somersaults over the greasy k'nishes
or dancing a jig without breaking the dishes.
Yes - on all other nights you sit nicely when dining -
So why on this night must it all be reclining?

⠠⠹⠑⠀⠗⠁⠞

ये रात दूसरी रातों से अलग क्यों है?

ทำไมคืนนี้ไม่เหมือนคืนอื่นๆ

ਇਹ ਰਾਤ ਦੂਜੀ ਰਾਤਾਂ ਤੋਂ ਅਲੱਗ ਕਿਉਂ ਹੈ?

Διὰ τὶ ἥδε ἡ νὺξ διαφέρει τῶν ἄλλων νυκτῶν

¿Por que es differente esta noche de las demas noches?

Чем отличается эта ночь от всех других ночей?

Bu gece neden bütün öbür gecelerden farklıdır?

Wat is het verschil tussen deze avond en alle andere avonden?

بماذا تختلف هذه الليلة عن كل الليالي الأخرى؟

爲什麼今晚與其他的夜晚不同？

どうして　今夜は他の夜と異なるのでしょうか？

𓂝𓏤𓇋𓊪𓏲𓏭𓈖 𓂧𓏏𓇋𓈖𓏏𓇋𓊪𓏲𓏭𓈖

TORAH SPEAKS THE LANGUAGE OF PEOPLE

Since *Ma Nishtana* was created to reflect children's actual questions about Seder night, it has been customary to encourage children and adults who do not know Hebrew to ask their questions in their native tongue - in Yiddish, Arabic, Ladino and a hundred other languages. This reflects the saying of the midrash that God spoke the Torah in 70 languages, so that each person could understand.

In that spirit, Murray Spiegel and Rickey Stein have collected *300 Ways to Ask the Four Questions,* the *Ma Nishtana* in different languages. Above are a few samples.

Can you guess where they are from?

Can anyone around the table translate *Ma Nishtana* into another language?

To check your answers see page 148-149.

YEHUDA AMICHAI

Seder night reflections: *"What is the difference?"* we asked,
"What makes this night different from all other nights?"
And most of us grew up and don't ask any more, while others
Continue to ask their whole lives just like they ask
"How are you?" or, *"What time is it?"* while continuing to walk on
Without hearing the answer. *"What's the difference?"* Every night
Like an alarm clock whose tick-tock calms and tranquilizes.
"What's the difference?" Everything changes. Change is God.

Seder night thoughts: "The Torah speaks of four sons
One who is wise, one who is wicked, one who is simple, and one
Who does not know how to ask. But it does not speak
About one who is good, nor about one who loves.
And this is a question that has no answer and if it did have an answer
I wouldn't want to know it. I, who have passed through all of the sons
In various combinations have lived my life, the moon has shone
Upon me without apparent cause and the sun has run its course and Passovers
Have passed without an answer. *"What's the difference? What has changed?"*
Change is God, and Death is his prophet.

HOW AM I DIFFERENT TONIGHT ?

After asking how this night is different from all other nights, you might want to take this opportunity to go around the table and have people share: How am I different tonight and this year from previous years? What has changed this year? This can be a wonderful way to mark the changes and differences in and around us, as well as a way to "catch up" with the many guests at the Seder table.

We Were Slaves עֲבָדִים הָיִינוּ

RETELLING OUR STORY

When, in time to come, your children ask you:
"What is the meaning of the decrees, laws, and rules that
Adonai our God has enjoined upon you?"
You shall say to your children:

עֲבָדִים הָיִינוּ לְפַרְעֹה בְּמִצְרַיִם,
וַיּוֹצִיאֵנוּ יְיָ אֱלֹהֵינוּ מִשָּׁם
בְּיָד חֲזָקָה וּבִזְרוֹעַ נְטוּיָה.

We were slaves to Pharaoh in Egypt

and Adonai freed us from Egypt

with a mighty hand and an outstretched arm.

Adonai produced before our eyes great and awful signs
and wonders in Egypt, against Pharaoh and all his
household. God freed us from there, so that God could
take us and give us the land that had been promised on
oath to our ancestors" (Deuteronomy 6:20-23).

The storytelling begins by re-entering the universe of slavery, as we ask ourselves: What was slavery like then? What is it like today?

Avadim Hayeenu is taken from Moshe's farewell speech to the Jewish people, as he prepares them for their arrival in the Promised Land. He commands them to retell their story of slavery and liberation in order to pass their identity on to the children of the next generation. That is what we do tonight.

LET MY PEOPLE GO | An African-American Spiritual

When Israel was in Egypt's land,
"Let My people go" (Exodus 5:1).
Oppressed so hard they could not stand,
"Let My people go."

Go down, Moses,
way down in Egypt's land,
Tell old Pharaoh:
"Let My people go."

Thus said the Lord, bold Moses said,
"Let My people go."
If not, I'll smite your first-born dead,
"Let My people go."
            Go down, Moses...

No more shall they in bondage toil,
"Let My people go."
Let them come out with Egypt's spoil,
"Let My people go."
            Go down, Moses...

THE FIRE OF CONCERN: MOSHE'S BURNING BUSH

Moses lived in a period of dictatorship. His people were slaves. The bosses made them work under a speed-up system, and committed horrible atrocities. Young Moses became curious about the Hebrew slaves, and one day went to the brickyards and saw an Egyptian boss hitting a Hebrew laborer. Moses was a powerful young man, and he lost his temper. He hit the boss and killed him! A fire had been kindled in Moses' heart, a fire of concern about his people and their suffering.

The next day he went back to the hot brickyards. Then he learned two things that those who try to help their fellow men often discover: first, that slaves often spend as much time and energy fighting each other as they do fighting their common oppressors, and second, that slaves do not always welcome their deliverers.

Moses found two Hebrews fighting each other. When he rebuked them, they turned on him and said, 'Who made you our boss? Do you mean to kill us as you did that Egyptian yesterday?'

Leon Baxter

Moses feared that they would tell the Egyptians that he killed the boss. He concluded that it might not be healthy to stay around those parts, so he ran away. In his new home he settled down to a nice comfortable life, raising a family and feeding the flocks of his father-in-law.

Only, after a while, God came into the picture, with a bush that burned and burned and did not stop burning. Moses had had a fire kindled in his heart once, but it went out, or at least died down. God is the Being whose heart does not stop burning. What was God all burned up about? The voice that came out of the bush said, "I have seen the affliction of my people that are in Egypt and have heard their cry by reason of their oppressors."

And the proof that God had entered into Moses was that he had to go back and identify himself with his enslaved people – organize them into Brickmakers' Union Number One – and lead them out of hunger and slavery into freedom and into "a good land, and a large one, a land flowing with milk and honey."

Abraham Johannes Muste (1885-1967), the grand old man of American radicalism and pacifism

THE DEPTH OF DEGRADATION

The degradation, the wrongs, the vices that grow out of slavery, are more than I can describe. They are greater than you would willingly believe.

My master met me at every turn, reminding me that I belonged to him. He told me I was his property; that I must be subject to his will in all things. My soul revolted against the mean tyranny. But where could I turn for protection? There is no shadow of law to protect the slave girl from insult, from violence, or even from death. All these are inflicted by fiends who bear the shape of men.

When they told me my new-born babe was a girl, my heart was heavier than it had ever been before. Slavery is terrible for men; but it is far more terrible for women. Superadded to the burden common to all, they have wrongs, and sufferings, and mortifications peculiarly their own...

God gave me a soul that burned for freedom and a heart nerved with determination to suffer even unto death in pursuit of liberty. The slave owners seem to satisfy their consciences with the doctrine that God created the Africans to be slaves. What a libel upon the heavenly Father, who "made of one blood all nations of men!" Slavery is a curse to the whites as well as to the blacks. It makes the white fathers cruel and sensual; the sons violent and licentious; it contaminates the daughters, and makes the wives wretched. And as for the colored race, it needs an abler pen than mine to describe the extremity of their sufferings, the depth of their degradation...

Harriet Jacobs, *Life of a Slave Girl, An Autobiography*, 1861. Born a slave in 1813 in North Carolina.

WE WERE SIXTIES REBELS

The authors of injustice and oppression in America are Pharaohs:

We name the Pharaohs in Congress who multiply the weapons.

We name the Pharaohs who condemn Black babies to die at twice the rate of whites.

We name the Pharaohs who poison the land and water.

In America we [Jews] have been both coerced and cajoled into abandoning the prophetic legacy. The American lifestyle tries to remake us in one dimension - bureaucratic, programmed, technological... flat... [But we demand] the survival of Judaism, not merely of a brood of suburban Bar Mitzvah boys and girls.

Arthur Waskow, *The Freedom Haggadah*, 1969

WE WERE ZIONIST PIONEERS

"We were slaves to Pharaoh in Egypt," to King Farouks and Nassers in Egypt. But "we went out from there" – with a popular national uprising, "with a strong hand" - working and laboring, "with an outstretched arm"– liberating ourselves.

And if our ancestors had not been liberated, "we and our children and our children's children, would still be slaves" – in exile.

Yitzhak Tabenkin, *Kibbutz Ein Harod Haggadah*, 1953

THE WAY WE WERE
20th Century Adaptations of "We were slaves"

Jews have seen the key to Jewish and universal liberation in many modern movements, and often wrote their own ideological adaptations of the Haggadah. Did these movements contribute to freedom or create new forms of enslavement? How would we write our own adaptation today?

WE WOMEN ARE STILL SLAVES

To our body image – guilt eating into our bodies and souls.

To our "super woman" ideals that scatter our energies everywhere.

To a selective memory of history that erases our foremothers.

To recalcitrant husbands who imprison us in dead marriages.

To our desire to be considered good little girls.

To society's concept of success – competitive, autonomous... and lonely.

To our misconception that feminism is just for and about women, that it denies deep and healthy relationships with the men in our lives.

Tanya Zion Waldoks, 2006

WE WERE COMMUNISTS

We were slaves to Capital, until the October Revolution [the Russian Bolshevik Revolution of 1917] "redeemed us with a strong hand" from the land of slavery.

If it weren't for the October Revolution, then we and our children and our children's children would still be slaves to Capital.

Today the revolution is only here, next year – a world revolution.

The Red Haggadah, 1927

WE WERE POLITICIANS

We were slaves to our passions for power, for career advancement, for political office, for secure income, and therefore we were slaves also to our voters.

Every party teaches its voters to recite: "All of us are wise." "Blessed is God, the Place of the World" – for all of this is to keep our place of work, a soft chair and a high office.

The Non Political Haggadah, Tel Aviv, 1947

More Storytelling כָּל הַמַּרְבֶּה

T H E   L O N G E R ,   T H E   B E T T E R

וְאִלּוּ לֹא הוֹצִיא הַקָּדוֹשׁ בָּרוּךְ הוּא
אֶת אֲבוֹתֵינוּ מִמִּצְרַיִם,
הֲרֵי אָנוּ וּבָנֵינוּ וּבְנֵי בָנֵינוּ
מְשֻׁעְבָּדִים הָיִינוּ לְפַרְעֹה בְּמִצְרָיִם.

If **God** had not taken
our ancestors out of Egypt,
then we would still be enslaved
to Pharaoh in Egypt, along with our children,
and our children's children.

וַאֲפִלּוּ
כֻּלָּנוּ חֲכָמִים,
כֻּלָּנוּ נְבוֹנִים,
כֻּלָּנוּ זְקֵנִים,
כֻּלָּנוּ יוֹדְעִים אֶת הַתּוֹרָה,
מִצְוָה עָלֵינוּ לְסַפֵּר בִּיצִיאַת מִצְרָיִם.

Even if
all of us **are wise,**
all of us **discerning,**
all of us **veteran scholars, and**
all of us **knowledgeable in Torah,**
it is still a mitzvah for us to retell
the story of the Exodus from Egypt.

וְכָל הַמַּרְבֶּה לְסַפֵּר
בִּיצִיאַת מִצְרָיִם הֲרֵי זֶה מְשֻׁבָּח.

So, the more and the longer,
one expands and embellishes the story,
the more commendable it is.

STORYTELLING IDEAS

The Haggadah recommends that parents go beyond the text of the Haggadah and improvise dramatically in retelling the story of the Exodus. However, the traditional Haggadah does not include a script for the storyteller nor does it even bring the appropriate Biblical chapters. So some parents tell the story in their own words. Others ask the children to retell what they have learned in school under three major headings:

What was it like to be a slave?

What do you know about Moshe as a baby and as a young man?

How did the Jews finally become free?

Before the Seder ask the children to prepare drawings to illustrate these themes and then to show and tell what they drew. Or look at the pictures and create a dialogue among the characters represented.

BIBLIODRAMA: FIRST-PERSON ACCOUNTS OF THE EXODUS

Though we all know the story of the Exodus, we need to bring it alive tonight. Invite the participants to think of a person or an object, then to retell part of the story from their character's/prop's point of view. For example: an Egyptian official during the plague of darkness, a Jewish child crossing the Red Sea, Moses' staff or basket, etc.

Here is one story of Moses' basket, as told to Peter Pitzele, creator of the Bibliodrama method:

> "I am the reed ark that carried Moses down the Nile."
> "Tell me more about yourself."
> "Well, what do you want to know?"
> "Who made you?"
> "Moses' mother made me."
> "Did she talk to you while she was making you? Or could you read her thoughts?"
> "Not her thoughts, her feelings. She was sad, and angry."
> "I see. And did you know what you were being made for?"
> "Yes. To carry the little infant down the Nile."
> "How did you feel about this assignment?"
> "It was a huge responsibility. I wanted Moses' mother to be very careful. To weave me well and to caulk me well. I did not want to leak, or tilt over."
> "And did she build you well?"
> "Yes, very well."
> "Yes. I want you to know what it felt like to carry him down the river. It was like being his mother."

And another group member said, "I never thought about the ark of papyrus, the basket, before as a kind of second mother, a womb. It made me realize how many times Moses was mothered and passed on. The little ark is like a metaphor for how transient his childhood must have felt for him."

Peter Pitzele, *Scripture Windows*

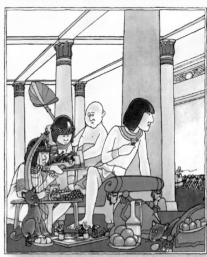

Leon Baxter

It was the Finger of God!

by the Religion Editor, Sigmund Freud, author of the forthcoming

Moses and Monotheism

The head of the Egyptian priests admitted publicly that the plagues are an act of the Jewish god, according to a report by the Akhenaten Association. This is the first time the priests have acknowledged the existence of a divine power other than themselves. What began as the Israelites' struggle for freedom might lead to a religious revolution, whose international ramifications remain to be seen.

TOMBS DESECRATED

The Egyptian Antiquities Authority (EAA) reported today that two mummies were stolen from Ramses' tomb – Tsofnat Paneiakh (alias Joseph) and a daughter of Ramses II. The EAA spokesperson says the Israelites are the main suspects in the theft.

LAND O'GOSHEN BAKERY

When time flies and the bread won't rise

INSTANT MATZA!

Weekly Horoscope

Leo: Nachshon Ben-Aminadav

head of the tribe of Judah, first to cross the Red Sea, is a classic Leo, determined and brave even though they are also reckless and hasty!

Leos jump to the head of the pack, making them natural leaders, yet drawing them into dangerous or embarrassing situations. After they leap without looking, they can find themselves knee-deep in mud, but the move can also be one that makes history!

Pest Control

Frogs, gnats and lice getting you down? Call Amenhetop for a free estimate today.

JOSHUA, THE CAMPING KING!

Big spring sale on all trekking equipment

Ask about our special desert survival kit:

■ **2 packages of bitter waters** desalination pills ■ **Unleavened trail mix** – from Gorp – the trail mix master ■ **Anti reflection UV** coated sunglasses, guaranteed to block out even Divine rays ■ **Battery operated GPS** – don't wander without it!

CONDO DEVELOPMENT

Get in on the ground floor of this new condo conversion project. Lovely views of the pyramids. Goshen area. Former slave dwellings can become your luxury home! **Call Ramses for details.**

The Hieroglyph Times

16 Nisan, 2560 | published in Egypt for 210 years | Cost: 1 dinar in Goshen | "All the news that is permitted to print" – by Ramses II

THE EXODUS BEGINS!

Final approval from the Pharaoh: Go!

The most heated meeting to date was concluded just yesterday between Moses Ben-Amram and the Pharaoh.

Hebrew sources revealed that the Pharaoh, in a familiar tactic, tried to renege on his agreement. It appeared that negotiations had reached a stalemate. Then came the fateful night of the 14th of Nisan. A mysterious plague left every Egyptian firstborn lifeless. An unearthly howl went up, never heard before.

"Out!" shouted the Egyptian people. "Out before we are all dead! Take our jewelry, take our dresses. But get out – Now!"

The palace capitulated and this morning more than 3,000,000 slaves headed for Egypt's border. After 210 years of slavery, drowning babies, deceit, and desperation, the Jews are free! Neither the Egyptians nor the Jews will forget this night.

Egypt to the Israelites: Return the stolen gold!

A class action lawsuit has been filed in international court against the Israelites by the Egyptians, who claim that the Jews used the confusion created by the "plague of the first-borns," to steal large quantities of gold on their way out of the country.

The Israelites' attorney said that the gold represents token compensation for years of enslavement at the hands of the Egyptians.

Our legal reporter adds: "When you set a slave free, do not send him empty handed."

(Deuteronomy 15:13-15)

Everything Must Go!

Great prices on household furnishings and heavy equipment! Moving away sale – bargains aplenty! Call now, ask for Aaron.

Situation Wanted

Speech therapist available afternoons and evenings. I got Moses to say "Let my People Go." I can get you to speak up too! Nefrititi - Therapist to the Stars.

Five Rabbis מַעֲשֶׂה בְּרַבִּי אֱלִיעֶזֶר

THE LONGEST SEDER

מַעֲשֶׂה בְּרַבִּי אֱלִיעֶזֶר וְרַבִּי יְהוֹשֻׁעַ
וְרַבִּי אֶלְעָזָר בֶּן עֲזַרְיָה וְרַבִּי עֲקִיבָא
וְרַבִּי טַרְפוֹן שֶׁהָיוּ מְסֻבִּין בִּבְנֵי
בְרַק, וְהָיוּ מְסַפְּרִים בִּיצִיאַת
מִצְרַיִם כָּל אוֹתוֹ הַלַּיְלָה, עַד שֶׁבָּאוּ
תַלְמִידֵיהֶם וְאָמְרוּ לָהֶם: "רַבּוֹתֵינוּ,
הִגִּיעַ זְמַן קְרִיאַת שְׁמַע שֶׁל שַׁחֲרִית".

A tale is told of Rabbi Eliezer, Rabbi Yehoshua, Rabbi Elazar son of Azarya, Rabbi Akiva and Rabbi Tarfon who dined (reclined) at the Seder in Bnai B'rak. The whole night long they spent retelling the story of the Exodus from Egypt, until their students arrived and announced to them: "Our masters, it is already time to recite the morning Sh'ma!"

אָמַר רַבִּי אֶלְעָזָר בֶּן עֲזַרְיָה: הֲרֵי אֲנִי כְּבֶן
שִׁבְעִים שָׁנָה, וְלֹא זָכִיתִי שֶׁתֵּאָמֵר יְצִיאַת
מִצְרַיִם בַּלֵּילוֹת עַד שֶׁדְּרָשָׁה בֶּן זוֹמָא, שֶׁנֶּאֱמַר:
"לְמַעַן תִּזְכֹּר אֶת יוֹם צֵאתְךָ מֵאֶרֶץ מִצְרַיִם כֹּל
יְמֵי חַיֶּיךָ"

"יְמֵי חַיֶּיךָ" - הַיָּמִים, "כָּל יְמֵי חַיֶּיךָ" - הַלֵּילוֹת.
וַחֲכָמִים אוֹמְרִים: "יְמֵי חַיֶּיךָ" - הָעוֹלָם הַזֶּה,
"כָּל יְמֵי חַיֶּיךָ" - לְהָבִיא לִימוֹת הַמָּשִׁיחַ.

Rabbi Elazar son of Azarya said: Even though I am like a man of seventy, I had never understood why the Exodus from Egypt should be mentioned at night-time [in the Sh'ma] , until Ben Zoma explained it to me using the verse:
"That you may remember the day when you came out of Egypt all the days of your life"
(Deuteronomy 16:3).

"The days of your life" means just the days, BUT "*all the days of your life*" means the nights as well! However the Rabbis explain: *"The days of your life"* means this life, BUT "*all the days of your life*" means the days of the Messiah as well!
(Mishna Brachot 1:5)

After we do our own storytelling, the Haggadah now recounts the story of the longest Seder ever, as a model for our own Seder.

This is an opportunity to recount other stories of successful and memorable Seders, throughout Jewish history, as well as in our own family experiences. Invite participants to share a special Seder memory from home or from their most unusual Seder.

SONGS OF FREEDOM IN A SYRIAN PRISON

On Thursday, April 2, 1970, an Israeli Phantom jet was shot down over a Damascus suburb. The pilot **Pini Nahmani** was imprisoned in the al-Mazza Prison in Damascus. In his secret diary he describes his Festival of Freedom:

It's hard to imagine the holiday atmosphere here: in the morning, we gave the cell a thorough scrubbing, something the concrete floor had never had. We drew a Seder plate on a piece of cardboard, with a Magen David in the middle, and a different item at each of the star's points. In the afternoon, we managed to give ourselves baths in ice-cold water, and then we put on our cleanest clothes.

These were difficult hours of soul searching. When you are a prisoner of war, the memories rise up and choke you. You think about home, trying to sense the smells and the holiday feeling at twilight. You know that your family and children, that the entire Jewish people, are waiting and hoping, while you're still here, tossing and turning, helpless, on your stinking mattress. Time crawls by at its own pace.

Two Haggadahs and some matza crumbs sent by the Chief Rabbi of Zurich gave us the feeling of a real Passover. When Boaz, the youngest among us - almost a kid - sang the four questions, tears welled up in my throat. But then came the singing! It was such a strange scene. In the most heavily-guarded prison of an enemy state, three Israeli prisoners are singing songs of the ancient holiday of liberty.

While we were still celebrating and reading the Haggadah, the guards appeared and demanded that we stop. It seemed that our singing had disturbed the ousted Syrian president in the next cell, Nur al-din Atassi. He had thrown us in jail and declared that "the Israeli pilots would grow old in a Syrian prison!" Now [after Hafez al-Assad, father of the present leader of Syria, seized power in a military coup] Nur was in the same boat we were. At any rate, we refused to stop, even when they threatened to throw us into solitary confinement as a punishment for making noise, for even that awful threat could not silence the sound of freedom.

We finished the Haggadah with *Had Gadya*, and went on singing other Israeli songs - Naomi Shemer's "Jerusalem of Gold" – just to continue the celebration long into the night and to avenge ourselves a little bit… I had never taken part in such a long Seder. We had to be taken prisoner in order to fulfill the Haggadah's description of the five rabbis in Bnai Brak: "The whole night long they spent retelling the story of the Exodus."

THE LAST ETHIOPIAN SEDER, 1991

From the eyewitness report of Micha Odenheimer, journalist and director of a program for Ethiopian olim.

"I brought you to Me on eagles' wings" (Exodus 19:4)

On Friday night, May 24, 1991, fourteen thousand four hundred Jews from Beita Yisrael crowded into the Israeli Embassy compound in Addis Ababa, the capital. They were caught between a nightmare and a dream, the danger of slaughter by the rebel army that encircled the capital and the opportunity to make aliyah to Israel at the last possible moment before the invasion by the rebels.

Months earlier the Jews of Ethiopia who had lived for centuries as farmers in the Gondar region abandoned their homes, sold their property and migrated – often by foot – 700 km south to the slums of the capital of the Marxist regime, hoping to leave from there to Israel.

Eight weeks earlier the priests (called *kesim*) celebrated at the Israeli Embassy their last Passover in Ethiopia. After purifying themselves in water they laid their hands on ten one-year-old sheep, blessed them, and then ritually slaughtered and roasted them. When the *kesim* honored me by offering me – an Ashkenazi Orthodox Jew – a piece of the lamb, I hesitated for a moment because their kashrut is different than my own. Yet I knew that eating the Pesach lamb has always been the symbol of inclusion in the Jewish community, so I expressed my solidarity with their Exodus and ate my first Paschal sacrifice.

Now, only weeks after Pesach, the final Exodus was to begin under the title "Operation Solomon." The Marxists who ruled the capital had made a deal with Israel for a $35,000,000 bribe

In less than 24 hours El Al passenger planes and Hercules transports took 14,400 people in the largest, longest, and fastest airlift of refugees in the history of the world; 40 journeys over 1,560 miles and back in 24 hours.

(paid by American Jewish philanthropists) to release the Jews in a massive airlift just days before the government fell.

At the Israeli embassy, 14,400 Jews spent all night long in darkness and exceptional calm and discipline. They experienced a mixture of fear and hope (reminiscent of the children of Israel in Egypt on the first Seder night).

That night the Ethiopian Jews passed from one station to another at the embassy grounds. First the head of the household's identity card was checked and his children counted off and given a sticker with the number of their bus to wear on their forehead. Then all their local money had to be thrown into a box, as demanded by the Ethiopian government. Afterwards all their possessions were relinquished, for lack of space in the planes. Only what they wore – their nicest clothes and gold jewelry – came with them, along with bread which was wrapped in their flowing garments.

I remembered the Biblical verses describing a similar "Night of Vigil" in which no one slept, on Passover evening in Egypt: *"The people took their dough before it was leavened...wrapped in their cloaks upon their shoulders. That was...a Night of Vigil"* (Exodus 13:9). Even the numbered stickers on the foreheads reminded me of the command, *"This shall serve you as a sign upon your hand and as a reminder on your forehead... that the Lord freed you from Egypt with a mighty hand."* (Exodus 13:9).

It's good the British don't know I hate matzos!

Passover Hunger Strike April 1946

THE HUNGER STRIKE SEDER, 1946

Golda Meir, Israel's first female prime minister, tells of one memorable Pesach Seder in the midst of the struggle against the British Mandate's restrictions on Jewish immigration.

On April 8, 1946, I received the following telegram from Italy:

"We are 1100 Jewish refugees. We sailed from Spezia for Palestine - our last hope. Police arrested us on board. We won't leave the ship! We demand permission to continue to Eretz-Israel. Be warned: we will sink with the ship if we are not allowed to continue to Palestine, because we cannot be more desperate."

The next day, the refugees went on a hunger strike. We asked them to stop because of the harsh conditions on board, and decided that we would take their place and fast until the ship was allowed to sail to Palestine. On the second day of the hunger strike, every Jew in Palestine over the age of 13 fasted. We suddenly felt that we were a single, united, people.

The third day of the hunger strike was Pesach Eve. Thousands of people carrying flowers came to Jerusalem to show their support. The chief rabbis, who joined our fast and presided over the unusual Seder, decided that everyone would eat a single piece of matza, no bigger than an olive. We put out cups of tea rather than wine for the hunger strikers.

We read from the Haggadah: *"Every generation must see itself as the one that left Egypt…the Lord saved not only our ancestors, but us, as well."* We repeat these words at Seder every year, but this time they took on a new meaning.

I will never forget my children joining me at the Jewish Agency for the Seder, which may have been their most important lesson in the suffering of the Jews, the love of Judaism, and the resilience of the Jewish people.

The day after the Seder, we were notified that the refugees had been allowed to enter Palestine. So, on the first day of Passover, the 101-hour fast ended.

DREAM FREEDOM, 2002

This is the story of how Jewish middle school students in Los Angeles became abolitionists – today in the 21st century:

It all began as a program to make the holiday of Passover more meaningful for the students at our school. The entire school, students and teachers, read Sonia Levitin's book *Dream Freedom* which chronicles the modern problem of slavery in Sudan, where Muslim gangs with army support take over Christian villages and sell men, women and children as slaves. Two weeks before Passover, the school convened to meet Francis Bok, a Sudanese slave who escaped to America. One student wrote: "*Before meeting Francis Bok, slavery seemed like*

a horrific nightmare, but I never imagined that the nightmare would stand right in front of me. To witness a slave was an enlightening experience, and I thank God every day that I am free. The whole concept of selling people like property and treating them like animals is the most horrendous and disturbing problem that faces our world today. I learned that 27,000,000 people are enslaved today. Now all my problems seem so miniscule. Today I am helping to free several in bondage."

It costs only $36 to free a slave, to buy their

freedom from the Sudanese captors. Many students made bracelets engraved with the name of a slave who had been recently captured. Others wrote a prayer for their Seder tables to remind us that we who were once slaves need to work for the freedom of others. In two weeks, the middle school students collected a whopping $14,700 - enough to free 411 slaves! As Jews, we know that we cannot remain silent while others have been abandoned into bondage.

Rabbi **Leah Kroll**, Milken Community High School of Stephen S. Wise Temple, Los Angeles

Four Children　אַרְבָּעָה בָּנִים

בָּרוּךְ הַמָּקוֹם, בָּרוּךְ הוּא.
בָּרוּךְ שֶׁנָּתַן תּוֹרָה לְעַמּוֹ יִשְׂרָאֵל,
בָּרוּךְ הוּא.

Blessed be God, Blessed be that One.
Blessed be the Giver of the Torah
to the people Israel,
Blessed be that One.

כְּנֶגֶד אַרְבָּעָה בָנִים דִּבְּרָה תוֹרָה:

The Torah alludes to Four Children:

אֶחָד חָכָם

One Wise or Thoughtful

וְאֶחָד רָשָׁע

One Wicked or Rebellious

וְאֶחָד תָּם

One Simple or Innocent

וְאֶחָד שֶׁאֵינוֹ יוֹדֵעַ לִשְׁאָל.

One Who Does Not Know How to Ask.

The midrash of the Four Children invites us to listen to each child's question and identify different character types.

Then the Rabbis turn the commandment of *v'heegadta* ("you shall tell") into a **mitzvah of dialogue** – with give and take on both sides. Successful dialogue means that each side, and especially the side anxious to "pass on the message," be keenly attentive to what the other is saying and feeling – to the particular personality of the child and his or her needs.

QUESTIONS OF THE FUTURE

In a future generation when/if [כִּי] your children ask:
"What do you mean by this Passover rite?" (Exodus 12:26-27).
The Rabbis read this verse as a "good news, bad news" joke:
"At that moment, bad news was brought to the Israelites:
that the Torah would be forgotten. Some say that good
news was brought to them: that they would have children
and children's children!" (Mechilta)

The good news arises if we read the Hebrew word כִּי as
"when your children ask you," and not as "if your children
ask you." There is an assurance of generations to come.
The bittersweet nature of questions has to do with
forgetting and the desire to know. Without forgetting, there
would be no questions.

Is this – the inevitability of forgetting – bad news? Or is it
good news, implying the constant rebirth of narratives,
responses to the questions of those in whom distance and
forgetting create desire? The issue is not decided, as so
many true questions are not decided.

Aviva Zornberg, *The Particulars of Rapture*

The Four Israeli Sons by Michel Kichka, 2004

TOO QUICK TO CATEGORIZE

It is tempting, and at times not altogether inappropriate,
to sort people into a few well-chosen "types." But I urge
a sense of the complexity of people on myself and on the
reader. William Carlos Willams, the American poet, once
talked of the "zeal" with which we "take to labels of all kinds."
"We crave certainty; we love to put a period at the end of
a sentence, and that is that. But take a look at people, a real
close look, and you'll find inconsistencies and contradictions
- and that's where a closer look is needed, not a category or
a definition that tells you, that reassures you: all right, you've
got it!"

Robert Coles, educator, *The Call of Service*

THE FOUR CHILDREN

WE are always proud, forever
speaking of the wise one, the wise child.
What about the bad one (recalling, of course,
Father Flanagan's "There's no such thing as a bad kid")?
If we have none of those, why are so many rabbis
making rounds in the Big Houses across our fair land?
Who are these ghosts in the minimum,
medium, and maximum prisons? Figments?
(We had our Uncle Simcha who hid out
with Grandpa for a few weeks. I think it was
Prohibition and he was mixed up with some,
shall we say, undesirable fellows.)
NOW comes the hard part, the special two -
"simple" and "unable-to-ask."
You may say "simple" means nice or "easygoing,"
the kid who likes everything, is happy, and
makes no demands. It's the one you refer to
now that he or she is grown up when you say,
"Joe (or Nancy) was an easy child." All right, then -
that's three out of four.
But that still leaves "the one who doesn't know how to ask."
I think the pictures in the Haggadah are wrong,
painting children so small.
They shift; they mislead. It doesn't mean:
"so young they can't formulate the words."
It means . . . We know what it means.
And if we just say it, with the pride of the first,
maybe this year more can come out of their hiding places.

Danny Siegel, poet and Tzedakah educator

The Wise Child   הֶחָכָם

חָכָם מַה הוּא אוֹמֵר:

Narrator:

What does the wise child say?

Otto Geismar, 1923

"מָה הָעֵדֹת
וְהַחֻקִים וְהַמִּשְׁפָּטִים,
אֲשֶׁר צִוָּה יי אֱלֹהֵינוּ אֶתְכֶם?"

Wise or Thoughtful Child:

"What are the testimonies,
the statutes, and the laws
which Adonai our God has
commanded you?" (Deuteronomy 6:20)

The midrash of the four
children provides the
script for a dialogue.
Let each character in
the dialogue be played
by a different Seder
participant.

Narrator:

**So, you teach the child all the
laws of Pesach, till the last one:**

וְאַף אַתָּה אֱמָר־לוֹ כְּהִלְכוֹת הַפֶּסַח:

The cast is as follows:
Narrator / Each of the
four children / Four
parents who answer.

First Parent:

"We do not conclude the eating
at the Pesach Seder with the
afikoman."
(Last Mishna in Pesachim, Chapter 10)

"אֵין מַפְטִירִין אַחַר הַפֶּסַח אֲפִיקוֹמָן."

Look at the parent or
child to whom you are
speaking. Try to add
facial expressions, hand
gestures and tone of
voice to portray your
character.

NOTE about the Parents' Answer:
Actually today we do conclude the Seder with the
afikoman, the matza we hid. But then, in the days of
the Mishna, "afikoman" meant in Greek the custom
of making after-dinner celebrations. The Rabbis
prohibited that kind of "afikoman."
This is, as you see, a sophisticated answer, fitting a
wise child.

THE WISE CHILD'S *REAL* QUESTION

> The truly wise question the wisdom of others – because they question their own wisdom as well; the foolish – because it is different from their own.
>
> Rabbi **Leopold Stein**, *Journey into the Self*, Germany, 19th C.

"What are the statutes and decrees and laws which Adonai our God commanded you?" (Deuteronomy 6:20) The wise son's question is *a real question*. On one level, it asks for information, it questions the meanings of a detailed list of laws. What makes [the wise child's question] a *real question*, however, is not its encyclopaedist categories of laws, but precisely the awkward word, *etchem* – "commanded *you*." This is awkward because it seems akin to the wicked son's terminology -"What is this ritual *to you*?" The wise son, too, asks a disturbing question, in which he opens up a distance between his father and himself.

The father and his generation were there; he was not. This distinction between generations is always true.

The wise son, however, articulates his question with exquisite care: ... "which *our* God commanded *you*." As Rashi says, "He does not exclude himself by the word, "*you*," because he says, "*our* God." "Our God" is the expression of relationship, of responsibility for the Other. He is both inside and outside, committed to God and His commandments, but not directly present at the original site of commandment.

Aviva Zornberg, *The Particulars of Rapture*

The Four Daughters by Michel Kichka, 2006

The Wicked Child הָרָשָׁע

רָשָׁע מַה הוּא אוֹמֵר:

Narrator:
Narrator:

What does the wicked child say?

"מָה הָעֲבדָה הַזֹּאת לָכֶם?"

Wicked or Alienated Child:

"Whatever does this service mean to you?" (Exodus 12:26)

'לָכֶם' - וְלֹא לוֹ.
וּלְפִי שֶׁהוֹצִיא אֶת עַצְמוֹ מִן הַכְּלָל - כָּפַר בָּעִקָּר.
וְאַף אַתָּה הַקְהֵה אֶת שִׁנָּיו וֶאֱמָר לוֹ:

Narrator:

This child emphasizes "you" and not him or herself! Since the child excludes him or herself from the community and rejects a major principle of faith, you should set his or her teeth on edge and say:

"בַּעֲבוּר זֶה עָשָׂה יי לִי בְּצֵאתִי מִמִּצְרָיִם."

Second Parent:

"It is because of this, that Adonai did for me when I went free from Egypt." (Exodus 13:8)

'לִי' - וְלֹא לוֹ.
אִלּוּ הָיָה שָׁם, לֹא הָיָה נִגְאָל.

Narrator:

"Me" and not that one over there! Had that one been there, s/he would not have been redeemed.

The Four Marx Brothers
by Richard Codor, 1981

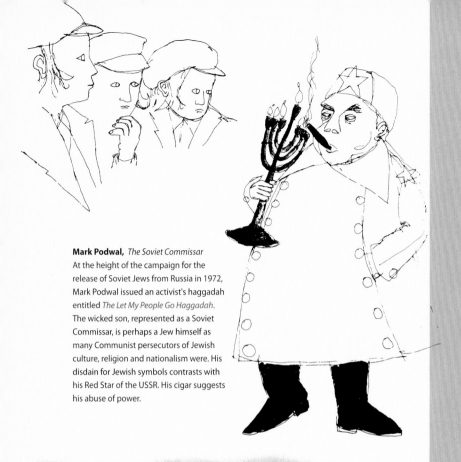

Mark Podwal, *The Soviet Commissar*
At the height of the campaign for the
release of Soviet Jews from Russia in 1972,
Mark Podwal issued an activist's haggadah
entitled *The Let My People Go Haggadah.*
The wicked son, represented as a Soviet
Commissar, is perhaps a Jew himself as
many Communist persecutors of Jewish
culture, religion and nationalism were. His
disdain for Jewish symbols contrasts with
his Red Star of the USSR. His cigar suggests
his abuse of power.

ASKING THE UNASKABLE QUESTION

*"Thinking again?" the Duchess asked, with another dig of her sharp
little chin. "I have a right to think," said Alice sharply, for she was
beginning to feel a little worried. "Just about as much right," said the
Duchess, "as pigs have to fly."*
Lewis Carroll*, Alice in Wonderland*

In many social worlds asking certain questions would be considered
traitorous, bait for the enemy. Such questions no one is permitted to
ask. In my first year at Yeshiva, a fellow student asked such a question.
He wanted to know whether the whole received tradition, written
and oral, had actually been given at Sinai. The rabbi's answer was
"Well, where do you think you are, young man? *The Reform rabbinical
seminary?"* Like the "wicked son" at the Passover Seder, the questioner
was responded to in anger and disdain.
Certain questions demonstrate that the questioner is marginal to
the community. He would have never made it out of Egypt. They
mark one as an outsider precisely because insiders don't ask this
sort of question. And such threatening questions are not unique to
traditional environments. They can be asked in the boardroom, in the
university classroom, and in the halls of state. One infraction might be
ignored, but repeated commitment to asking an inappropriate why is
an invitation to social marginalization and potentially to eviction from
the community.
Rabbi **Steve Greenberg**, *Wrestling with God and Men*

THE ARROGANT CHILD

This child is not asking a question
like the others but making
a statement as it says in the Torah:
"When your children come to tell
you: What is this service to you?"
(Exodus 12:26) The tone is arrogant
and the intent is to ridicule the
ceremony. Instead of asking "why,"
the child asks sarcastically:
What is this service for? This
tiresome, bothersome Haggadah
ruins the festive atmosphere and
postpones the meal!
Rabbi **Shimon Chavillo**, Italy, 17th C

WHO ARE YOU CALLING "WICKED"?

The very term "*rasha*"– is difficult to translate: "wicked" and "evil" are very
harsh, uncompromising terms for a child. "Rebellious," "mischievous,"
"recalcitrant," "chutzpadik," "impolite," "*vilde khaya,*" "naughty," "troublesome,"
"difficult," "problematic" or "alienated" are also possible.
What would you suggest? What different kinds of children are portrayed
by the various translations? Do you think the harsh parent described in the
Haggadah would behave differently had the label been different?

The Simple Child   הַתָּם

Narrator:

What does the simple child ask?

תָּם מַה הוּא אוֹמֵר:

Simple or Naïve Child:

"What is this?" (Exodus 13:14)

"מַה זֹּאת?"

Narrator:

And you say to that child:

וְאָמַרְתָּ אֵלָיו:

Third Parent:

[Let me tell you an awesome tale.]

**"With a mighty hand Adonai
brought us out of Egypt,
out of the house of bondage."**

(Exodus 13:14)

"בְּחֹזֶק יָד הוֹצִיאָנוּ יי מִמִּצְרַיִם, מִבֵּית עֲבָדִים."

LOOSE CONNECTIONS

The simple child who is clueless about Judaism may have a "loose connection." The Jerusalem theater-educator Joyce Klein once directed a musical play about Israeli teenagers who have an undefined sense of Jewish identity, an amorphous question with no firm answer. She was inspired by a house call by her Israeli electrician who was summoned to fix her flickering light fixture. While standing on her dining room table examining the short circuit and the frayed wires, he pronounced his diagnosis: "You have a problem: Loose connections!" Then he began to philosophize: "Actually all of us Jews share that problem of loose connections, poor communication among people and a disrupted flow of energy between our past and our future."

Joyce turned that insight into a performance in which a teenager is asked: "What connects you to the Jewish people?"

"Perhaps holidays? Holocaust? Israel? Family? Ethics?"

"I don't know," shrugged the teenager.

Can you answer that simple yet profound question? To what do you connect?

BEWARE OF SOPHISTICATION

One must keep one's distance from people who are wise in their own eyes and think they know great wisdoms of how to serve God. For all these are great foolishness and are not needed in order to worship the Creator. For the main thing is purely naivete, simplicity, and faith in God…even though simple ones must be sure not to act like fools. One can achieve great happiness through naivete, faith and complete simplicity.

Rebbe **Nahman of Bratzlav**, Ukraine, 19th C.

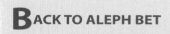

Rony Oren, *The Animated Haggadah*, 1985

BACK TO ALEPH BET

When a child learns the shapes of the Hebrew letters for the first time, there is a fresh revelation in Heaven concerning these letters. And this fresh revelation, occurring in Heaven through the child's learning of the letters, is drawn downwards, so the child draws down upon himself a fresh revelation as to the meaning of the shapes of the letters.

This is not the case with adults, who are too familiar with the shapes of the letters. When we look at them we are not learning anything new, so we do not have God teaching us anything directly.

When the Talmud describes "children" who explain the mystical meanings in the shapes of the letters, it is actually referring to holy people who can still approach the text as children. They bring out new revelations even in the shape of the letters, and not just in the meaning of the text. They can still learn like children, and so are able to look at the *alef* and *beth* and *gimmel* and ask, "Why is the leg of the *gimmel* stretched out toward the *dalet*?"

Rabbi **Kalonymus Kalman** of Pieasezna, the Hasidic Rebbe of the Warsaw Ghetto

LOVE QUESTIONS WITHOUT ANSWERS LIKE LOCKED DOORS

Be patient towards all that is unsolved in your heart and try to love the questions themselves like locked rooms and like books written in a foreign language. Do not now look for the answers. They cannot now be given to you because you could not live them. It is a question of experiencing everything. At present you need to *live* the questions now. Perhaps you will gradually, without even noticing it, find yourself experiencing the answer, some distant day.

Maria Rainer Rilke, *Letters to a Young Poet*, Austria, 1922

The Child Who Does Not Know How to Ask

שֶׁאֵינוֹ יוֹדֵעַ לִשְׁאֹל

Narrator:

וְשֶׁאֵינוֹ יוֹדֵעַ לִשְׁאֹל

As for the child who does not know how to ask,

אַתְּ פְּתַח לוֹ,

you should prompt the child.

שֶׁנֶּאֱמַר: "וְהִגַּדְתָּ לְבִנְךָ בַּיוֹם הַהוּא לֵאמֹר,

The Torah says: "You shall tell your child on that day."

[Don't wait for the child to take the initiative. Start the story, your story, and hopefully this silent child will listen, absorb and identify with you].

Fourth Parent:

בַּעֲבוּר זֶה עָשָׂה יְיָ לִי בְּצֵאתִי מִמִּצְרָיִם.״

"It is because of this, that Adonai did for me when I went free from Egypt."
(Exodus 13:8)

WHERE DID YOU GO? OUT. WHAT DID YOU DO? NOTHING

The title of Robert Paul Smith's classic book *Where Did You Go? Out. What Did You Do? Nothing* captures the withdrawal and boredom that adult questions so frequently evoke in children. Both on the street and in the classroom, adults assume that it is their right to engage children in questions: *How are your parents? What grade are you in now? What caused the destruction of the Second Temple? Who was the first Jew?* and the ubiquitous, *What did you do on your summer vacation?* Parents who speak this way regularly find that their children respond as if to an interrogation and consequently tell as little as possible. Children are placed on the defensive. Tension is raised which stands in the way of thinking and communication.

The child who does not want to communicate is perhaps the Fourth Child. This child may not ask because the child wants to avoid painful conversations with the parent. If that child neither asks nor answers but sits silently as the parents lecture, then he or she avoids greater embarrassment and tiresome interrogation. Perhaps that child has been silenced by those in authority, probing and testing for faults. Questions are often threats to authority or ways to assert authority. They play on a field of power relations between parent and child, ruler and subject. That is why they often lead not to dialogue or exploration of knowledge but to rhetorical putdowns and defensive shutting down of information exchanges. The fourth child sidesteps these battles.

Based on **Joseph Lukinsky** and **Lifsa Schachter**

A THUNDEROUS SILENCE

Open up the children who have not learned to ask. Lead them on the path to becoming a questioning personality, one who inquires about the way of the world. Open them up so they can formulate their own questions. For without questions your ready-made answers remain inert and there is no common ground between you. The silence of the child can be thunderous. The silence of the one who does not know how to ask may be the result of not having found an appropriate address to express queries. Deeply meaningful silences can issue forth secrets that resound throughout the whole world. Model for the child; show them adults who know how to ask of themselves questions. As the Rabbis said: "If the child and the spouse are unable to ask, let the parents ask themselves" (T.B. Pesachim 115a). Then there is a good chance that the child will learn to ask as well.

Yariv Ben Aharon, kibbutz author and educator

The Four Books by David Wander, 1988

IN PRAISE OF THE UNQUESTIONING PERSONALITY

No! I don't agree with the advice of the Haggadah here. The Haggadah says open the child up to critical thinking. In my judgment the parent should be silent. Just kiss this child on the forehead for faithfully maintaining loyalty to those sanctified traditions. The love of knowledge, the philosophical quest is important, but the supreme wisdom is to accept the treasures of the past without second guessing, without evaluating their historical origins and their pragmatic utility. It is essential to cherish and preserve that kind of respectful wisdom and not to tarnish it with unnecessary talk.

Zeev Jabotinsky, founder of the Revisionist Zionist Movement (later the Likud)

Four Generations

FOUR GENERATIONS IN ISRAEL

While the Haggadah urges us to create dialogue and continuity from parent to child, the ideological changes in Jewish life over the last 100 years in Israel have often involved revolting against one's parents' ideals in belief, in dress and even in body image. Each child is identified not by what they ask but what they read. The so-called wise child, the stereotype of the pre-Zionist ultra Orthodox, is a woman not concerned with a slim figure or stylish eyeglasses. Her daily reading is Psalms. The rebellious child is the Zionist intellectual reading the modern novelist Amos Oz. The simple child is of the third generation, which lacks knowledge and ideology. Her reading matter is a newspaper that says in the words of the Haggadah – "*Ma Zot* - What is this?" Last and still least is the little girl under the table who does not know how to read. She holds her potty training book upside down. Its name – *Pot of Pots* - is a pun on the Biblical love songs read on Pesach – *Song of Songs*.

Illustration by **Michel Kichka**

FOUR GENERATIONS IN NORTH AMERICA

One might identify four generations – since the great emigration of Eastern European Jews to the New World began in the 1880s. The first generation of immigrants is the WISE child who knows and feels comfortable with Jewish tradition. The second generation is the REBEL who in the name of progress and Westernization rejects their parents' Judaism after having imbibed it at home. The third generation is assimilated. There is little knowledge and little resentment, but there is still SIMPLE curiosity about the customs of their grandparents.

Finally, a fourth generation, without knowledge or even mild acquaintance, is born. They DO NOT KNOW HOW TO ASK. They might be called "orphans in history" lacking any of the resources of Jewish wisdom against which to struggle and from which to draw personal meaning.

As a child, growing up on Manhattan's East Side, I lived among Jewish WASPs. My father had changed his name from "Cohen" to "Cowan" when he was 21. So I was brought up to think of myself as a "Cowan" – the Welsh word for stonecutter, not a "Cohen" – a member of the Jewish priesthood. My family celebrated Christmas and always gathered for an Easter dinner of ham and sweet potatoes. Though they never converted to Christianity my parents sent me to an Episcopalian prep school with a mandatory chapel service. In those years, I barely knew what a Passover Seder was. I didn't know anyone who practiced "archaic" customs such as keeping kosher or lighting candles Friday night. When I fell in love and married Rachel, a New England Protestant whose ancestors came here in the 17th century, it didn't matter in the least that we were formally an interfaith marriage. I had become an orphan without a history.

Paul Cowan, *An Orphan in History*, courtesy of his wife, Rabbi Rachel Cowan, Institute for Jewish Spirituality.

Four Biblical Daughters

Rabbi **Einat Ramon**, Schechter Rabbinical Seminary, Israel

The Torah speaks of Four Daughters: one possessing wisdom of the heart, one rebellious, one naïve and one who cannot ask questions.

MIRIAM, the daughter possessing wisdom of the heart, what does she say?
According to the Midrash, young Miriam confronted her father Amram who had vowed to refrain from procreation because of Pharaoh's decree to destroy all male newborns (Talmud Bavli, Sotah 12).
"Father, your decree is harsher than Pharoah's. He will destroy all the males, but you will destroy all the females and males. The decree of the wicked Pharoah may or may not be fulfilled, but your decree will for sure be realized." Miriam's father heeded his daughter. SO we will follow in her steps with drums and dancing, spreading her prophecy among the nations.

TAMAR, the rebellious daughter, what does she say?
Tamar was accused of adultery. She had been married to two of Judah's sons who died without producing offspring, so Judah was obligated to give her his third son in marriage so she could give life to her heirless husbands. But Judah refused, so Tamar dressed as a prostitute, Judah solicited her and without realizing it made his daughter-in-law pregnant, thus guaranteeing the tribe's survival. However Judah sought to have Tamar burned as a prostitute.
"Father-in-law," said Tamar, "recognize" the tyranny of man's rule over women and the hypocrisy of double standards. She rebelled against authority and Judah admitted: "*She is more righteous than I.*" SO we can enjoy no freedom until we have challenged unjust ways (Genesis 38:26).

RUTH, the simple and pure daughter, what does she say?
"Naomi, my mother-in-law: *Wherever you go, I shall go, and wherever you rest your head, there I will rest mine. Your people are mine, and your God my God*" (Ruth 1:16).
SO we must demonstrate simple and ingenuous loyalty.

THE BEAUTIFUL CAPTIVE, the daughter who cannot ask, who will speak for her?
The Torah permits a soldier conquering an enemy to take a woman captive as a wife, but only after she has been allowed to mourn the loss of her mother and father. Only her silent weeping is heard, as it is says, "*and she wept for her father and mother*" (Deuteronomy 21:13).
SO we will be her mouthpiece and she will be our judge. So we will return her to her mother's house and we will "*proclaim liberty in the land for all its [enslaved] inhabitants*" (Leviticus 25:10). The silent weeping that erupts from this dark reality is a call to action for the cause of freedom and liberty of every man and woman born in the image of God.

STARTER CONVERSATIONS: THE PARENTS' FOUR QUESTIONS

The Haggadah suggests various types of children that ask questions of their parents. Tonight let us reverse the process and ask our children about **how they feel and think**.
To get started, imagine you have just overheard a snippet of a parent-child exchange.
Ask a pair of volunteers to read responsively one exchange. Now open the forum to anyone who wishes to step in and speak to or in the name of the child or the parent.

> Children begin by loving their parents, after a time they judge them, rarely, if ever, do they forgive them.
>
> **Oscar Wilde**, 1890

DEAR CURIOUS CHILD

Parent: You are always asking such great questions. You are so curious and eager to learn about Judaism and about your family history. But I have a question or two for you. First, what or who turned you on to learning? Second, is it a secret burden to be the family's "good kid"?

Wise child: First, Grandma was my inspiration to learn something new every moment. She was so patient – listening to me and looking things up. Together we wondered about the mysteries of the world.
Second, I guess I can reveal to you that it is not always easy to be the studious "goody goody." Sometimes I just want to be ordinary. I try to sidestep unwanted praise – being spoken about in proud superlatives is embarrassing. I do not want to be a *nakhas*-producing machine. But I do appreciate your quiet pride in my achievements.

DEAR ANGRY CHILD

Parent: Okay, maybe I have gone overboard with my "tough love." Perhaps I have followed the Haggadah's parents in excluding their "wicked" child. But I know how **hurt** parents feel because you too have spoken to me at times with such hutzpah, putting down "your whole Seder thing." But I do not know how you feel beneath the skeptical façade. Talk to me – I promise not to be judgmental. After all, I too was a rebel against my parents and their Judaism.

Angry child: Your Judaism is fine for you, but not for me! You still do not hear me: I do not want to be here, at this table. This you call the "Holiday of Freedom"? Huh? Freedom for whom? Not for me! I am here because you make me, and to tell you the truth many of the adults at this table right now feel the same way! This is your Seder, not mine!

DEAR SWEET CHILD

Parent: I must tell you what a joy (and a relief) it is to have a child as easy as you. I am always happy to listen to your questions. Still sometimes I worry: will you ever become more critical and independent minded like your older siblings?

Simple child: I love you too, but it is not always so simple to be your "simple" child. In many Jewish families kids like me are considered a disappointment. But not all of us can be "the best and the brightest." I cannot read the Hebrew and probably never will. So please do us both a favor and stop asking me to read out loud at every Seder. I see what my siblings have achieved, but I have my own way of doing things. Please do not compare us, neither positively nor negatively.

DEAR QUIET CHILD

Parent: Talking comes so easily to me that I don't always understand what is hidden in your head and in your heart. How do I get through to you?

The child who does not know how to ask: If I were suddenly to open my mouth I would tell you: Remember, still waters run deep. At this table verbal dueling dominates too often. I would ask you to learn my language in which I am quite articulate. I am comfortable in the physical language of art and dance... Listen to me speaking the language of movement, of music, or color. Can you learn the eloquence of silence? You may discover that I too am a "wise" child whose deepest insights can never be reduced to words.

52

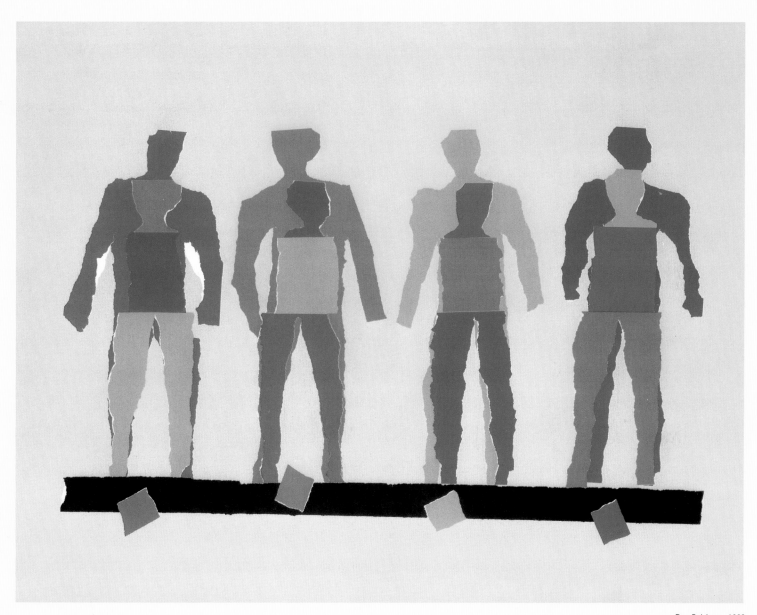

Dan Reisinger, 1982

"We each have all the four children within us"

Rabbi **Israel Salanter**, founder of the Musar Movement, Lithuania, 19th C.

וְהִגַּדְתָּ לְבִנְךָ

YOU SHALL TELL YOUR CHILD

"וְהִגַּדְתָּ לְבִנְךָ בַּיּוֹם הַהוּא לֵאמֹר:
'בַּעֲבוּר זֶה עָשָׂה יי לִי בְּצֵאתִי מִמִּצְרָיִם'".

"You shall tell your child *on that day*: 'It is *because of this*, that Adonai did for me, when I went free from Egypt.'" (Exodus 13:8)

"וְהִגַּדְתָּ לְבִנְךָ" – יָכוֹל מֵרֹאשׁ חֹדֶשׁ?
תַּלְמוּד לוֹמַר "בַּיּוֹם הַהוּא".
אִי "בַּיּוֹם הַהוּא", יָכוֹל מִבְּעוֹד יוֹם?
תַּלְמוּד לוֹמַר "בַּעֲבוּר זֶה" –
"בַּעֲבוּר זֶה" לֹא אָמַרְתִּי, אֶלָּא בְּשָׁעָה
שֶׁיֵּשׁ מַצָּה וּמָרוֹר מֻנָּחִים לְפָנֶיךָ.

Could this verse mean that you should begin to tell the story at the beginning of the month of Nisan? No, for the verse explicitly states "on that day" (of the Exodus).

Could that mean that we start when it is still daytime? No, for the verse explicitly states: "because of this."

"*This*" must refer to a time when matza and maror are laid before you [only on Seder night].

When is the best time for telling the Exodus story? The answer is implicit in the verse used to answer the fourth child. The best time is Passover night itself, for the parent can use edible and visual aids to tell the story.

A great storyteller uses an animated style and appeals to all of the child's senses. This is how the Haggadah wants the Exodus story to be told.

| **MAGGID** | Ma Nishtana | Avadim Slaves | Five Rabbis | **Four Children** | Idolatry | Arami Symposium | Ten Plagues | Dayenu | Pesach | Dor vaDor | Hallelujah |

54

A LEGACY OF LUGGAGE

Judaism imposes a vital task on the parents: to tell the children their people's story. What the child does with this past, no parent can decree. **Parents provide their children with luggage.** Whether the child will open up the suitcases and use their contents is beyond the reach of parents. They have no right to enter the child's future. Parents must aim at instilling memories that haunt the child an entire lifetime; their bequest is a weight of generations, an awareness that one's biography began with Abraham and Sarah.

Rabbi **David Hartman**, Jerusalem philosopher

Grandfather and grandson prepare for their Exodus from their home in Tiblisi, Georgia, Former Soviet Union, to Israel. Over 2,000,000 Jews from the Former Soviet Union have made this journey since 1990.

Photographer: **Aliza Orbach**, 1991

YEHUDA AMICHAI

My father was a god and did not know it. He gave me
The Ten Commandments neither in thunder nor in fury; neither in fire nor in cloud
But rather in gentleness and love. And he added caresses and kind words
And he added "I beg you," and "please."
And he sang "keep" and "remember" the Shabbat
In a single melody and he pleaded and
cried quietly between one utterance and the next,
"Do not take the name of God in vain," do not take it, not in vain,
I beg you, "do not bear false witness against your neighbor."
And he hugged me tightly and whispered in my ear
"Do not steal. Do not commit adultery. Do not murder."
And he put the palms of his open hands
On my head with the Yom Kippur blessing.
"Honor, love, in order that your days might be long
On the earth." And my father's voice was white like the hair on his head.
Later on he turned his face to me one last time
Like on the day when he died in my arms and said,
I want to add Two to the Ten Commandments:
The eleventh commandment – "Thou shall not change."
And the twelfth commandment – "Thou must surely change."
So said my father and then he turned from me and walked off
Disappearing into his strange distances.

COMMUNICATION ACROSS
THE GENERATION GAP

Tomorrow, when your child asks you. (Exodus 13:14)

Tomorrow's generation is always so unpredictably different than today's. The Torah spoke to immigrants who passed in a mere three generations from slavery in Egypt, to wandering in the desert, and then became farmers and shepherds in the Promised Land. God commanded parents to tell their children stories of what it was like back in the old country, "back when I was a child." But it would also be good for parents to ask their children what is unique about the "tomorrow" generation.

What are the generational gaps between those at the table? How has childrearing changed? Women's roles? Political and economic experience? Technology? Jewish life? What can we learn from and about one another from these gaps?

מתחלה עובדי עבודה זרה

FROM SERVING IDOLS TO SPIRITUAL LIBERATION

מִתְּחִלָּה עוֹבְדֵי עֲבוֹדָה זָרָה הָיוּ אֲבוֹתֵינוּ,

וְעַכְשָׁיו קֵרְבָנוּ הַמָּקוֹם לַעֲבֹדָתוֹ, שֶׁנֶּאֱמַר:

"וַיֹּאמֶר יְהוֹשֻׁעַ אֶל כָּל הָעָם:

כֹּה אָמַר יי אֱלֹהֵי יִשְׂרָאֵל –

בְּעֵבֶר הַנָּהָר יָשְׁבוּ אֲבוֹתֵיכֶם מֵעוֹלָם

– תֶּרַח אֲבִי אַבְרָהָם וַאֲבִי נָחוֹר –

וַיַּעַבְדוּ אֱלֹהִים אֲחֵרִים.

וָאֶקַּח אֶת אֲבִיכֶם, אֶת אַבְרָהָם,

מֵעֵבֶר הַנָּהָר

וָאוֹלֵךְ אוֹתוֹ בְּכָל אֶרֶץ כְּנָעַן;

וָאַרְבֶּה אֶת זַרְעוֹ וָאֶתֵּן לוֹ אֶת יִצְחָק.

וָאֶתֵּן לְיִצְחָק אֶת יַעֲקֹב וְאֶת עֵשָׂו.

וָאֶתֵּן לְעֵשָׂו אֶת הַר שֵׂעִיר לָרֶשֶׁת אֹתוֹ,

וְיַעֲקֹב וּבָנָיו יָרְדוּ מִצְרָיִם."

In the beginning our ancestors were idol worshippers.
But now God has brought us near to serve Adonai.

The leader:

Joshua said to the people: "Thus said Adonai, the God of Israel: Long ago, your ancestors, including Terah, father of Abraham and Nahor, lived beyond the Euphrates and worshipped other gods. But I took your father Abraham from beyond the Euphrates and led him through the whole land of Canaan and multiplied his offspring. I gave him Isaac, and to Isaac I gave Jacob and Esau... Then Jacob and his children went down to Egypt."
"Then I sent Moses and Aaron, and brought plagues on Egypt after which I freed you – I freed your ancestors – from Egypt. Now, therefore, serve Adonai with undivided loyalty... Or, if you are loath to serve Adonai, choose this day other gods to serve. But I and my family will serve Adonai."

All:

In reply, the people declared, "Far be it from us to forsake Adonai and serve other gods!
For it was Adonai our God who brought us and our ancestors up from the land of Egypt, the house of bondage, and who performed these miracles before our very eyes..."
Now we too will serve Adonai, for Adonai is our God" (Joshua 24: 1-18).

The Haggadah offers two versions of the Exodus story. The Talmudic Rabbi, Shmuel, emphasized political enslavement ("We were slaves in Egypt"). Now we turn to his colleague, Rav, who tells a story of spiritual servitude.

Rav's version is drawn from Joshua's farewell speech to the nation of Israel. Joshua feared that the new generation in Israel might assimilate into the local pagan cultures. So he told them the story of Abraham's liberation from idolatry. That personal struggle for freedom and enlightenment can be relevant to each of us.

I AM FREE OF IDOLS

I had a very difficult childhood. I was stoned. I was called a Christ killer. And yet as a Jew I am never subdued or undone.
As a Jew I am free. I feel enormously grateful to be a Jew. I feel free, facing the whole wide world in my Jewishness. I may not be able to say what God is, who God is, how God is; I can make no definitive statement, no attributive statement about the Source of Being.

But I can say what the Source is not. I'm free of idols, I'm not going to fall for false gods, false ideas. You can see through such a device, you can know an idol instantly, because you have been taught Torah. You know how to make a distinction between reality and illusion, between the actual and the fraudulent. Judaism is a training toward intellectual freedom and expansiveness and insight. That is how Jewishness, and also the spiritual force of restored Jerusalem and Israel, nourish and support and enliven me. They have helped me come through.

Cynthia Ozick, American novelist

At the Seder the Jews of Djerba, Tunisia, traditionally recount the story of young Abraham rebelling against his father and breaking the idols.

JEWISH BY CHOICE

We should ask ourselves what to do with our historic inheritance. In every generation, Jews have had to make a decision to remain Jewish. The Jewish people have survived for thousands of years because millions of Jews, over dozens of generations, have made personal decisions to uphold their identity.
The Torah, the *mitzvot*, the languages spoken, the collective memory, the ways of life, the creative works – all these were sustained first and foremost by the decision that every Jew made privately: to stay a Jew and not to leave.

Identity has meaning only when it can be abandoned; only when a person is allowed to leave; only when each individual makes the decision, freely, to keep his or her identity and not to change it.

Amos Oz, Israeli novelist

FREEDOM BEGINS WITH IMAGINATION

I think the first thing I smelled in literature was freedom. You could contemplate other realities freely. When you're with a book nobody butts in... So I think that in the beginning, I came to literature because it fed the need for a more capacious environment. As Saul Bellow says, "Look at me, going everywhere!" You didn't have to stay on Leslie Street in Newark. You didn't have to stay in your bedroom at home; you could be anywhere. You could go wherever you wanted and you could be whatever you wanted to be. And that's pretty wonderfully heady.

Philip Roth, American novelist

A FRIGHTENED PERSON CANNOT BE FREE

Contemporary man is an unfree being because he is insecure. Man is a social animal and cares about public opinion. Modern man does all he can in order to win favor in the eyes of the public. Even those who are legally free men, who are not slaves, are in bondage to nature, to society, to restrictive phobias, superstitions, and prejudices.

There is only one way for man to free himself from all his restrictions, from all his fears, from all his phobias. Surrender to God frees man from his serfdom to his fellow man. Modern man is not free – a frightened person cannot be free. Terror and fear mean captivity for man.

Rabbi **Joseph B. Soloveitchik**, *Festival of Freedom*

WHY HAVE YOU CHANGED THE HOLY WAYS OF YOUR FATHER?

Once a young Hassidic rebbe inherited the leadership of his father's hassidim. He immediately made many changes and innovations in the group's practice. The elders hastened to send a delegation of dignitaries to the young rabbi, to talk some sense into him. "Why have you changed the holy ways of your father?"

"On the contrary – I am following directly in my father's path: just as he, upon inheriting the leadership, made many changes from his father's path, so have I!"

There is a delicate balance between continuity and innovation between generations. On one hand, we want to conserve our parents' memory and traditions, their values and stories. On the other, we have over the years made many changes from their way of life – be it by open revolt or in gentle steps.

What have I changed, and what have I conserved, from my parent's path?

So show me a person who is not a slave!
One is addicted to passions, another to
money, a third to honor and all of them to fear.

Seneca, Stoic philosopher and political leader, Rome, 1st C.

▮ BREAK, THEREFORE I AM A JEW

Before I even knew how to read, I could already recite by heart the story of Avraham shattering the idols. The story was a great hit at my kindergarten. Many times, we put on the story of the great idol "boutique" of father Terah with the stupid people who came to buy idols from the brave and "wise son" Avraham who made fun of everybody, shattered the idols and escaped to the forest where he found the true God. The role of Avraham was, of course, my favorite. Why? Not only because of the opportunity to laugh at the stupid grown ups but in the main, because of the license to break, shatter and hit in the middle of this rather prim and proper kindergarten. Avraham is not just "a good Jewish boy" who is simply following the path laid out for him by God.

Each of us loves our rebellious ancestor differently and re-imagines him in our own fashion: The monotheists among us see in our Avram the inventor of monotheism. The rebels among us see in him the father of all young rebels and iconoclasts. The revolutionaries among us see in him the young man who first conceived the idea of building a new world. The yeshiva boys among us see in him someone who left the vanities of this world for a life of learning Torah in the legendary Beit Midrash of Shem and Ever. And the *halutzim* [Zionist pioneers] among us see in him the first young Zionist who left his parents' home, a promising career and a homeland and went to redeem the Promised Land.

I break, therefore, I am a Jew. I leave my homeland and my parents' home, therefore I am a rooted Jew.

Today I am no longer young, but I don't give up on my obligation to create from within the tradition, and my right to rebel against it from its depths. There is a rich creative life after the death of my childhood God. There is no more complete God than a broken God. It is a great pleasure "to renew our days of old" and to return to our bookshelves filled with broken tablets and shattered idols. It is a great pleasure to make puzzles from all these pieces of ourselves, who have been created – thank God – in the broken image of God.

Ari Elon, Israeli educator and midrash writer

בָּרוּךְ שׁוֹמֵר הַבְטָחָתוֹ לְיִשְׂרָאֵל

K E E P I N G   T H E   P R O M I S E

בָּרוּךְ שׁוֹמֵר הַבְטָחָתוֹ

לְיִשְׂרָאֵל, בָּרוּךְ הוּא.

שֶׁהַקָּדוֹשׁ בָּרוּךְ הוּא חִשַּׁב אֶת הַקֵּץ,

לַעֲשׂוֹת כְּמָה שֶׁאָמַר לְאַבְרָהָם אָבִינוּ

בִּבְרִית בֵּין הַבְּתָרִים, שֶׁנֶּאֱמַר:

"וַיֹּאמֶר לְאַבְרָם: יָדֹעַ תֵּדַע

כִּי גֵר יִהְיֶה זַרְעֲךָ

בְּאֶרֶץ לֹא לָהֶם.

וַעֲבָדוּם, וְעִנּוּ אֹתָם - אַרְבַּע מֵאוֹת שָׁנָה.

וְגַם אֶת הַגּוֹי, אֲשֶׁר יַעֲבֹדוּ, דָּן אָנֹכִי.

וְאַחֲרֵי כֵן יֵצְאוּ בִּרְכֻשׁ גָּדוֹל."

Blessed is the One who keeps the Promise to Israel. The Holy One calculated the end of our exile and acted just as promised to Abraham our Father at the Covenant between the Pieces: "God said to Abram: You should know that your seed will be strangers in a land not their own. The people (of that land) will enslave and afflict them for four hundred years. But that nation, whom they serve, I will judge. Afterwards (your seed) will go out with great wealth."

(Genesis 15: 13-14)

After recalling Abraham's spiritual journey to God (p. 56) and his ascent to Eretz Yisrael, the Haggadah will recount the descent of his great grandchildren to Egyptian slavery ("The Wandering Aramean," p. 64). But first the Haggadah reassures us, as God did to Abraham, that there is a Divine pledge to maintain Jewish continuity whatever the ups and downs of history.

Wherever a Jew is persecuted – that means you

A Jew, in my vocabulary, is someone who regards himself as a Jew, or someone who is forced to be a Jew. A Jew is someone who acknowledges his Jewishness. If he acknowledges it publicly, he is a Jew by choice. If he acknowledges it only to his inner self, he is a Jew by the force of his destiny. If he does not acknowledge any connection with the Jewish people either in public or in his tormented inner being he is not a Jew, even if religious law defines him as such because his mother is Jewish. A Jew, in my unhalakhic opinion, is someone who chooses to share the fate of other Jews, or who is condemned to do so. Moreover: to be a Jew almost always means to relate mentally to the Jewish past, whether the relation is one of pride or gloom or both together, whether it consists of shame or rebellion or pride or nostalgia.

Moreover: to be a Jew almost always means to relate to the Jewish present, whether the relation is one of fear or confidence, pride in the achievement of Jews or shame for their actions, an urge to turn them away from their path or a psychological need to stick to their path.

And finally: to be a Jew means to feel that wherever a Jew is persecuted for being a Jew – that means you.

Amos Oz, Israeli novelist

Next Year...

I remember my grandfather's house, when we lived in Turkey. We would celebrate a big, splendid Passover. When grandfather read *"Blessed is the One who keeps the promise..."* in the Haggadah, he would get up and open the window. He would stick out his head and look left and right, as if he were seeing the view for the first time. Afterwards, he would pull his head back in, sigh, and say to the family: "Another year in exile..."

Yaakov Shneor, Kibbutz Be'erot Yitzhak

Abraham's Promise: Children like the Stars in the Sky
(Genesis 15:5)
by Ephraim Moses Lilien

The Generation of the Exodus and our Generation

Experience of the world must always be brought to the reading of Torah. This century's history makes it far more difficult to read the opening chapters of Exodus with composure... The parallels between ancient Israelites and ourselves in respect to the demands of history are striking – far more so, in fact, than most of us would wish. Like us, the Children of Israel faced (and had to face down) a reality that was nothing short of terrifying. Pharaoh tried to erase their existence, and in a variety of ways – culminating at the Sea – attempted to block the Israelites' path to Sinai. Hitler came dangerously close a mere half century ago to annihilating the Jews, killing many of our own ancestors, relatives, and friends in the process. ...The Israelites of course did manage with God's assistance to reach the place of faith and covenant, and if we too get there nonetheless, it is thanks in large part to the fact that we, like they, have been witness to a remarkable liberation. For me, as for many Jews of this generation, Jewish history has meant above all Holocaust and Israel. The latter does not justify the former. Israel can never make sense of the Holocaust, but it does help me to overcome its impact. Both have been crucial to the formation of my adult Jewish identity.

Arnold Eisen, Chancellor, Jewish Theological Seminary

וְהִיא שֶׁעָמְדָה

STANDING UP FOR US

וְהִיא שֶׁעָמְדָה לַאֲבוֹתֵינוּ וְלָנוּ.

שֶׁלֹּא אֶחָד בִּלְבַד עָמַד עָלֵינוּ לְכַלּוֹתֵנוּ,

אֶלָּא שֶׁבְּכָל דּוֹר וָדוֹר עוֹמְדִים עָלֵינוּ לְכַלּוֹתֵנוּ,

וְהַקָּדוֹשׁ בָּרוּךְ הוּא מַצִּילֵנוּ מִיָּדָם.

V'hee she-am-da,
la-a-vo-tei-nu v'la-nu,
sheh-lo eh-khad beel-vad,
amad alei-nu l'kha-lo-tei-nu
eh-la sheh-b'khol dor va-dor
om-deem a-lei-nu l'kha-lo-tei-nu,
v'ha-ka-dosh ba-rukh hu
ma-tzee-lei-nu mee-ya-dam.

This promise has stood us and our parents in good stead .
For not only has one enemy stood over us to annihilate us.
But in every generation enemies have stood over us to annihilate us.
Yet the Holy One keeps the promise to save us from their hands.

Cover the matza, raise your cup and sing together, acknowledging God's commitment to our survival.

Afterwards, set the cup down and uncover the matza for the continuation of Maggid.

IN EVERY GENERATION OUR ENEMIES SEEK TO ANNIHILATE US

1400 -1200 BCE Slavery in Egypt **722** BCE Kingdom of Israel destroyed and Ten Tribes exiled by Assyria **586** BCE First Temple destroyed and exile by Babylonia (Tisha B'Av) **167** BCE Religious persecution by Antiochus, Greek-Syria (Hanukkah) **70** CE Second Temple destroyed by Romans **135** Bar Kochba Revolt suppressed by Rome **627** Arabian Jewish tribes killed by Mohammed **873** Forced baptism of Byzantine Jews **992** Limoges' Jews expelled from France for witchcraft **1007** Egyptian Jews persecuted because Arabic translation of the Haggadah praises the drowning of the Egyptian ruler (Pharaoh) **1096** First Crusade: Jews murdered **1141** Forced conversion of Jews of Spain by Muslim tribes **1144** First blood libel in Norwich, England **1147** Second Crusade **1189** Third Crusade **1215** Pope Innocent III orders Jews to wear distinctive badge or clothes **1242** Talmud burned in Paris **1290** Jews expelled from England **1306** Jews expelled from France **1348** Black Plague blamed on the Jews **1391** Spanish Inquisition, riots and forced conversions **1492** Jews expelled from Spain by Ferdinand and Isabella **1495** Jews expelled from Lithuania **1496** Jews expelled from Portugal **1500** Jews expelled from Provence **1510** Jews expelled from Napoli **1536** Jews expelled from Saxony, Germany **1597** Jews expelled from Milan **1648** Ukrainian Jews slaughtered in Cossack's Rebellion led by Chmielnitzki **1736** Iranian Jews killed or forcibly converted **1840** Blood libel of Damascus **1881** Wave of pogroms in Russia **1894** Alfred Dreyfus arrested in France as spy **1903** Pogroms in Kishinev, Russia **1929** Pogroms in Mandate Palestine **1935** Nuremberg Laws in Germany **1938** Kristalnacht – synagogues burned, leaders deported to Dachau in Germany **1942** Wannsee Conference in Berlin decides on the Final Solution.

Arami Oved Avi   אֲרַמִי אֹבֵד אָבִי

THE WANDERING JEW: A SYMPOSIUM

"אֲרַמִי אֹבֵד אָבִי,

וַיֵּרֶד מִצְרַיְמָה וַיָּגָר שָׁם בִּמְתֵי מְעָט,

וַיְהִי שָׁם לְגוֹי גָּדוֹל, עָצוּם וָרָב.

וַיָּרֵעוּ אֹתָנוּ הַמִּצְרִים וַיְעַנּוּנוּ,

וַיִּתְּנוּ עָלֵינוּ עֲבֹדָה קָשָׁה.

וַנִּצְעַק אֶל יי אֱלֹהֵי אֲבֹתֵינוּ,

וַיִּשְׁמַע יי אֶת קֹלֵנוּ,

וַיַּרְא אֶת עָנְיֵנוּ וְאֶת עֲמָלֵנוּ וְאֶת לַחֲצֵנוּ.

וַיּוֹצִיאֵנוּ יי מִמִּצְרַיִם בְּיָד חֲזָקָה וּבִזְרֹעַ נְטוּיָה,

וּבְמֹרָא גָּדֹל, וּבְאֹתוֹת וּבְמֹפְתִים.

וַיְבִאֵנוּ אֶל הַמָּקוֹם הַזֶּה;

וַיִּתֶּן לָנוּ אֶת הָאָרֶץ הַזֹּאת,

אֶרֶץ זָבַת חָלָב וּדְבָשׁ."

"Today I want to tell Adonai, our God, how I have come to be in the land Adonai promised our ancestors, to give to us." (Deuteronomy 26:3).

All:

"My ancestor was a wandering Aramean.
He descended to Egypt and resided there in small numbers.
He became a nation – great, powerful and numerous.
Then the Egyptians treated us badly. They persecuted us and subjected us to hard labor.
We cried out to Adonai, the God of our ancestors. God heard our voice. God saw our persecution,
our labor and our oppression.
God took us out of Egypt – with a strong hand and an outstretched arm, with awesome power, signs and wonders.
Then God brought us to this place and gave us this land,
a land of milk and honey." (Deuteronomy 26:1-10).

Tonight's script is the telling of our national autobiography as wandering Jews. We go from migration down to exploitation, and then up from rags to riches and finally to homecoming.

The text we use was once recited by heart by every Jew, when bringing first fruits of the homeland to the Temple.

Michel Kichka: To the Land of Milk (3% fat) and Honey

Historically, the Promised Land was known for goat milk and date honey. But the artist takes the more popular understanding and identifies this Divine prophecy with Israeli products found daily in every grocery store.
Can you identify the various stages of the Pesach story in this illustration?

THE SEDER AND THE TEACHING COMMUNITY

The Seder is celebrated by a community within which one shares not only one's material goods, but also one's selfhood, spiritual treasures, knowledge, experiences, aspirations, and hopes.

The Seder community is a teaching community that practices the highest form of *hesed* [love, kindness and giving]... To foster this community, Hazal, the Sages, demanded that Torah be taught at every meal (Mishna Avot 3:3)... On the Seder night, every Jewish home becomes a teaching community, a didactic fellowship, a school where a class of disciples is instructed in Judaism.

Rabbi **Joseph B. Soloveitchik**, *Festival of Freedom*

צֵא וּלְמַד מַה בִּקֵּשׁ לָבָן
הָאֲרַמִי לַעֲשׂוֹת לְיַעֲקֹב אָבִינוּ:
שֶׁפַּרְעֹה לֹא גָזַר אֶלָּא עַל הַזְּכָרִים
וְלָבָן בִּקֵּשׁ לַעֲקֹר אֶת הַכֹּל,
שֶׁנֶּאֱמַר:

"אֲרַמִי אֹבֵד אָבִי."

Go out and learn
what (awful) plans
Lavan the Aramean
had for Jacob our
Father:
While Pharaoh
intended to kill only
the boys,
Lavan sought to
uproot the whole of
Jacob's family, the
children of Israel.
This is the hidden
meaning of the verse,
the Aramean (Lavan)
sought to exterminate
my father (Jacob).

(Deuteronomy 26:5)

"Go out and learn" is the official invitation to Jewish study, to the rabbinic symposium which we are encouraged to join this evening. Recapitulating phrase by phrase the story of migration recited on the previous page, we add rabbinic elaborations (Midrash).

Some families read every word, some skip to the Ten Plagues p.78, and others choose just one phrase and one theme to trigger their own discussions about one of these themes:

Assimilation and Identity p. 69

Birth and Genocide p. 71

Oppression and Resistance p. 73

Women and Liberation p. 75

THE ETHIOPIAN JOURNEY TO THE LAND OF ISRAEL

Shlomo Gronich and the Sheba Choir, the Ethiopian Immigrant Band
Words: Chaim Idissis

The moon is watching from above
On my back is a light bag of food
The desert beneath me has no end ahead
And my mother promises my little brothers
"A little more, a little more
lift up your legs, a last push
towards Jerusalem"

The moonlight stood fast
Our bag of food was lost.
The endless desert
Cries of jackals
And my mother comforts my little brothers
"A little bit more, a little more
soon we'll be redeemed
we won't stop going
to the land of Israel"

And at night bandits attacked
With a knife and a sharp sword
In the desert, the blood of my mother
The moon is my witness and I promise my brothers
"A little bit more, a little more
The dream will be fulfilled
One last effort before we get to Jerusalem"

THE EXODUS – TAKE TWO

During the 1980's, the Jews of Ethiopia sought to emigrate to Israel, though it was illegal, by crossing the border to the Sudan on a long journey on foot. Police guards, thieves and the desert often made this a march of death. The popular Israeli song (above) describes this courageous migration toward the Promised Land.

Later in 1991, during Operation Solomon (named after King Solomon who hosted the Queen of Sheba, which is today's Ethiopia), Israeli Air Force Hercules cargo planes picked up almost 15,000 Ethiopian Jews from the capital city of Addis Ababa.
Several months later, there were still stragglers from distant agricultural areas bringing up the rear of this massive Exodus. Here they are shown carrying all their possessions and their younger children on their backs on a fifteen day trek to a collection center.

Photograph by **Aliza Orbach**, 1992

"וַיֵּרֶד מִצְרַיְמָה וַיָּגָר שָׁם בִּמְתֵי מְעָט,
וַיְהִי שָׁם לְגוֹי גָּדוֹל, עָצוּם וָרָב."

"Israel (Jacob) descended to Egypt, resided there in small numbers, and there became a nation – great, powerful and numerous."

(Deuteronomy 26:5)

וַיֵּרֶד מִצְרַיְמָה

אָנוּס עַל פִּי הַדִּבּוּר.

"ISRAEL DESCENDED TO EGYPT"

compelled by the Divine word, to fulfill the prophecy of God to Abraham that "your descendants will be strangers in a land not their own, where they will be enslaved and persecuted..." (Genesis 14:13).

וַיָּגָר שָׁם

מְלַמֵּד שֶׁלֹּא יָרַד יַעֲקֹב אָבִינוּ לְהִשְׁתַּקֵּעַ בְּמִצְרַיִם - אֶלָּא לָגוּר שָׁם.
שֶׁנֶּאֱמַר: "וַיֹּאמְרוּ אֶל פַּרְעֹה: 'לָגוּר בָּאָרֶץ בָּאנוּ,
כִּי אֵין מִרְעֶה לַצֹּאן אֲשֶׁר לַעֲבָדֶיךָ, כִּי כָבֵד הָרָעָב בְּאֶרֶץ כְּנָעַן.
וְעַתָּה יֵשְׁבוּ נָא עֲבָדֶיךָ בְּאֶרֶץ גֹּשֶׁן'."

"ISRAEL RESIDED THERE"

temporarily. Jacob our Father never intended to settle permanently in Egypt. Jacob's family made that clear from the onset. "*They said to the Pharaoh (who reigned in the days of Joseph): we have come merely to reside in this land, for there is no pasture for your servants' sheep. For the famine in the land of Canaan is very heavy. Therefore, please permit your servants to stay in the land of Goshen* (within Egypt, where grazing is good)" (Genesis 47:4).

בִּמְתֵי מְעָט

כְּמָה שֶׁנֶּאֱמַר:
"בְּשִׁבְעִים נֶפֶשׁ יָרְדוּ אֲבֹתֶיךָ מִצְרָיְמָה,
וְעַתָּה שָׂמְךָ יְיָ אֱלֹהֶיךָ כְּכוֹכְבֵי הַשָּׁמַיִם לָרֹב."

"IN SMALL NUMBERS"

Jacob arrived in Egypt. Moshe reminds us that: "*with only seventy persons, your ancestors descended to Egypt. Yet now Adonai your God has made you as numerous as the stars of the sky*" (Deuteronomy 10:22).

וַיְהִי שָׁם לְגוֹי

מְלַמֵּד שֶׁהָיוּ יִשְׂרָאֵל מְצֻיָּנִים שָׁם.

"THERE ISRAEL BECAME A NATION"

recognizable, distinctive, standing out from the others.

Assimilation and Identity

"I, as practically all Soviet Jews, was absolutely assimilated. I knew nothing about our language, about our history, about our religion. But the pride of being a Jew, the pride for our State of Israel after the Six Day War, made me feel free from that big Soviet prison."

Nathan Sharansky, former Prisoner of Zion and Israeli Minister

Being a Stranger

Imagine the life of an immigrant. Ask those who have been a stranger in a new location to retell their story: How does one feel after being uprooted? About being a newcomer? What aspects of the identity of origin are preserved, hidden or changed? Do you ever feel really at home?

GOY GADOL – WHAT IS A "GREAT NATION"?

One aspect of a *goy gadol*, a great nation, is that it distinguishes itself in the area of righteousness: "*And what* goy gadol *is there that has statutes and ordinances so righteous as this law?*" (Deuteronomy 4:8). The people as such, as well as the individuals who comprise it, possess a developed sense of and fine sensitivity to justice. Instinctively, they cannot tolerate evil; they hate discriminatory practices and chicanery. If a nation is emotionally capable of approving of injustice, it cannot lay claim to greatness, no matter how powerful it is militarily and economically, or however ingenious it is in matters of science and technology. Real greatness consists in the innate quality of fairness and righteousness, in the spontaneous indignation whenever one is confronted with hypocrisy and selfishness...

If asked what characterizes Jewish morality, I would answer with a single Yiddish word: *rahmanus*. The English translations of mercy, compassion, sympathy, or empathy do not capture its full meaning. *Rahmanus* refers to the exceptionally tender and warm approach of one individual to another. The word *rahamim* in Hebrew is derived from *rehem*, the womb; it means the love of a mother for her child. The fact that in Egypt the Jews were exposed to all kinds of chicanery and humiliation, the fact that they were treated there like objects, not people, engendered in the Jewish people sensitivity and tenderness toward their fellow man.

Rabbi **Joseph B. Soloveitchik**, *Festival of Freedom*

> Freedom never comes on a silver platter. It's never easy...
> Whenever you break out of Egypt you better get ready for stiff backs.
> You better get ready for some homes to be bombed.
> You better get ready for some churches to be bombed.
> You better get ready for a lot of nasty things to be said about you,
> because you are getting out of Egypt.
>
> **Rev. Martin Luther King**, Jr.

גָּדוֹל, עָצוּם

כְּמָה שֶׁנֶּאֱמַר:

"וּבְנֵי יִשְׂרָאֵל פָּרוּ וַיִּשְׁרְצוּ וַיִּרְבּוּ וַיַּעַצְמוּ בִּמְאֹד מְאֹד

וַתִּמָּלֵא הָאָרֶץ אֹתָם."

"A NATION – GREAT AND POWERFUL"

emerged at an incredible pace. *"The children of Israel were fruitful and swarmed, and multiplied and became very, very powerful. The land was filled with them"* (Exodus 1:7).

וָרָב

כְּמָה שֶׁנֶּאֱמַר: "רְבָבָה כְּצֶמַח הַשָּׂדֶה נְתַתִּיךְ,
וַתִּרְבִּי וַתִּגְדְּלִי וַתָּבֹאִי בַּעֲדִי עֲדָיִים,
שָׁדַיִם נָכֹנוּ וּשְׂעָרֵךְ צִמֵּחַ, וְאַתְּ עֵרֹם וְעֶרְיָה."

"A NUMEROUS NATION" also means "full-grown."

The prophet captures God's nurturing of Israel in Egypt with graphic imagery. *"I let you grow like the plants of the field. You continued to grow up until you attained womanhood, until your breasts became firm, and your hair flourished. Yet you were still naked"* (Ezekiel 16:7) – (spiritually).

"וַיָּרֵעוּ אֹתָנוּ הַמִּצְרִים וַיְעַנּוּנוּ,

וַיִּתְּנוּ עָלֵינוּ עֲבֹדָה קָשָׁה."

"The Egyptians treated us badly, they persecuted us and imposed hard labor on us" (Deuteronomy 26:6).

וַיָּרֵעוּ אֹתָנוּ הַמִּצְרִים

כְּמָה שֶׁנֶּאֱמַר: "הָבָה נִתְחַכְּמָה לוֹ;
פֶּן יִרְבֶּה, וְהָיָה כִּי תִקְרֶאנָה מִלְחָמָה -
וְנוֹסַף גַּם הוּא עַל שׂנְאֵינוּ
וְנִלְחַם בָּנוּ וְעָלָה מִן הָאָרֶץ."

"THE EGYPTIANS TREATED US BADLY" –

they "bad-mouthed" our loyalty. Pharaoh set the ominous tone when exhorting his people: *"Let us outsmart them so that they may not increase. Otherwise, in the event of war, they will join our enemies, fight against us and expel us from the land"* (Exodus 1:10).

Birth and Genocide

SEXTUPLETS

"And the children of Israel were fruitful and swarmed and multiplied and increased very, very, very much. The land was filled with them" (Exodus 1:7).

This is an explosion of life, an almost surrealistic description of the spawning of a nation. It is a celebration of the fullness of life, burgeoning and uncontained. This reading is a fulfillment of God's promise to Jacob: *"Fear not to go down to Egypt, for I will make you there into a great nation"* (Genesis 46:3).

The redundant expressions of fertility have been read as denoting multiple births. In the midrashic readings, there is a miraculous, even a whimsical sense of the outrageous victory of life over death: these, for instance, take the six expressions of fertility (they were fruitful, they swarmed, they multiplied, they increased, very, very much) to indicate that each woman gave birth to sextuplets ("six to a belly").

The affirmation of life contained in these pounding synonyms intimates, in its very excess, a transcendent order of meaning: *"Even though Joseph and his brothers died,* their God did not die, *but the children of Israel were fruitful and multiplied..."* The midrash here wants to decipher the cascade of births not only as blessing but as the "survival of God." In some way that is not fully explained here, God expresses His undimmed vitality in the language of physical fertility.

Aviva Zornberg, *The Particulars of Rapture*

WHEN THE GOING GETS TOUGH

"In every generation we [women] must look upon ourselves as if we [were the women who] came out of Egypt."

The actions of the women of the Exodus story, the "righteous women of that generation," are memorable and praiseworthy; but they are not extraordinary, not limited merely to a few heroines of the past. We all have seen the strength of women in adversity. Women fight to keep their families together in times of war, economic deprivation, and epidemics. Reticent, dependent women "who never balanced a checkbook" turn into superwomen when they have to nurse ailing husbands or raise their families alone because of widowhood or divorce. All the strengths and talents that have been invisible – even to the woman herself – start coming to the fore. It is as if women are turned inside out by trouble: when the going gets tough, it seems, women get going.

Tikvah Frymer Kensky, Bible scholar and educator

NO MORE JEWISH CHILDREN

February 5, 1942:
Today the Gestapo in Vilna announced:
"FROM TODAY ON, NO MORE JEWISH CHILDREN ARE TO BE BORN"
The impact of the order on the ghetto is indescribable. Everyone cited the first Sedrah in Exodus in which Pharaoh had forbidden the birth of male children. The Pharaoh of the twentieth century is far more cruel – no births whatsoever!
When I came to the ghetto later I found that my wife had had a baby in a ghetto hospital. But I saw the hospital surrounded by Germans and a black car standing before the door...
In the evening when the Germans had left, I went to the hospital and found my wife in tears... When she had had her baby, the Jewish doctors of the hospital had already received the order that Jewish women must not give birth; and they had hidden the baby, together with other newborn children, in one of the rooms.
But when the Germans came to the hospital, they heard the cries of the babies. They broke open the door and entered the room. When my wife heard that the door had been broken, she immediately got up and ran to see what was happening to the child. She saw one German holding the baby and smearing something under its nose. Afterwards he threw it on the bed and laughed. When my wife picked up the child, there was something black under his nose. When I arrived at the hospital, I saw that my baby was dead. He was still warm.

Poet **Abraham Suzkever**, testimony before the International Military Tribunal in Nuremberg, February 27, 1946.

וַיְעַנּוּנוּ

כְּמָה שֶׁנֶּאֱמַר: "וַיָּשִׂימוּ עָלָיו שָׂרֵי מִסִּים לְמַעַן עַנֹּתוֹ בְּסִבְלֹתָם. וַיִּבֶן עָרֵי מִסְכְּנוֹת לְפַרְעֹה: אֶת פִּתֹם וְאֶת רַעַמְסֵס."

"THEY PERSECUTED US"

"They put task masters over Israel to conscript their labor in order to persecute them with their burdens. They built for Pharaoh the garrison cities of Pitom (House of the god Atum) and Ra-meses (Domain of the Son of the Sun god, Ra)" (Exodus 1:11).

וַיִּתְּנוּ עָלֵינוּ עֲבֹדָה קָשָׁה

כְּמָה שֶׁנֶּאֱמַר: "וַיַּעֲבִדוּ מִצְרַיִם אֶת בְּנֵי יִשְׂרָאֵל בְּפָרֶךְ."

"THEY IMPOSED HARD LABOR ON US"

"The Egyptians worked the children of Israel harshly (be-farekh)" (Exodus 1:13)
– degrading us with back-breaking and spirit-crushing labor.

"וַנִּצְעַק אֶל יי אֱלֹהֵי אֲבֹתֵינוּ, וַיִּשְׁמַע יי אֶת קֹלֵנוּ, וַיַּרְא אֶת עָנְיֵנוּ וְאֶת עֲמָלֵנוּ וְאֶת לַחֲצֵנוּ."

"We cried out to Adonai, the God of our fathers, God heard our voice, saw our persecution, our labor, and our oppression" (Deuteronomy 26:7).

וַנִּצְעַק אֶל יי אֱלֹהֵי אֲבֹתֵינוּ

כְּמָה שֶׁנֶּאֱמַר: "וַיְהִי בַיָּמִים הָרַבִּים הָהֵם – וַיָּמָת מֶלֶךְ מִצְרַיִם. וַיֵּאָנְחוּ בְנֵי יִשְׂרָאֵל מִן הָעֲבוֹדָה וַיִּזְעָקוּ! וַתַּעַל שַׁוְעָתָם אֶל הָאֱלֹהִים מִן הָעֲבֹדָה."

"WE CRIED OUT TO ADONAI"

This was the turning point:
"After many, many days, the king of Egypt died. The children of Israel groaned from under the labor and CRIED OUT in protest. Their cry for help rose up to God from their labor" (Exodus 2:23).

וַיִּשְׁמַע יי אֶת קֹלֵנוּ

כְּמָה שֶׁנֶּאֱמַר: "וַיִּשְׁמַע אֱלֹהִים אֶת נַאֲקָתָם, וַיִּזְכֹּר אֱלֹהִים אֶת בְּרִיתוֹ, אֶת אַבְרָהָם, אֶת יִצְחָק וְאֶת יַעֲקֹב."

"GOD HEARD OUR VOICE"

just as it says in Exodus: *"God HEARD their moans and God remembered the Divine covenant with Abraham and Isaac and Jacob"* (Exodus 2:24).

Oppression and Resistance

PICK YOUR DEFINITION OF SLAVERY/FREEDOM

Review the quotes, pick one that speaks to you and share your choice with others:

To be free, to be able to stand up and leave everything behind – without looking back. To say Yes!

Dag Hammarskjold, United Nations Secretary General, 1953

No man can put a chain about the ankle of his fellow man without at last finding the other end fastened about his own neck.

Frederick Douglas, former slave, Washington, DC, 1883

We have confused the free with the "free and easy."

Adlai Stevenson, Presidential contender, 1956

It is often safer to be in chains than to be free.

Franz Kafka, *The Trial*, Prague, 1925

To be liberated – that is easy. To be a free person – that is very hard.

Andre Gide, French author, 20th C

Liberty means responsibility. That is why most men dread it.

George Bernard Shaw, Irish playwright, 20th C

None are more hopelessly enslaved than those who falsely believe they are free.

Goethe, German poet, *Faustus*, 19th C

No human being is free who is not master of himself.

Epicetitus, Greek philosopher, Rome, 1st C

OPPRESSION AND RESISTANCE

Slavery is like Playing Checkers

Risky...very risky. For a slave woman to love anything that much was dangerous, especially if it was her children she had settled on to love. The best thing was to love just a little bit; everything, just a little bit, so when they broke its back, or shoved it in a croaker sack, well, maybe you'd have a little love left over for the next one...

Men and women were moved around like checkers. Anybody [the grandmother] Baby Suggs knew, let alone loved, who hadn't run off or been hanged, got rented out, loaned out, bought up, brought back, stored up, mortgaged, won, stolen or seized. So Baby's eight children had six fathers. What she called the nastiness of life was the shock she received upon learning that nobody stopped playing checkers just because the pieces included her children. Halle, she was able to keep the longest. Twenty years. A lifetime. Given to her, no doubt, to make up for hearing that her two girls, neither of whom had their adult teeth, were sold and gone and she had not been able to wave goodbye. To make up for coupling with a straw boss for four months in exchange for keeping her third child, a boy, with her – only to have him traded for lumber in the spring of the next year and to find herself pregnant by the man who promised not to and did. That child she could not love and the rest she would not. "God take what He would," she said. And He did, and He did, and He did...

Toni Morrison, African-American novelist, Nobel laureate, *Beloved*

"GO OUT AND LEARN" FROM PHARAOH'S DAUGHTER

Go out and learn: What did Pharaoh's daughter wish to teach the children of Israel when she felt compassion for one of the Hebrew boys and brought him up as her son?

That all who raise an orphan boy or girl in their homes is regarded by the Torah as if they gave birth to that child" (Talmud Megillah 13a).

Therefore the Holy One said to Pharaoh's daughter: "Moshe was not your son, yet you raised him, so too you are not my daughter by birth but I will call you my daughter, Bat-ya."

(Midrash Leviticus 1:3)

From this we learn that "there are righteous Gentiles who have a portion in the world-to-come" (Tosefta Sanhedrin 13:2). In every generation the Divine *Shekhina* spreads its wings over us and raises up men and women from the Jewish people and from the nations of the world whose courage and spiritual strength save us from arbitrariness, from terror and from indifference that "rise against us to annihilate us."

Rabbi **Einat Ramon**, Schechter Rabbinical Seminary, Jerusalem

וַיַּרְא אֶת עָנְיֵנוּ

זוֹ פְּרִישׁוּת דֶּרֶךְ אֶרֶץ, כְּמָה שֶׁנֶּאֱמַר: "וַיַּרְא אֱלֹהִים אֶת בְּנֵי יִשְׂרָאֵל וַיֵּדַע אֱלֹהִים."

"GOD SAW OUR PERSECUTION"

The root *"oni"* (persecution) is similar to *"ona"* (marital intimacy), thus hinting at Pharaoh's policy of enforced abstention from *"ona"* (sexual intercourse).

Perhaps that is delicately intimated when it says that: *"God saw the children of Israel, and God knew"* (Exodus 2:25) (their marital suffering, for knowledge has sexual overtones as in *"Adam knew his wife Eve"* [Genesis 4:1]).

וְאֶת עֲמָלֵנוּ

אֵלוּ הַבָּנִים,

כְּמָה שֶׁנֶּאֱמַר: "כָּל הַבֵּן הַיִּלּוֹד הַיְאֹרָה תַּשְׁלִיכֻהוּ וְכָל הַבַּת תְּחַיּוּן."

"OUR LABOR"

refers to the sons – the lost fruits of our "labor" who were drowned in Egypt. Pharaoh proclaimed: *"Every son who is born shall be cast into the Nile, while every daughter shall live"* (Exodus 1:22).

וְאֶת לַחֲצֵנוּ

זֶה הַדְּחַק,

כְּמָה שֶׁנֶּאֱמַר: "וְגַם רָאִיתִי אֶת הַלַּחַץ אֲשֶׁר מִצְרַיִם לֹחֲצִים אֹתָם."

"OUR OPPRESSION"

refers to "the pressure which the Egyptians applied to them" (Exodus 3:9).

Women and Liberation

Simon Solomon, **Miriam's Mission** (England, 1860).

Rushing river of days,

Cradle every parent's child in your waters.

We launch our babes in fragile baskets,

Moses multiplied by millions, released from muddy shores.

We squint to see around your bends

As our hearts are carried away.

We toss small sticks to float behind baskets, our prayers.

Meg Riley

PHARAOH'S DAUGHTER DILEMMA

Why did God give the responsibility of Moses' rearing to an Egyptian woman and the daughter of Pharaoh? Who was this woman?

I can imagine a young woman dissatisfied with the life and values bequeathed her by her father. It is a life without substance, though every physical need was filled and every material desire satisfied. She has reached that critical moment in life where dissatisfaction has become unbearable and action is required. The only problem (and it is always the problem): she doesn't know what to do. It is at such times that God presents us with an opportunity to act, if we recognize it as such. She sees a basket among the reeds beside the river. The closed basket looks like a tiny coffin. Does it contain the body of a dead Jewish boy? She does not turn and walk away from the possible horror, but orders the basket brought to her. The midrash records that one of the slave girls said: "Your Highness, it is the general rule that when a king makes a decree, his own family will obey that decree even if everyone else transgresses it. But you are flagrantly disobeying your father's command?" Yes, because her need for an identity separate from her father's was much greater.

The basket is brought to her and instead of ordering the slave girl to open it, Batya knows that she must be responsible for her act, and the text records this remarkable line: *"And she opened it, and saw it, even the child."* (Exodus 2:6) To open is one of the most important and difficult spiritual acts we are asked to do. Only when we open can the new present itself. But opening means forsaking the comfort of the familiar to enter the unknown.

Julius Lester, African-American convert, social activist and professor of Jewish Studies

"God took us out of Egypt, with a strong hand and an outstretched arm, with awesome power, signs and wonders" (Deuteronomy 26:8).

"וַיּוֹצִאֵנוּ יי מִמִּצְרַיִם! בְּיָד חֲזָקָה וּבִזְרֹעַ נְטוּיָה, וּבְמֹרָא גָּדֹל, וּבְאֹתוֹת וּבְמֹפְתִים."

"GOD TOOK US OUT"

וַיּוֹצִאֵנוּ יי מִמִּצְרַיִם

Not by the hands of an angel, **Not** by the hands of a messenger, But the Blessed Holy One alone. Just as the Torah says, *"I will pass through the land of Egypt, and I will strike down every first born in Egypt, both human and beast, I will execute judgment on all the gods of Egypt, I am God"* (Exodus 12:12).

לֹא עַל יְדֵי מַלְאָךְ, וְלֹא עַל יְדֵי שָׂרָף, וְלֹא עַל יְדֵי שָׁלִיחַ, אֶלָּא הַקָּדוֹשׁ בָּרוּךְ הוּא בִּכְבוֹדוֹ וּבְעַצְמוֹ, שֶׁנֶּאֱמַר: "וְעָבַרְתִּי בְאֶרֶץ מִצְרַיִם בַּלַּיְלָה הַזֶּה, וְהִכֵּיתִי כָל בְּכוֹר בְּאֶרֶץ מִצְרַיִם מֵאָדָם וְעַד בְּהֵמָה, וּבְכָל אֱלֹהֵי מִצְרַיִם אֶעֱשֶׂה שְׁפָטִים. אֲנִי יי."

"וְעָבַרְתִּי בְאֶרֶץ מִצְרַיִם בַּלַּיְלָה הַזֶּה" - אֲנִי וְלֹא מַלְאָךְ,
"וְהִכֵּיתִי כָל בְּכוֹר בְּאֶרֶץ מִצְרַיִם" - אֲנִי וְלֹא שָׂרָף,
"וּבְכָל אֱלֹהֵי מִצְרַיִם אֶעֱשֶׂה שְׁפָטִים" - אֲנִי וְלֹא הַשָּׁלִיחַ,
"אֲנִי יי" - אֲנִי הוּא וְלֹא אַחֵר.

"WITH A STRONG HAND"

בְּיָד חֲזָקָה

refers to an epidemic of animal disease (*dever*) – the fifth plague. *"The hand of Adonai will strike your livestock in the fields – the horses, the donkeys, the camels, the cattle, and the sheep – with a very severe disease"* (Exodus 9:3).

זוֹ הַדֶּבֶר, כְּמָה שֶׁנֶּאֱמַר: "הִנֵּה יַד יי הוֹיָה בְּמִקְנְךָ אֲשֶׁר בַּשָּׂדֶה, בַּסּוּסִים, בַּחֲמֹרִים, בַּגְּמַלִּים, בַּבָּקָר וּבַצֹּאן, דֶּבֶר כָּבֵד מְאֹד."

An Outstretched Arm: According to an Afghani Jewish custom, the leader of the Seder raises the bone (*zeroa*) from the Seder plate as a symbol of God's outstretched arm (*zeroa*).

"WITH AN OUTSTRETCHED ARM"

וּבִזְרֹעַ נְטוּיָה

refers to God's sword [as a metaphor for the plague of the first born] just as it does elsewhere: *"David woke up and saw the angel of Adonai standing between heaven and earth, with a drawn sword in his hand, **outstretched** against Jerusalem"* (I Chronicles 21:16).

זוֹ הַחֶרֶב, כְּמָה שֶׁנֶּאֱמַר: "וְחַרְבּוֹ שְׁלוּפָה בְּיָדוֹ, נְטוּיָה עַל יְרוּשָׁלָיִם."

"WITH AWESOME POWER"

וּבְמֹרָא גָּדֹל

refers to the revelation of God's power to our very eyes. That is just what Moshe tells Israel: *"Did a god ever before attempt to come and extract one nation for himself from the midst of another nation by prodigious acts, by signs and wonders, by war, by a strong hand, an outstretched arm and awesome power, as Adonai your God did for you in Egypt before your very eyes?"* (Deuteronomy 4:34).

זֶה גִּלּוּי שְׁכִינָה, כְּמָה שֶׁנֶּאֱמַר: "אוֹ הֲנִסָּה אֱלֹהִים לָבֹא לָקַחַת לוֹ גוֹי מִקֶּרֶב גּוֹי בְּמַסֹּת בְּאֹתֹת וּבְמוֹפְתִים וּבְמִלְחָמָה וּבְיָד חֲזָקָה וּבִזְרוֹעַ נְטוּיָה וּבְמוֹרָאִים גְּדֹלִים, כְּכֹל אֲשֶׁר עָשָׂה לָכֶם יי אֱלֹהֵיכֶם בְּמִצְרַיִם לְעֵינֶיךָ."

"WITH SIGNS"

וּבְאֹתוֹת

זֶה הַמַּטֶּה, כְּמָה שֶׁנֶּאֱמַר: "וְאֶת הַמַּטֶּה הַזֶּה תִּקַּח בְּיָדֶךָ, אֲשֶׁר תַּעֲשֶׂה בּוֹ אֶת הָאֹתֹת."

refers to the staff, as God told Moshe: *"Take the staff in your hand to do signs with it"* (Exodus. 4:17).

"WITH WONDERS"

וּבְמֹפְתִים

זֶה הַדָּם, כְּמָה שֶׁנֶּאֱמַר: "וְנָתַתִּי מוֹפְתִים בַּשָּׁמַיִם וּבָאָרֶץ..."

"... דָּם וָאֵשׁ וְתִימְרוֹת עָשָׁן."

refers to the plagues of blood, fire and smoke that are recalled by the prophet Joel: *"Before the great and terrible day of Adonai comes, I will set wonders in the sky and on earth . . . blood, fire, pillars of smoke!* **Da-am** (drop of wine) *va-eish* (drop) *v'teemrot ashan* (drop)! *The sun shall turn to darkness and the moon into blood"* (Joel 3:3).

God's Finger and the Sixteen Drops
It is a medieval custom to dip one's finger in the Seder's second cup of wine and to remove sixteen drops of wine. As each plague is recited we decrease our own joy, drop by drop, as we recall the enemy's pain. Besides the ten plagues, the extra six drops correspond to the three prophetic plagues mentioned by the prophet Joel – blood, fire and smoke – and the three word abbreviation of the ten plagues invented by Rabbi Yehuda – *d'tzakh, adash, b'akhab*.

דָּבָר אַחֵר: "בְּיָד חֲזָקָה" – שְׁתַּיִם; "וּבִזְרֹעַ נְטוּיָה" – שְׁתַּיִם; "וּבְמֹרָא גָּדֹל" – שְׁתַּיִם; "וּבְאֹתוֹת" – שְׁתַּיִם; "וּבְמֹפְתִים" – שְׁתַּיִם.

> **"No slave ever escaped Egypt" (Midrash Mekhilta).**
> **What makes release possible? What is the turning point in the history**
> **of this unarticulated misery? And what is the secret of redemption?**
> **Aviva Zornberg**

THE HUMAN ROLE IN THE REDEMPTION

History, Judaism says, cannot move or progress without the individual. God waits for man if there is something to be done. He does nothing until man initiates action. God waits for man, for a single person, to accept responsibility and initiate the process of *ge'ulah*, of redemption. It is strange. On the one hand, God is the *Go'el Yisrael*, our redeemer and liberator; however, God wills man to become His *shali'ah* [his messenger or representative] in the drama of *ge'ulah*, the personalistic *shali'ah* with whom God will walk.

God will not desert him, but God alone does not want to take the initiative. The Jewish people have been waiting a long time for the *Mashi'ah* – a human being like us who will initiate the process of *ge'ulah*. God wants an individual great in knowledge, in morality, in prophecy, to be a participant in the drama of *ge'ulah*. God wills man to emerge as a great being through his acceptance of the *shelihut*, mission. Not the collective, but the individual, seizes the initiative. *"It came to pass in the course of those many days, that the king*

of Egypt died, and the children of Israel sighed by reason of the bondage and their cry rose up to God ... and God saw their affliction, and God knew" (Exodus 2:23-25). God was ready, the people were ready, the time had passed, *ge'ulah* was possible, and God could have taken them out in a split second. But God had to wait for someone. Immediately, in the next verse, Moses is mentioned: *"Now Moses kept the flock of Jethro"* (Exodus 3:1).

Rabbi **Joseph B. Soloveitchik**, *Festival of Freedom*

The Ten Plagues

עֶשֶׂר הַמַּכּוֹת

אֵלּוּ עֶשֶׂר מַכּוֹת שֶׁהֵבִיא
הַקָּדוֹשׁ בָּרוּךְ הוּא עַל הַמִּצְרִים
בְּמִצְרַיִם, וְאֵלּוּ הֵן:

The Blessed Holy One brought **Ten Plagues** on the Egyptians in Egypt. These are the ten:

It is **customary** to spill a drop of wine from our cup of joy for each plague that God had to bring on the stubborn Egyptian oppressors until they agreed to release Israel from slavery.

דָּם	Da-am	Blood
צְפַרְדֵּעַ	Tz'far-dei-ah	Frogs
כִּנִּים	Kee-neem	Lice
עָרוֹב	Ah-rov	Wild beasts
דֶּבֶר	Deh-ver	Cattle plague
שְׁחִין	Sh'kheen	Boils
בָּרָד	Ba-rad	Hail
אַרְבֶּה	Ar-beh	Locusts
חֹשֶׁךְ	Kho-shech	Darkness
מַכַּת בְּכוֹרוֹת.	Ma-kat B'kho-rot	Death of the Firstborns

The **Rabbis debated** about our attitude to the Ten Plagues: On the one hand, they were a necessary instrument of liberation and a just punishment for Egyptian cruelty. Yet, on the other, they involved the suffering of fellow human beings, Divine creations in the image of God. **"We celebrate the Exodus from Egypt, not the downfall of the Egyptians,"** said Rabbi Simcha Cohen.

רַבִּי יְהוּדָה הָיָה נוֹתֵן בָּהֶם סִמָּנִים:

Rabbi Yehuda used to abbreviate them as an acrostic:

בְּאַחַ"ב.   עַד"שׁ   דְּצַ"ךְ

D-Tza-Kh (drop)   A-Da-Sh (drop)   B'-A-Kha-B (drop)

Ten Horrors
The artist has integrated all ten plagues into one simultaneous collage. Two plagues are represented by details of famous contemporary painters. Can you find them?

Can you discover which plague was accidentally left out?

כַּמָּה מַכּוֹת לָקוּ הַמִּצְרִים עַל הַיָּם?

MULTIPLYING THE TEN PLAGUES: THREE NUMERICAL RIDDLES

רַבִּי יוֹסֵי הַגְּלִילִי אוֹמֵר: מִנַּיִן אַתָּה אוֹמֵר שֶׁלָּקוּ הַמִּצְרִים בְּמִצְרַיִם עֶשֶׂר מַכּוֹת וְעַל הַיָּם לָקוּ חֲמִשִּׁים מַכּוֹת? בְּמִצְרַיִם מַה הוּא אוֹמֵר – "וַיֹּאמְרוּ הַחַרְטֻמִּים אֶל פַּרְעֹה: אֶצְבַּע אֱלֹהִים הוּא", וְעַל הַיָּם מַה הוּא אוֹמֵר – "וַיַּרְא יִשְׂרָאֵל אֶת הַיָּד הַגְּדֹלָה אֲשֶׁר עָשָׂה יי בְּמִצְרַיִם, וַיִּירְאוּ הָעָם אֶת יי, וַיַּאֲמִינוּ בַּיי וּבְמֹשֶׁה עַבְדּוֹ". כַּמָּה לָקוּ בְּאֶצְבַּע? עֶשֶׂר מַכּוֹת. אֱמֹר מֵעַתָּה: בְּמִצְרַיִם לָקוּ עֶשֶׂר מַכּוֹת וְעַל הַיָּם לָקוּ חֲמִשִּׁים מַכּוֹת.

RABBI YOSSI the Galilean posed the riddle: "How do you know that God struck the Egyptians with only 10 blows in Egypt, while God struck them with 50 blows at the Red Sea?"

Solution: In Egypt God used 1 finger just as "the Egyptian magicians said to Pharaoh: This (plague) is the finger of God" (Exodus 8:15). But at the Red Sea, God used the whole hand. "Israel saw the great hand that God used against Egypt" (Exodus 14:31). Logically, if 1 finger produced 10 plagues in Egypt, then a whole hand (5 fingers) produced 50 plagues at the Red Sea.

רַבִּי אֱלִיעֶזֶר אוֹמֵר: מִנַּיִן שֶׁכָּל מַכָּה וּמַכָּה שֶׁהֵבִיא הַקָּדוֹשׁ בָּרוּךְ הוּא עַל הַמִּצְרִים בְּמִצְרַיִם הָיְתָה שֶׁל אַרְבַּע מַכּוֹת? שֶׁנֶּאֱמַר: "יְשַׁלַּח בָּם חֲרוֹן אַפּוֹ, עֶבְרָה וָזַעַם וְצָרָה, מִשְׁלַחַת מַלְאֲכֵי רָעִים." "עֶבְרָה" – אַחַת, "וָזַעַם" – שְׁתַּיִם, "וְצָרָה" – שָׁלֹשׁ, "מִשְׁלַחַת מַלְאֲכֵי רָעִים" – אַרְבַּע. אֱמֹר מֵעַתָּה: בְּמִצְרַיִם לָקוּ אַרְבָּעִים מַכּוֹת וְעַל הַיָּם לָקוּ מָאתַיִם מַכּוֹת.

RABBI ELIEZER posed the riddle: "How do you know that each of the 10 plagues in Egypt was really 4 plagues rolled into one?"

Solution: In Psalms 78:49 God's burning anger at the Egyptians is described with 4 extra synonyms: (1) "wrath;" (2) "indignation;" (3) "trouble;" and (4) "a band of deadly messengers." Each of the plagues must have 4 dimensions. In sum, God struck 40 blows (4x10) in Egypt (using just one finger) and 200 blows (4x10x5) at the Sea (using his whole hand).

רַבִּי עֲקִיבָא אוֹמֵר: מִנַּיִן שֶׁכָּל מַכָּה וּמַכָּה שֶׁהֵבִיא הַקָּדוֹשׁ בָּרוּךְ הוּא עַל הַמִּצְרִים בְּמִצְרַיִם הָיְתָה שֶׁל חָמֵשׁ מַכּוֹת? שֶׁנֶּאֱמַר: "יְשַׁלַּח בָּם חֲרוֹן אַפּוֹ, עֶבְרָה וָזַעַם וְצָרָה, מִשְׁלַחַת מַלְאֲכֵי רָעִים." "חֲרוֹן אַפּוֹ" – אַחַת, "עֶבְרָה" – שְׁתַּיִם, "וָזַעַם" – שָׁלֹשׁ, "וְצָרָה" – אַרְבַּע, "מִשְׁלַחַת מַלְאֲכֵי רָעִים" – חָמֵשׁ. אֱמֹר מֵעַתָּה: בְּמִצְרַיִם לָקוּ חֲמִשִּׁים מַכּוֹת וְעַל הַיָּם לָקוּ חֲמִשִּׁים וּמָאתַיִם מַכּוֹת.

RABBI AKIBA posed the riddle: "How do you know that each of the 10 plagues in Egypt was really 5 plagues rolled into one?"

Solution: In Psalms 78:49 5 synonyms for anger one expressed in each plague: "(God) inflicted: (1) God's burning anger upon them; (2) wrath; (3) indignation; (4) trouble; and (5) a band of deadly messengers." In sum, God struck 50 blows (5x10) in Egypt (using just one finger) and 250 blows at the Red Sea (using God's whole hand).

THE TEN FEARS

The plagues God visited on the Egyptans in Egypt seem to me to be a parade of people's greatest fears. They are a mythological show of the power of the living vs. primal fear.

Starting from the blood of birth and of death, through primal human fears of small creatures (lice) and large ones (wild beasts), fear of financial ruin (locusts), fear of the dark (losing direction and meaning), we face the greatest fear: the fear for our children's lives – loss of the future.

Tonight, a night to commemorate the past, we seek the mercy of God's protection, look out from our places at a world full of fears and dangers – and pray for another quiet year.

Shai Zarhi, Israeli educator

FROGS ON PHARAOH'S HEAD

One morning when Pharaoh awoke in bed
There were frogs on his head and frogs on his bed
Frogs on his nose and frogs on his toes
Frogs here, frogs there,
Frogs were jumping everywhere.

Shirley Cohen

PESACH MATH RIDDLES: COMPUTE IN YOUR HEAD

A = Number of Moshe's siblings x number of years in desert x (number of days Moshe spent on Mount Sinai without eating – number of tablets of law)

B = (Books of Torah – number of tribes) x (number of plagues x number of days of *bris*) + (number of cups x number of questions x number of children)

Bonus Question:

C = number of rabbis in all-nighter in Bnei Brak (squared) + (months Moshe was hidden by his mother x number of animals mentioned in Had Gadya) + number of verses in Dayenu

See answers on page 148-149.

Dayeinu דַּיֵּנוּ

כַּמָּה מַעֲלוֹת טוֹבוֹת לַמָּקוֹם עָלֵינוּ!

אִלּוּ הוֹצִיאָנוּ מִמִּצְרַיִם, וְלֹא עָשָׂה בָהֶם שְׁפָטִים,

דַּיֵּנוּ.

| Ee-lu | ho-tzee-anu mee-Meetz-ra-yeem, |
| | v'lo asa va-hem sh'fa-teem, **Da-yeinu** |

אִלּוּ עָשָׂה בָהֶם שְׁפָטִים, וְלֹא עָשָׂה בֵאלֹהֵיהֶם,

דַּיֵּנוּ.

| Ee-lu | asa va-hem sh'fa-teem, |
| | v'lo asa vei-lo-hei-hem, **Da-yeinu** |

אִלּוּ עָשָׂה בֵאלֹהֵיהֶם, וְלֹא הָרַג אֶת בְּכוֹרֵיהֶם,

דַּיֵּנוּ.

| Ee-lu | asa vei-lo-hei-hem, |
| | v'lo ha-rag et b'kho-rei-hem, **Da-yeinu** |

אִלּוּ הָרַג אֶת בְּכוֹרֵיהֶם, וְלֹא נָתַן לָנוּ אֶת מָמוֹנָם,

דַּיֵּנוּ.

| Ee-lu | ha-rag et b'kho-rei-hem, |
| | v'lo natan la-nu et ma-mo-nam, **Da-yeinu** |

אִלּוּ נָתַן לָנוּ אֶת מָמוֹנָם, וְלֹא קָרַע לָנוּ אֶת הַיָּם,

דַּיֵּנוּ.

| Ee-lu | natan la-nu et ma-mo-nam, |
| | v'lo kara la-nu et ha-yam, **Da-yeinu** |

Dayeinu commemorates a long list of miraculous acts God did for us, any one of which would have been pretty amazing just by itself. For example, *"Had God only taken us out of Egypt but not punished the Egyptians - it would have been enough."* Dayeinu, translated liberally, means, "Thank you, God, for overdoing it."

דַּיֵּינוּ

אילו	דַּיֵּינוּ ✓
אילו	דַּיֵּינוּ ✓
אילו	דַּיֵּינוּ ✓
אילו	דַּיֵּינוּ ✓
אילו	דַּיֵּינוּ
אילו	דַּיֵּינוּ
אילו	דַּיֵּינוּ
אילו	דַּיֵּינוּ
אילו	דַּיֵּינוּ
אילו	דַּיֵּינוּ
אילו	דַּיֵּינוּ
אילו	דַּיֵּינוּ
אילו	דַּיֵּינוּ

אִלּוּ קָרַע לָנוּ אֶת הַיָּם, וְלֹא הֶעֱבִירָנוּ בְתוֹכוֹ בֶּחָרָבָה,

דַּיֵּינוּ.

Ee-lu ka-ra la-nu et ha-yam, v'lo he-eh-vee-ra-nu
b'to-kho beh-kha-ra-va, **Da-yeinu**

אִלּוּ הֶעֱבִירָנוּ בְתוֹכוֹ בֶּחָרָבָה, וְלֹא שִׁקַּע צָרֵינוּ בְּתוֹכוֹ,

דַּיֵּינוּ.

Ee-lu heh-eh-vee-ra-nu v'to-kho beh-kha-ra-va,
v'lo shee-ka et tza-rei-nu b'to-kho, **Da-yeinu**

אִלּוּ שִׁקַּע צָרֵינוּ בְּתוֹכוֹ, וְלֹא סִפֵּק צָרְכֵּנוּ בַּמִּדְבָּר אַרְבָּעִים שָׁנָה,

דַּיֵּינוּ.

Ee-lu shee-ka et tza-rei-nu b'to-kho, v'lo see-peik tzor-kei-nu
ba-meed-bar ar-ba-eem shana, **Da-yeinu**

אִלּוּ סִפֵּק צָרְכֵּנוּ בַּמִּדְבָּר אַרְבָּעִים שָׁנָה, וְלֹא הֶאֱכִילָנוּ אֶת הַמָּן,

דַּיֵּינוּ.

Ee-lu see-peik tzor-kei-nu ba-meed-bar
ar-ba-eem sha-na, v'lo heh-eh-khee-la-nu et ha-man, **Da-yeinu**

אִלּוּ הֶאֱכִילָנוּ אֶת הַמָּן, וְלֹא נָתַן לָנוּ אֶת הַשַּׁבָּת,

דַּיֵּינוּ.

Ee-lu heh-eh-khee-la-nu et ha-man,
v'lo na-tan la-nu et ha-Shabbat **Da-yeinu**

אִלּוּ נָתַן לָנוּ אֶת הַשַׁבָּת, וְלֹא קֵרְבָנוּ לִפְנֵי הַר סִינַי,

דַּיֵּנוּ.

Ee-lu na-tan la-nu et ha-Shabbat, v'lo ker-va-nu leef-nei har See-nai, Da-yeinu

אִלּוּ קֵרְבָנוּ לִפְנֵי הַר סִינַי, וְלֹא נָתַן לָנוּ אֶת הַתּוֹרָה,

דַּיֵּנוּ.

Ee-lu ker-va-nu leef-nei har See-nai, v'lo na-tan la-nu et ha-Torah, Da-yeinu

אִלּוּ נָתַן לָנוּ אֶת הַתּוֹרָה, וְלֹא הִכְנִיסָנוּ לְאֶרֶץ יִשְׂרָאֵל,

דַּיֵּנוּ.

Ee-lu na-tan la-nu et ha-Torah, v'lo heekh-nee-sa-nu l'Eretz Yisrael, Da-yeinu

אִלּוּ הִכְנִיסָנוּ לְאֶרֶץ יִשְׂרָאֵל, וְלֹא בָּנָה לָנוּ אֶת בֵּית הַבְּחִירָה,

דַּיֵּנוּ.

Ee-lu heekh-nee-sa-nu l'Eretz Yisrael, v'lo ba-na la-nu et beit ha-b'khee-ra, Da-yeinu

עַל אַחַת כַּמָּה וְכַמָּה, טוֹבָה כְפוּלָה וּמְכֻפֶּלֶת לַמָּקוֹם עָלֵינוּ: שֶׁהוֹצִיאָנוּ מִמִּצְרַיִם, וְעָשָׂה בָהֶם שְׁפָטִים, וְעָשָׂה בֵאלֹהֵיהֶם, וְהָרַג אֶת בְּכוֹרֵיהֶם, וְנָתַן לָנוּ אֶת מָמוֹנָם, וְקָרַע לָנוּ אֶת הַיָּם, וְהֶעֱבִירָנוּ בְתוֹכוֹ בֶּחָרָבָה, וְשִׁקַּע צָרֵינוּ בְתוֹכוֹ, וְסִפֵּק צָרְכֵּנוּ בַּמִּדְבָּר אַרְבָּעִים שָׁנָה, וְהֶאֱכִילָנוּ אֶת הַמָּן, וְנָתַן לָנוּ אֶת הַשַׁבָּת, וְקֵרְבָנוּ לִפְנֵי הַר סִינַי, וְנָתַן לָנוּ אֶת הַתּוֹרָה, וְהִכְנִיסָנוּ לְאֶרֶץ יִשְׂרָאֵל, וּבָנָה לָנוּ אֶת בֵּית הַבְּחִירָה לְכַפֵּר עַל כָּל עֲוֹנוֹתֵינוּ.

Each one of these good things would have been enough to earn our thanks. Dayeinu! GOD took us out of Egypt, punished the oppressors, and humiliated their gods, exposing their futility. God killed their first born (when the Egyptians refused to release Israel, God's first born) and gave us some of the Egyptians' wealth, just reparations for our forced labor. God divided the Red Sea for us, bringing us across on dry land, while drowning our pursuers in the sea. God supplied our needs for forty years in the desert - feeding us manna. God granted us the Shabbat and brought us to Mount Sinai to receive the Torah. God ushered us into Eretz Yisrael and later built us a Temple, the chosen place to atone for our crimes and misdemeanors.

THE AFGHANI ONION FREE-FOR-ALL

From our seat around the Seder table, it's easy for us to sing "Dayeinu" and claim that "each one of these good things would have been enough to earn our thanks." But for those who are in the middle of the process of liberation it is much harder to constantly be appreciative, especially during 40 years of desert wanderings. In fact, our ancestors were infamous for their lack of appreciation, their selective memory about the slavery in Egypt, their stubbornness and complaints:

"We fondly remember the fish that we could eat in Egypt at no cost, along with the cucumbers, melons, leeks, onions and garlic. But now our spirits are dried up, with nothing but the manna before our eyes…" (Numbers 11:5-6)

Some families, following the Afghani and Persian custom, pull out green onions and the occasional leek, and – upon getting to the ninth stanza about the manna – whip each other lightly with the green onion stalks, every time they sing the refrain "Da-yeinu." It is doubtful that this custom will ease our ancestral stubbornness, but it'll definitely give the participants a lively and memorable evening!

Dan Reisinger, Campaign for the release of Russian Jewry, 1969

רַבָּן גַּמְלִיאֵל הָיָה אוֹמֵר:
כָּל שֶׁלֹּא אָמַר שְׁלֹשָׁה דְּבָרִים אֵלּוּ בַּפֶּסַח,
לֹא יָצָא יְדֵי חוֹבָתוֹ, וְאֵלּוּ הֵן:

Rabban Gamliel **used to say:**
"All who have not explained the significance of three things during the Pesach Seder have not yet fulfilled their duty."
The three are:

פֶּסַח, מַצָּה וּמָרוֹר.

the Pesach **lamb, the** matza **and the** maror."

Leader points at (but does not raise) the roasted bone:

פֶּסַח שֶׁהָיוּ אֲבוֹתֵינוּ אוֹכְלִים בִּזְמַן
שֶׁבֵּית הַמִּקְדָּשׁ הָיָה קַיָּם, עַל שׁוּם מָה?

"*Pesach Al Shum Ma?*" – **The** Pesach **lamb (that our ancestors ate in the days of the Temple) – why did we used to eat it?**

All:

עַל שׁוּם שֶׁפָּסַח הַקָּדוֹשׁ בָּרוּךְ הוּא
עַל בָּתֵּי אֲבוֹתֵינוּ בְּמִצְרַיִם, שֶׁנֶּאֱמַר:
"וַאֲמַרְתֶּם: זֶבַח פֶּסַח הוּא לַיי,
אֲשֶׁר פָּסַח עַל בָּתֵּי בְנֵי יִשְׂרָאֵל בְּמִצְרַיִם
בְּנָגְפּוֹ אֶת מִצְרַיִם – וְאֶת בָּתֵּינוּ הִצִּיל.
וַיִּקֹּד הָעָם וַיִּשְׁתַּחֲווּ".

To remind ourselves that God passed over our ancestors' houses in Egypt (at this very hour on this very date). Moshe instructed us: "*When your children ask you, 'What do you mean by this ceremony?' you shall say: 'It is the Passover offering to Adonai, because God passed over the houses of Israel in Egypt when God struck the Egyptians, but saved our houses!'*" (Exodus 12:26-27).

Before leaving the Maggid, we go over the major themes of the story one more time, as mandated by Rabban Gamliel, the leader of the Jewish people in the time that the Haggadah was composed. These themes are epitomized in three of Pesach's strongest symbols: The Pesach lamb, the matza and the maror. More than just symbolic table decorations **for the centerpiece**, these are **"edible symbols,"** essential foods, whose significance must be internalized verbally, and later orally, by all the participants in the Seder.

Why these three? The Pesach lamb, matza and maror constituted the original menu in the Egyptian Seder: "They *shall eat the meat* (of the lamb) . . . *roasted over the fire, with matza and with maror*" (Exodus 12:8).

Ask a participant to become the "Quiz master," asking the questions, while the others all reply together.

Gamliel's Beachside Souvenirs

Barbeque Lamb
take home orders

Israeli Express Travelers Checks Accepted Here!

Diet shmura matza

Organic Maror

cigares PHARAON

Rabban Gamliel's Souvenir Kiosk

Rabban Gamliel, the main framer of the Rabbinic Seder, returns to the Haggadah as a jovial beach-bum, a souvenir-shop-owner in the Sinai desert, now a major tourist destination. To make sure one never forgets that long "vacation" in Egypt, he is selling souvenirs, just as what we eat at the Seder are edible tokens of the past – Pesach, matza and maror. Gamliel offers diet matzas, family size manna, organic maror and a *Bedikat Hametz* kit with flashlight and feather for finding crumbs of *hametz*.

THE SHARED MEAL: BUILDING A COMMUNITY

"If the household is too little for a lamb, let him and his neighbor next to his house take it" (Exodus 12:3- 4).

A new fellowship was formed around the paschal lamb; a new community sprang into existence. Being together, living with each other, sharing something many possess in common was made possible by the ceremonial of the paschal lamb. The Halakhah coined the term *havurah* with reference to the group gathering for this ceremonial. Eating together is a great medium of communication between individuals. Therefore, everything is shared.

The slave suddenly realizes that the little he has saved up for himself, a single lamb, is too much for him. The slave spontaneously does something he would never have believed he was capable of doing, namely, he knocks on the door of the neighbor he had never noticed, inviting him to share the lamb with him and to eat together. No wonder our Seder commences with the declaration, "*Ha lahma anya*, This is the bread of poverty." Whatever we possess, even if it is just the bread of the poor, is too much for us, and we invite all to come and eat with us: "Let all who are hungry come and eat."

Planned meals in which many participate are the mold in which togetherness, community-mindedness, and relatedness are fashioned... I want the thou to share my joy and the pleasure I derive from partaking of the food given to me by the Almighty. In the invitation, there is sympathetic understanding for and response to the other self's needs and cravings. It demonstrates that I think not exclusively of myself, that while I am driven by a biological impulse to some action, I refuse to take this action alone. Rather, I take it in community with others, who either do not have the means necessary for gratifying their physical needs or hate to be alone and quest for sociability and togetherness.

"You shall rejoice before the Lord your God: you, your son, your manservant, your maidservant, the Levite... the stranger, the orphan, and the widow that are in your midst" (Deuteronomy 16:11).

Rabbi **Joseph B. Soloveitchik**, *Festival of Freedom*

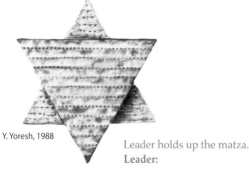

Y. Yoresh, 1988

מַצָּה זוֹ שֶׁאָנוּ אוֹכְלִים, עַל שׁוּם מָה?

עַל שׁוּם שֶׁלֹּא הִסְפִּיק בְּצֵקָם שֶׁל אֲבוֹתֵינוּ לְהַחֲמִיץ עַד שֶׁנִּגְלָה עֲלֵיהֶם מֶלֶךְ מַלְכֵי הַמְּלָכִים, הַקָּדוֹשׁ בָּרוּךְ הוּא וּגְאָלָם, שֶׁנֶּאֱמַר: "וַיֹּאפוּ אֶת הַבָּצֵק אֲשֶׁר הוֹצִיאוּ מִמִּצְרַיִם עֻגֹת מַצּוֹת, כִּי לֹא חָמֵץ, כִּי גֹרְשׁוּ מִמִּצְרַיִם וְלֹא יָכְלוּ לְהִתְמַהְמֵהַּ, וְגַם צֵדָה לֹא עָשׂוּ לָהֶם".

מָרוֹר זֶה שֶׁאָנוּ אוֹכְלִים, עַל שׁוּם מָה?

עַל שׁוּם שֶׁמֵּרְרוּ הַמִּצְרִים אֶת חַיֵּי אֲבוֹתֵינוּ בְּמִצְרַיִם, שֶׁנֶּאֱמַר: "וַיְמָרֲרוּ אֶת חַיֵּיהֶם בַּעֲבֹדָה קָשָׁה, בְּחֹמֶר וּבִלְבֵנִים וּבְכָל עֲבֹדָה בַּשָּׂדֶה, אֵת כָּל עֲבֹדָתָם אֲשֶׁר עָבְדוּ בָהֶם בְּפָרֶךְ".

Leader holds up the matza.
Leader:

"Matza Al Shum Ma?" – This matza! Why do we eat it?

All:

To remind ourselves that even before the dough of our ancestors in Egypt had time to rise and become leavened, the Ruler of rulers, the Holy One, was revealed and redeemed them.
The Torah says: *"They baked unleavened cakes of the dough that they had taken out of Egypt, for it was not leavened, since they had been driven out of Egypt and could not delay; nor had they prepared any provisions for themselves"* (Exodus 12:39).

Leader raises maror from the Seder plate.
Leader:

"Maror Al Shum Ma?" - This maror! Why do we eat it?

All:

To remind ourselves that the Egyptians embittered our ancestors' lives: *"They embittered their lives with hard labor, with mortar and bricks (construction) and with all sorts of field labor (agriculture). Whatever the task, they worked them ruthlessly"* (Exodus 1:14).

Sweetening the Bitterness of Slavery

As a lesson from our bitter experience in Egypt, where Pharaoh oppressed the Jews with "harsh labor," the Torah forbids a Jew from forcing a slave to do "harsh labor" (Leviticus 25:46). As Maimonides explains:

> What is harsh labor?
>
> It is labor that has no limit or a job that is not needed, but rather has been conceived only to keep the slave from resting...
>
> One cannot say to one's slave: "Dig in this place" if there is no need for it. Even the command to heat up a cup of water, or to cool one, if it isn't needed, it is forbidden.
>
> (Mishne Torah, Legislation regarding Slaves 1:6).

Though he acknowledged that slavery was a legal part of the economic system in the Bible and even in his own era in Egypt, Maimonides recommends that slave owners and, by analogy, employers treat those working for them in ways much more humane than even the law might allow:

> It is pious and it is wise to be compassionate and to seek justice, not to add to the burden on one's slave and not to cause the slave distress...The earliest Rabbis would share the very same foods they ate with their slaves, making sure the slaves ate before the master's own meal. Also the master should never humiliate the slave with violence, physical or verbal, nor should one shout or show anger to a slave. Rather speak always politely and be attentive to their complaints... Strive to behave like God showing compassion to all God's creatures. (ibid., 9:8)

My First Matza in Eretz Yisrael. Photograph by **Yossi Roth**, 1985

MARGE PIERCY

Matzoh

Flat you are as a door mat
and as homely.
No crust, no glaze, you lack
a cosmetic glow.
You break with a snap.
You are dry as a twig split from an oak
in midwinter.

You are bumpy as a mud basin
in a drought.
Square as a slab of pavement,
you have no inside
to hide raisins or seeds.
You are pale as the full moon
pocked with craters.

What we see is what we get,
honest, plain, dry
shining with nostalgia
as if baked with light instead of heat.
The bread of flight and haste
in the mouth you
promise, home.

In Every Generation בְּכָל דּוֹר וָדוֹר

IDENTIFYING WITH THE EXODUS

בְּכָל דּוֹר וָדוֹר חַיָּב אָדָם
לִרְאוֹת אֶת עַצְמוֹ כְּאִלּוּ הוּא יָצָא מִמִּצְרַיִם,
שֶׁנֶּאֱמַר: "וְהִגַּדְתָּ לְבִנְךָ בַּיּוֹם הַהוּא לֵאמֹר,
בַּעֲבוּר זֶה עָשָׂה יי לִי בְּצֵאתִי מִמִּצְרָיִם."

All say together:

In every generation one is obligated to see oneself as one who personally went out from Egypt. Just as it says: "You shall tell your child on that very day: 'It is because of this that God did for me when I went out from Egypt.'" (Exodus 13:8)

לֹא אֶת אֲבוֹתֵינוּ בִּלְבַד גָּאַל
הַקָּדוֹשׁ בָּרוּךְ הוּא מִמִּצְרַיִם,
אֶלָּא אַף אוֹתָנוּ גָּאַל עִמָּהֶם, שֶׁנֶּאֱמַר:
"וְאוֹתָנוּ הוֹצִיא מִשָּׁם, לְמַעַן הָבִיא אֹתָנוּ,
לָתֶת לָנוּ אֶת הָאָרֶץ אֲשֶׁר נִשְׁבַּע לַאֲבוֹתֵינוּ."

Not only were our ancestors redeemed by the Holy One, but even we were redeemed with them. Just as it says: "God took us out from there in order to bring us and to give us the land God swore to our ancestors." (Deuteronomy 6:23)

The Sephardi Haggadah text, following Maimonides, reads: "One is obligated to SHOW oneself...". Invite the participants to *show* in various ways that they themselves left Egypt. Use physical gestures, body posture, dramatic tone of voice, facial expressions, or costumes to show how one feels about one's newly granted freedom.

> **"The Exodus from Egypt occurs in every human being, in every era, in every year and even on every day."**
>
> Rabbi **Nachman of Bratslav**

Commemorating the Freedom for Soviet Jewry campaign, this stamp from 1972 coincided with the arrival of the first wave of Soviet Jews to Israel. God's command to Pharoah "Let My People Go" appears in Russian as well as Hebrew, English and Arabic. Today over 1,000,000 Russian speaking Jews live in Israel and one of every five soldiers is a Russian immigrant. Design by M. Pereg.

Passover Vacations in the Sinai by **Michel Kichka**

For many Israelis, the Pesach holiday period is actually a time to go down into Egypt – for a vacation in the Sinai, that is. This Israeli family going off to the Sinai may or may not recognize that the camel caravan they have encountered is populated by they themselves, some 3200 years ago.

The point of Pesach is to bring us literally "to see ourselves as if we went out of Egypt," to see ourselves as the direct descendants of the Jews of the Exodus, to see the stories of our lives as Exodus stories in their own right.

THE WANDERING, TIME-TRAVELING, JEW

It was fate that delivered me and my contemporaries into this great era, when the Jews returned to and re-established their homeland. I am no longer a wandering Jew who migrates from country to country, from exile to exile. But all Jews, in every generation must regard themselves as if they had been there, in previous generations, places, and events. Therefore, I am still a wandering Jew, but not along the far-flung paths of the world. Now I migrate through the expanses of time, from generation to generation, down the paths of memory.

I was a slave in Egypt. I received the Torah at Mount Sinai. Together with Joshua and Elijah, I crossed the Jordan River. I entered Jerusalem with David (circa 1000 BCE), was exiled from it with King Zedekiah (586 BCE), and did not forget it by the rivers of Babylon. And when the Lord returned the captives of Zion (538 BCE), I dreamed among the builders of its ramparts. I fought the Romans (66-70 CE) and was banished from Spain (1492). I was bound to the stake in Mainz. I studied Torah in Yemen and lost my family in Kishinev (Russia, 1903). I was incinerated in Treblinka (1942), rebelled in Warsaw (1943), and emigrated to the Land of Israel, the country from which I had been exiled and where I had been born, from which I come and to which I return.

I am a wandering Jew who follows in the footsteps of his forbearers, and just as I escorted them there and then, so do my forbearers accompany me and stand here with me today. And just as memory forces us to participate in each day and every event of our past, so does the virtue of hope force us to prepare for each day of our future.

Ezer Weizman, founder of the Israeli Air force and Israeli President, in an address to the German Bundestag, 1996. Speech written by Israeli novelist Meir Shalev.

Hallelujah הַלְלוּיָה

A NEW SONG TO FREEDOM

לְפִיכָךְ אֲנַחְנוּ חַיָּבִים לְהוֹדוֹת, לְהַלֵּל,
לְשַׁבֵּחַ, לְפָאֵר, לְרוֹמֵם, לְהַדֵּר, לְבָרֵךְ, לְעַלֵּה
וּלְקַלֵּס לְמִי שֶׁעָשָׂה לַאֲבוֹתֵינוּ וְלָנוּ אֶת כָּל
הַנִּסִּים הָאֵלּוּ:

הוֹצִיאָנוּ מֵעַבְדוּת לְחֵרוּת, מִיָּגוֹן לְשִׂמְחָה,
וּמֵאֵבֶל לְיוֹם טוֹב, וּמֵאֲפֵלָה לְאוֹר גָּדוֹל,
וּמִשִּׁעְבּוּד לִגְאֻלָה.
וְנֹאמַר לְפָנָיו שִׁירָה חֲדָשָׁה:

הַלְלוּיָה!

הַלְלוּיָה!

הַלְלוּ עַבְדֵי יי, הַלְלוּ אֶת שֵׁם יי!
יְהִי שֵׁם יי מְבֹרָךְ מֵעַתָּה וְעַד עוֹלָם!
מִמִּזְרַח שֶׁמֶשׁ עַד מְבוֹאוֹ מְהֻלָּל שֵׁם יי.
רָם עַל כָּל גּוֹיִם יי, עַל הַשָּׁמַיִם כְּבוֹדוֹ.
מִי כַּיי אֱלֹהֵינוּ? הַמַּגְבִּיהִי לָשָׁבֶת,
הַמַּשְׁפִּילִי לִרְאוֹת בַּשָּׁמַיִם וּבָאָרֶץ.
מְקִימִי מֵעָפָר דָּל, מֵאַשְׁפֹּת יָרִים אֶבְיוֹן,
לְהוֹשִׁיבִי עִם נְדִיבִים, עִם נְדִיבֵי עַמּוֹ.
מוֹשִׁיבִי עֲקֶרֶת הַבַּיִת אֵם הַבָּנִים שְׂמֵחָה.

הַלְלוּיָה!

Leader:

THEREFORE we owe it to God: to thank and to
sing, to praise and to honor, to bless and to acclaim
the One who has done all these wonders for our
ancestors and for us.

God took us from slavery to freedom,
from sorrow to joy, from mourning to festivity,
from a thick darkness to a great light,
from enslavement to redemption!

All:

Let us sing before God, a new song.

Hallelujah!

Hallelujah!

Servants of Adonai, give praise; praise the name of Adonai.

Let the name of Adonai be blessed now and forever.

From east to west the name of Adonai is praised.

Adonai rules high above all nations; God's glory is above the heavens.

Who is like Adonai our God, who is enthroned on high,

Yet sees what is below, in heaven and on earth?

God raises the poor from the dust, lifts up the needy from the garbage heap

and seats them among the greats of God's people.

God seats the childless woman at home

as a happy mother of children.

Hallelujah! (Psalm 113)

After covering all the
matza at the table,
everyone raises their
second cup of wine in a
toast to liberation and
to the Liberator.

After the toast and
before drinking the
second cup, the first
part of Hallel (Psalms
113-114) is sung. The
rest of Hallel will
follow after the meal is
completed.

On the signs:

HALLELUJAH!
Traffic is flowing at Praise-the-Lord Junction

Next exit - 40 years

Egypt-State Line

YEHUDA AMICHAI

And what is the continuity of my life? I am like one who left Egypt.
The Red Sea is split in two and I cross on dry ground
With two walls of water – on my right and on my left.
Behind me – Pharaoh's soldiers and horsemen.
Before me – the wilderness
And, perhaps, the Promised Land.
This is the continuity of my life.

GO TELL IT ON THE MOUNTAIN

We've got some difficult days ahead. But it really doesn't matter with me now. Because I've been to the mountaintop. Like anybody, I would like to live a long life. Longevity has its place. But I'm not concerned about that now. I just want to do God's will. And he's allowed me to go up to the mountain. And I've looked over, and I've seen the Promised Land.
I may not get there with you, but I want you to know tonight that we as a people will get to the Promised Land. So I'm happy tonight. I'm not fearing any man. Mine eyes have seen the glory of the coming of the Lord!

Martin Luther King, final speech delivered the night before his assassination just a few weeks before Passover (Memphis, 1968)

בְּצֵאת יִשְׂרָאֵל מִמִּצְרַיִם — When Israel went out from Egypt,

בֵּית יַעֲקֹב מֵעַם לֹעֵז, — The house of Jacob departed from a foreign people,

הָיְתָה יְהוּדָה לְקָדְשׁוֹ — Judah became God's holy one,

יִשְׂרָאֵל מַמְשְׁלוֹתָיו. — Israel, God's domain.

הַיָּם רָאָה וַיָּנֹס — The sea saw them and fled,

הַיַּרְדֵּן יִסֹּב לְאָחוֹר. — The Jordan ran backward,

הֶהָרִים רָקְדוּ כְאֵילִים — Mountains skipped like rams,

גְּבָעוֹת - כִּבְנֵי צֹאן. — Hills like lambs.

מַה לְּךָ הַיָּם כִּי תָנוּס — What alarmed you, sea, that you fled,

הַיַּרְדֵּן תִּסֹּב לְאָחוֹר, — Jordan, that you ran backward,

הֶהָרִים תִּרְקְדוּ כְאֵילִים — Mountains, that you skipped like rams,

גְּבָעוֹת - כִּבְנֵי צֹאן? — Hills, like lambs?

מִלִּפְנֵי אָדוֹן חוּלִי אָרֶץ — Tremble, earth, at the presence of Adonai,

מִלִּפְנֵי אֱלוֹהַּ יַעֲקֹב, — at the presence of the God of Jacob,

הַהֹפְכִי הַצּוּר אֲגַם מָיִם — Who turned the rock into a pool of water,

חַלָּמִישׁ - לְמַעְיְנוֹ מָיִם! — Flint into a fountain. (Psalm 114)

B'tzeit Yis-ra-el, mee-Meetz-rai-eem, Beit Ya-a-kov, mei-am lo-eiz
Hai-ta Ye-hu-da l'kod-sho, Yisra-el mam-sh'lo-tav.
Ha-yam ra-a va-ya-nos, ha-Yar-den yee-sov l'a-khor.
Heh-ha-reem rak-du kh'ei-leem, g'va-ot keev-nei tzon
Ma-l'kha ha-yam, kee-ta-noos, ha-Yar-den, tee-sov l'akhor.
Heh-ha-reem, teer-k'du kh'ei-leem, g'va-ot keev-nei tzon.
Mee-leef-nei A-don, khu-lee aretz, mee-leef-nei, Elo-ha Ya-a-kov
Ha-hof-khee ha-tzur, agam ma-yeem, kha-la-meesh, l'mai-no ma-yeem.

SECOND CUP כּוֹס שְׁנִיָּה

A TOAST TO REDEMPTION

בָּרוּךְ אַתָּה יי אֱלֹהֵינוּ מֶלֶךְ הָעוֹלָם,

אֲשֶׁר גְּאָלָנוּ וְגָאַל אֶת אֲבוֹתֵינוּ מִמִּצְרַיִם,

וְהִגִּיעָנוּ לַלַּיְלָה הַזֶּה לֶאֱכָל בּוֹ מַצָּה וּמָרוֹר.

כֵּן יי אֱלֹהֵינוּ וֵאלֹהֵי אֲבוֹתֵינוּ,

הַגִּיעֵנוּ לְמוֹעֲדִים וְלִרְגָלִים אֲחֵרִים

הַבָּאִים לִקְרָאתֵנוּ לְשָׁלוֹם,

שְׂמֵחִים בְּבִנְיַן עִירֶךָ וְשָׂשִׂים בַּעֲבוֹדָתֶךָ.

וְנֹאכַל שָׁם מִן הַזְּבָחִים וּמִן הַפְּסָחִים

אֲשֶׁר יַגִּיעַ דָּמָם עַל קִיר מִזְבַּחֲךָ לְרָצוֹן,

וְנוֹדֶה לְךָ שִׁיר חָדָשׁ עַל גְּאֻלָּתֵנוּ וְעַל פְּדוּת נַפְשֵׁנוּ.

בָּרוּךְ אַתָּה יי,   גָּאַל יִשְׂרָאֵל.

בָּרוּךְ אַתָּה יי אֱלֹהֵינוּ מֶלֶךְ הָעוֹלָם,

בּוֹרֵא פְּרִי הַגָּפֶן.

Blessed are You, Adonai our God, Ruler of the Universe, who redeemed us and redeemed our ancestors from Egypt, and who brought us to this night to eat matza and maror.

Adonai, our God and God of our ancestors, may You bring us in peace to future holidays. May we celebrate them in your rebuilt city, and may we be able to eat the Pesach lamb and the other sacrifices offered on the altar. We will thank you for our redemption.

Blessed are You, the Redeemer of Israel.

Blessed are You, Adonai our God, Ruler of the Universe, Creator of the Fruit of the Vine.

Ba-rukh ata Adonai / Elo-hei-nu me-lekh ha-olam / bo-rei pree ha-gafen.

We conclude the long Maggid section (storytelling) by drinking the second cup of wine, the Cup of Redemption.

Recline on a pillow to the left and drink at least half the second cup of wine.

Some families pour a "Miriam's Cup" of water, commemorating her feminine presence and leadership at the Exodus.

MIRIAM'S CUP

Miriam's Cup, filled with spring water, evokes the miracles of the past and present, complementing Elijah's Cup, which is filled with wine to represent our hope for redemption. Miriam, a prophet and a leader of the people, is always associated with miracles by water. Her name, "*Mir-yam*," contains the Hebrew word for "sea." As a child, Miriam watched over her baby brother in the Nile when he was rescued by the Pharaoh's daughter. After the miracle of the parting waters of the Red Sea, Miriam leads the women in song and dance with their tambourines. The midrash asserts that a well of water accompanied the children of Israel through the desert because of the characteristic optimism and faith of Miriam. When Miriam is stricken with leprosy, Moses pleads with God for her healing, incanting a short, powerful, rhyming staccato prayer:

"אנא אל נא רפא נא לה" "*ana El-na refa-na la.*" "*God please, heal her, please!*" (Numbers 12:13). Thus Miriam's well, which legend reports had been filled with the waters of the firmament at creation, became associated with healing. When Miriam dies, the earth goes into mourning and "*the community is without water*" (Numbers 20:1-2), and so the tradition speculates that Miriam's well departed with her death (BT Taanit 9a), though it subsequently returned and remains with us to this day.

Some people use Miriam's Cup as an opportunity to pray for healing or to express gratitude for everyday blessings, like water.

Lori Lefkovitz, professor of Gender and Judaism, Reconstructionist Rabbinical School

Betsy Teutsch, Miriam's Tambourine (Psalm 150)

WHO IS THIS GIRL STANDING AMONG THE REEDS?

"*And his sister stood afar off, to witness what would be done to him.*" (Exodus 2:4)

The Exodus of the Children of Israel from Egypt was, according to the Rabbis, a typical case of "behind every great man, there is a greater woman." Had the women not accelerated the salvation of the entire population, the men would not have had the gumption to depart from the house of slavery and embark on the long journey to freedom. In fact the foundation story of the birth of the Jewish people as a nation is accompanied by a woman, who was there and not there, a woman whose name and actions mark her as a rebel, but who also earned the title "prophetess."

Who is this girl standing among the reeds who, with her eyes burning, gazes at the small basket of bulrushes as it drifts with the current into the broad river? She is little Miriam. Six years old, no more, standing and watching over her brother cradled by the murky water, where lurking crocodiles wait to ambush smuggled Jewish babies. Her tiny feet are soaked with mud. Her knees and thighs are scratched by the reeds. The burning Egyptian sun beats down on her head. She is responsible for him, for when her father Amram – in light of Pharoah's decrees – gave up and wanted to divorce his wife, it was his daughter Miriam who convinced him to take back Yocheved and thus brought about Moshe's birth. Perhaps that is why she was called *Mir*-iam, from the Hebrew root meaning to rebel. But she was also called prophetess because she prophesied that Moshe would save them all.

Years later, at the miracle of the parting of the Red Sea, her brother sang the great, epic song: "*I will sing to Adonai for God has triumphed gloriously.*" The men sang after him in response. And then, all of a sudden, Miriam's voice was heard again. She took the timbrel in her hand, and sang to herself. The women – who until now had stood off to the side – burst into song and dance.

One can hear, through the laconic description, the storm of mass emotion raging in the women's dance. All of the senses, all of the urges, all of the silenced voices of the maidens, the women and the mothers who had suffered double slavery – erupted like a cascade of water in this singing. All of Miriam's daring, revolutionary *joie de vivre* flowed through the melody and the dance that responded to her brother's song. This is how Hebrew women's song was born, echoing with the voices of innumerable women.

Avirama Golan, Israeli novelist and journalist

Rakhtza, Motzi, Matza　רָחְצָה, מוֹצִיא, מַצָּה

EATING THE MATZA

בָּרוּךְ אַתָּה יי אֱלֹהֵינוּ מֶלֶךְ הָעוֹלָם,

אֲשֶׁר קִדְּשָׁנוּ בְּמִצְוֹתָיו וְצִוָּנוּ

עַל נְטִילַת יָדַיִם.

Blessed **are You, Adonai our God,**

Ruler of the Universe, who sanctified us

by commanding us to wash our hands.

Ba-rukh ata Adonai / Elo-hei-nu me-lekh ha-olam / asher keed'sha-nu b'meetz-vo-tav / v'tzee-va-nu / al netilat yadayim.

בָּרוּךְ אַתָּה יי אֱלֹהֵינוּ מֶלֶךְ הָעוֹלָם,

הַמּוֹצִיא לֶחֶם מִן הָאָרֶץ.

Blessed **are You, Adonai our God,**

Ruler of the Universe, who extracts

bread from the earth.

Ba-rukh ata Adonai / Elo-hei-nu me-lekh ha-olam / ha-mo-tzee le-khem meen ha-aretz.

בָּרוּךְ אַתָּה יי אֱלֹהֵינוּ מֶלֶךְ הָעוֹלָם,

אֲשֶׁר קִדְּשָׁנוּ בְּמִצְוֹתָיו וְצִוָּנוּ

עַל אֲכִילַת מַצָּה.

Blessed **are You, Adonai our God,**

Ruler of the Universe, who sanctified us

by commanding us to eat matza.

Ba-rukh ata Adonai / Elo-hei-nu me-lekh ha-olam / asher keed'sha-nu b'meetz-vo-tav / v'tzee-va-nu / al akhee-lat matza.

The Seder meal opens with the ceremonial eating of Pesach's three symbols: Matza, Maror and Haroset.

In preparation for eating the matza, we wash our hands – this time reciting the blessing.

Often volunteers will wash and dry the hands of the participants, so that they don't have to rise from their seats. Having our hands washed by someone else is part of the Seder night experience of liberty and nobility

This is the one time during Pesach in which one is obligated to eat matza. It must be plain matza, without eggs or other ingredients that might enrich this bread of poverty.

Take the matzot in hand and recite the usual blessing for all forms of bread – the "motzi" – and the special blessing for matza – "al akheelat matza."

Take some of the top and middle matza, and eat while reclining (to the left). You may dip the matza in salt or haroset. Some rabbis require that at least 1/2 – 2/3 of a standard machine-made matza be eaten.

Samizdat: A Do-It-Yourself Haggadah in Russia

It was about a month before Pesach and we wanted to do a proper Seder but we had no Haggadahs and it was still forbidden for Jews to celebrate the Seder or to purchase Haggadahs. So I decided to try even if I endanger myself. I disguised myself as a Russian Orthodox priest, entered the church, went to the library and took out a Haggadah. But how would I obtain seven more copies? So I drafted several Jewish friends and we decided to found our own little publishing house for Haggadahs. The danger was enormous: If we were caught, we would be sent to Siberia, and I don't wish that on anyone.

Now we needed paper. So one at a time we entered stores to buy white paper – two sheets each visit. If we had purchased more, it would have aroused suspicion. Then we found an ancient machine press. I told my neighbors that I was going on vacation for a week, but actually I went down to the basement of my apartment building – so no one would hear the noise of the machine. It was hot and crowded there... there was very little water... several times someone knocked at the door and my heart stopped beating. But with great effort we succeeded in printing six more copies of the Haggadah. We had one for every two families. Making a Seder was also illegal, so we gathered in the basement and did the clandestine Seder there.

Of course now that we are in Israel everything is different...

Nadia Tauterastein

Appeared in "HaDoar" Hebrew Newspaper, New York, Pesach 1935.

A Blessing for Hametz, Instead of Matza , 1944

Right before Pesach 1944 the Jews of Rotterdam, Netherlands, were deported to Bergen Belsen along with Rabbi Aharon Davids. Though they wanted to refrain from eating Hametz, there was no alternative source of nourishment at the concentration camp. When their rabbi conducted the Seder and they arrived at the blessing for eating Matza, he reached over, picked up a slice of bread and prayed:

> Our Father in heaven, You know that it is our desire to do your will and we wish to celebrate Pesach, to eat Matza and to observe the prohibition on Hametz. Yet that is what causes our hearts to ache, for the enslavement prevents us and our lives are in danger.
>
> So we prepare ourselves to perform the mitzvah of "*You shall live by them*" (Leviticus 18:5) – "To live" – by the laws, not to die by them (Babylonian Talmud Yoma 85a). We will listen to the Biblical warning: "*Beware and guard your lives very much*" (Deuteronomy 4:9). So we pray to you to keep us alive and to redeem us swiftly – so we may observe your laws and do your will and serve you with a complete integrity of the heart.

"Amen" answered the congregation, as they fulfilled the mitzvah of eating matza – with a piece of bread.

As retold by Shani Harel, R. Davids' granddaughter. R. Davids was murdered in the camps, but his wife and daughters survived and made aliyah. Their family recites this prayer annually.

Maror מָרוֹר

בָּרוּךְ אַתָּה יי אֱלֹהֵינוּ מֶלֶךְ הָעוֹלָם,
אֲשֶׁר קִדְּשָׁנוּ בְּמִצְוֹתָיו וְצִוָּנוּ
עַל אֲכִילַת מָרוֹר.

Blessed are You, Adonai our God,
Ruler of the Universe who has
sanctified us by commanding us
to eat maror.

Ba-rukh ata Adonai / Elo-hei-nu me-lekh ha-olam / asher kee-d'sha-nu b'meetz-vo-tav/
v'tzee-va-nu / al akhee-lat maror.

Take an ounce of raw maror, dip it in a bit of **haroset** (but not so much that it eradicates the bitter taste). **Recite** the blessing, eat and savor the maror, but do not recline! **Reclining** is a custom of the free, while **maror** and **haroset** remind us of persecution.

Korekh כּוֹרֵךְ

HILLEL'S SANDWICH

זֵכֶר לַמִּקְדָּשׁ כְּהִלֵּל.
כֵּן עָשָׂה הִלֵּל בִּזְמַן
שֶׁבֵּית הַמִּקְדָּשׁ הָיָה קַיָּם:
הָיָה כּוֹרֵךְ מַצָּה וּמָרוֹר
וְאוֹכֵל בְּיַחַד,
לְקַיֵּם מַה שֶּׁנֶּאֱמַר:
"עַל מַצּוֹת וּמְרֹדִים
יֹאכְלֻהוּ".

This sandwich is eaten in memory of
Pesach in the Temple as Hillel used to
celebrate it. He would sandwich the
Pesach lamb between matza and marror,
and eat them all together in order to
observe the law:

"You shall eat it (the Pesach sacrifice)
on matzot and maror" (Numbers 9:11).

Prepare a matza sandwich with maror and haroset in between, reminiscent of Hillel, the 1st C. BCE inventor of the **delicatessen sandwich**. Eat it while reclining to the left. Eating the sandwich tonight reminds us of the way life combines moments of suffering (maror) and of relief (matza), enslavement and freedom.

Afterwards, continue with Shulkhan Orekh, the festive meal concluded by eating the Afikoman as dessert.

Tanya Zion, 1997

MAROR EATING CONTEST

An enjoyable way to experience the bitterness of the maror is by conducting a "maror eating contest": Each brave participant takes a sizable portion of sharp maror, and immediately after reciting the blessing pops it into their mouths and begin to chew... The first to redden, tear or fume is the loser. The winner can get a plate of sweet haroset or a hint for finding the afikoman.

וְצִוָּנוּ עַל אֲכִילַת מָרוֹר

BITTERSWEET HAROSET

Haroset's texture symbolizes the accursed mortar used to build the cities of Egypt. But why is this symbol of the bitterness of slavery sweetened with the fruits, nuts and spices mentioned in the *Song of Songs*, the Bible's great love song? The Rabbis read this poetry as the expression of love between God and Israel, expressed most concretely in taking Israel out of Egypt. So, *Song of Songs*, full of images of youthful, spring-time love, is traditionally sung on Pesach, often on Seder night.
Rabbi Akiva declared that the day that this love song was given to Israel was as great as the day the Torah was given at Sinai.

The Rebbe of Slonim explains: If the Torah was the only document given to us at the Exodus, then we could only relate to God as a lawgiver, as the one owed obedience. It would be as if we were still slaves having merely replaced one master with another. However, once the *Song of Songs* was given, our relationship became one of lovers, with mutual feelings, hopes, dreams and demands. Like the lovers in *Song of Songs,* we need to seek each other out, sometimes finding, often missing one another. The taste of the haroset reminds us that our relationship with God should be a love story: sticky but sweet.

HAROSET TASTE TEST

Around the world various haroset recipes have been created, using varied ingredients such as: mustard, banana, vinegar, and in some Judeo-Spanish communities even some scrapes of brick!
Taste and compare a few traditional recipes for haroset – some are sweet while others are tangy or savory.

HAROSET RECIPES

MYSTICAL
(HaAri, Rabbi Yitzchak Luria, Safed, 16th C.)
7 sorts of chopped nuts and fruits mentioned in the *Song of Songs*: walnuts, dates, figs, pomegranates, grapes, apples, pears, and 3 spices like ginger, cinnamon sticks, and sweet spike nard.

YEMENITE
(Rav Kapakh, 20th C)
1 cup raisins,
1/3 cup each figs, almonds, walnuts
½ cup sesame
1/3 cup cinnamon sticks
1 pinch black pepper, cumin, and ginger
Blend in food processor and mix with red wine.

MOROCCAN HAROSET SYRUP
1 cup "Silan" Date Honey
1/2 cup chopped walnuts

ASHKENAZI EASTERN EUROPEAN
1/2 cup chopped almonds and walnuts
2 chopped apples
1 teaspoon cinnamon
red wine to bind the ingredients

Tzafun צָפוּן

EATING THE HIDDEN AFIKOMAN

זֵכֶר לְקָרְבַּן פֶּסַח
הַנֶּאֱכָל עַל הַשֹּׂבַע.

This matza is a reminder of the Pesach sacrifice in the days of the Temple which was eaten on a full stomach!

The Afikoman, the other half of the middle matza which was hidden at the beginning of the Seder, must now be eaten. Its taste lingers as the last food eaten at the Seder.

At this point the leaders of the Seder "discover to their dismay" that the Afikoman has been "stolen" by the children. Knowing that it must be eaten at the end of the meal, the leaders must bargain for its return.

It is recommended that Jewish prizes be offered (a book or game) as well as the promise of some money. Some families ask the children to give 10% of their Afikoman prize to a **Tzedakah** of their choice and to announce the beneficiary at this point. The adults may be solicited for **matching gifts**.

THE AFIKOMAN GAME: RULES AND VARIATIONS

How do we make sure the children don't lose interest during a long Seder night?

Rabbi Elazar says: "Snatch matza one from the other, in order to make sure the children don't fall asleep" (Talmud Pesachim 109a). R. Elazar's tip quickly became today's afikoman game: The half matza broken in Yakhatz at the beginning of the Seder is placed in a secure place, for the Seder cannot end until the "afikoman" is eaten after the meal. Thus whoever steals the afikoman is in a great bargaining position, often negotiating for a gift before relinquishing the precious matza. When there are many children, hide more than one matza to avoid conflict and disappointment.

Some families reverse the treasure hunt, asking the children to hide the afikoman and turning the parents into the matza snatchers. Iraqi Jews tie the afikoman to the back of one of the younger children who must stay awake and guard it, while the other children wait for the young guardian to nod off – allowing a quick snatch to take place and a new guardian to be entrusted with the matza. Whoever holds the coveted piece at the end of the evening is awarded the prize.

LEONARD COHEN

BROKEN UNTO YOU

All my life is broken unto you, and all my glory soiled unto you.
Do not let the spark of my soul go out in the even sadness.
Let me raise the brokenness to you, to the world where the breaking is for love.
Do not let the words be mine, but change them into truth.
With these lips instruct my heart, and let fall into the world what is broken in the world.

Lift me up to the wrestling of faith. Do not leave me where the sparks go out, and the jokes are told in the dark, and new things are called forth and appraised in the scale of the terror. Face me to the rays of love, O source of light,
or face me to the majesty of your darkness,
but not here, do not leave me here,
where death is forgotten, and the new thing grins.

YEHUDA AMICHAI

IN SEARCH OF THE LOST FACE

Tzafun, the Hebrew term for Afikoman, means the hidden one. The same word is used in the Torah to describe Moshe, hidden as a baby by his mother and ultimately uncovered and adopted by Pharaoh's daughter. The Israeli poet laureate turns a search for a lost relationship into a poem about Moshe's personal quest

Moshe, our teacher, saw the face of God only once
And forgot. He did not want to see the desert
Nor, even the promised land, but only the face of God.
He struck the rock in the fury of his longings.
He climbed Mt. Sinai and descended. He shattered the two
Tablets of the Covenant and made a Golden Calf. He searched
In fire and cloud. But he remembered only
The strong hand of God and his outstretched arm
But not his face. Just like one who wants
To remember the face of a loved one but cannot.

He made for himself a 'mug shot' taking from the face
Of God, the face of the burning bush and the face of
Pharaoh's daughter as she leaned over him when he was an infant in the basket,
And he distributed the picture to all the tribes of Israel
And throughout the wilderness. But no one had seen
And no one recognized. And only at the end of his life
On Mt. Nebo, he saw, and died with a kiss from the face of God.

Birkat HaMazon בָּרֵךְ

THE BLESSING AFTER THE MEAL

שִׁיר הַמַּעֲלוֹת.

Shir HaMaalot: Song of Laughter

בְּשׁוּב יי אֶת שִׁיבַת צִיּוֹן

When Adonai restores the fortunes of Zion,

הָיִינוּ כְּחֹלְמִים.

we will see it as in a dream:

אָז יִמָּלֵא שְׂחוֹק פִּינוּ

our mouths will be filled with laughter,

וּלְשׁוֹנֵנוּ רִנָּה.

our tongues, with songs of joy.

אָז יֹאמְרוּ בַגּוֹיִם:

Then the nations will say:

הִגְדִּיל יי לַעֲשׂוֹת עִם אֵלֶּה,

"Adonai has done great things for them!"

הִגְדִּיל יי לַעֲשׂוֹת עִמָּנוּ,

Yes, Adonai will do great things for us

הָיִינוּ שְׂמֵחִים.

and we will be so happy.

שׁוּבָה יי אֶת שְׁבִיתֵנוּ

Restore our fortunes, Adonai,

כַּאֲפִיקִים בַּנֶּגֶב.

as the rain suddenly fills up dry riverbeds in the Negev.

הַזֹּרְעִים בְּדִמְעָה,

Those who plant seeds in tears

בְּרִנָּה יִקְצֹרוּ.

will reap with songs of joy.

הָלוֹךְ יֵלֵךְ וּבָכֹה

Now they go walking and weeping,

נֹשֵׂא מֶשֶׁךְ הַזָּרַע,

carrying the seed-bag, then they will come back

בֹּא יָבֹא בְרִנָּה, נֹשֵׂא אֲלֻמֹּתָיו.

singing for joy, carrying their sheaves of wheat. (Psalm 126)

Sheer ha–ma–alot.
B'shuv Adonai et sheev-at Tzion / ha-yeenu k'khol-meem.
Az y'ma-lei s'khok pee-nu / u'l-sho–nei–nu reena.
Az yo-m'ru va–goyim / heeg–deel Adonai la–asot eem eleh.
Heeg–deel Adonai / la–asot eemanu / ha–yee–nu s'mei-kheem.
Shuva Adonai / et sh'vee–tei–nu / ka–afee–keem ba–negev.
Ha–zor–eem b'deem–a / b'reena yeek–tzo-ru.
Ha–lokh yei–lekh u–va-kho/ no–sei meshekh hazara.
Bo yavo v'ree-na, no–sei alu–mo-tav.

After the meal we thank God not only for the food but for all the Divine gifts we have received. These blessings are recited over the third cup of wine which we pour now but drink only at the end of *Birkat HaMazon*.

For three or more adults (post bar-mitzvah) the **Invitation** (*mezuman*) is said. For ten or more, add to the invitation the word "*Eloheinu*," our God, since God's presence dwells in community.

The Invitation to Gratitude

Leader (raises the cup and begins):

רַבּוֹתַי נְבָרֵךְ / מִשְׁפַּחְתִּי נְבָרֵךְ /
חֲבֵרַי נְבָרֵךְ

Kha-vei-rai n'va-rekh.

All:

יְהִי שֵׁם יי מְבֹרָךְ מֵעַתָּה וְעַד עוֹלָם.

Y'hee sheim Adonai
m'vo-rakh mei-ata v'ad olam.

Leader (repeats):

יְהִי שֵׁם יי מְבֹרָךְ מֵעַתָּה וְעַד עוֹלָם.

Y'hee sheim Adonai m'vo-rakh
mei-ata v'ad olam.

Leader (adds the words in
parentheses when there is a minyan):

בִּרְשׁוּת כָּל הַמְסוּבִּים, נְבָרֵךְ
(אֱלֹהֵינוּ) שֶׁאָכַלְנוּ מִשֶּׁלוֹ.

Beer-shoot, n'va-rekh (Eloheinu)
she-akhal-nu mee-shelo.

All:

בָּרוּךְ (אֱלֹהֵינוּ) שֶׁאָכַלְנוּ מִשֶּׁלוֹ
וּבְטוּבוֹ חָיִינוּ.

Ba-rukh (Eloheinu) she-akhal-nu
mee-shelo, uv'tu-vo kha-yeenu.

Leader (repeats):

בָּרוּךְ (אֱלֹהֵינוּ) שֶׁאָכַלְנוּ מִשֶּׁלוֹ
וּבְטוּבוֹ חָיִינוּ.

Ba-rukh (Eloheinu) she-akhal-nu
mee-shelo, uv'tu-vo kha-yeenu.

All:

בָּרוּךְ הוּא וּבָרוּךְ שְׁמוֹ.

Ba-rukh hu u-varukh sh'mo.

First Blessing: Food for the Whole World

בָּרוּךְ אַתָּה יי אֱלֹהֵינוּ מֶלֶךְ
הָעוֹלָם, הַזָּן אֶת הָעוֹלָם כֻּלּוֹ
בְּטוּבוֹ, בְּחֵן בְּחֶסֶד וּבְרַחֲמִים.
הוּא נוֹתֵן לֶחֶם לְכָל בָּשָׂר, כִּי
לְעוֹלָם חַסְדּוֹ. וּבְטוּבוֹ הַגָּדוֹל
תָּמִיד לֹא חָסַר לָנוּ וְאַל יֶחְסַר
לָנוּ מָזוֹן לְעוֹלָם וָעֶד, בַּעֲבוּר
שְׁמוֹ הַגָּדוֹל, כִּי הוּא אֵל זָן
וּמְפַרְנֵס לַכֹּל וּמֵטִיב לַכֹּל, וּמֵכִין
מָזוֹן לְכָל בְּרִיּוֹתָיו אֲשֶׁר בָּרָא.
בָּרוּךְ אַתָּה יי, הַזָּן אֶת הַכֹּל.

Ba-rukh ata Adonai Elo-hei-nu /
me-lekh ha-olam / Ha-zan et ha-olam
ku-lo b'tuvo / b'khen, b'khesed,
u-v'ra-kha-meem / Hu no-ten
le-khem l'khol ba-sar / kee- l'olam
khas-do / Uv-tu-vo ha-gado /
ta-meed lo khasar lanu / v'al yekh-sar
lanu ma-zon / l'olam va-ed / ba-avur
she-mo ha-gadol / kee-hu Eil zan
um-far-neis la-kol / U-mei-teev
la-kol / u-mei-kheen ma-zon / l'khol
bree-yo-tav asher ba-ra / Barukh ata
Adonai / **ha-zan et ha-kol.**

Blessed are You, Adonai
our God, Ruler of the
universe, who nourishes
the whole world. Your
kindness endures forever.
May we never be in want
of food, for God provides
for all the creatures
which God has created.
Blessed are You, Adonai,
who feeds all.

OUR MOUTHS WILL FILL WITH LAUGHTER

Being Jewish has taught me how to laugh!
First and foremost to laugh at myself and at
my situation. More important, to laugh in
order to act in the world. This is not to say
we are to make fun of someone or make
light of our fate. Rather, one is not to take
oneself too seriously, but to take one's
responsibilities very seriously.

Laughter opens the door to hope and
healing. It opens up new possibilities.
Listen to what's funny to children and it will
reveal a new world and a new generation.
The first Jewish child born was called
"Yitzchak" (one will laugh).

Laughter – we pack it in our luggage, we
season our Friday night soup with it. Often
it is mixed with tears. We have fought
despair relentlessly. Laughter is one of our
secret weapons.

Rabbi **Naamah Kelman**, first woman ordained in Israel,
Hebrew Union College

Second Blessing: For the Good Land and its Fruits

נוֹדֶה לְךָ יי אֱלֹהֵינוּ עַל שֶׁהִנְחַלְתָּ לַאֲבוֹתֵינוּ אֶרֶץ חֶמְדָּה טוֹבָה וּרְחָבָה, וְעַל שֶׁהוֹצֵאתָנוּ יי אֱלֹהֵינוּ מֵאֶרֶץ מִצְרַיִם, וּפְדִיתָנוּ מִבֵּית עֲבָדִים, וְעַל בְּרִיתְךָ שֶׁחָתַמְתָּ בִּבְשָׂרֵנוּ, וְעַל תּוֹרָתְךָ שֶׁלִּמַּדְתָּנוּ, וְעַל חֻקֶּיךָ שֶׁהוֹדַעְתָּנוּ, וְעַל חַיִּים חֵן וָחֶסֶד שֶׁחוֹנַנְתָּנוּ, וְעַל אֲכִילַת מָזוֹן שָׁאַתָּה זָן וּמְפַרְנֵס אוֹתָנוּ תָּמִיד, בְּכָל יוֹם וּבְכָל עֵת וּבְכָל שָׁעָה.

וְעַל הַכֹּל יי אֱלֹהֵינוּ אֲנַחְנוּ מוֹדִים לָךְ וּמְבָרְכִים אוֹתָךְ, יִתְבָּרַךְ שִׁמְךָ בְּפִי כָל חַי תָּמִיד לְעוֹלָם וָעֶד, כַּכָּתוּב: "וְאָכַלְתָּ וְשָׂבָעְתָּ וּבֵרַכְתָּ אֶת יי אֱלֹהֶיךָ עַל הָאָרֶץ הַטּוֹבָה אֲשֶׁר נָתַן לָךְ."

בָּרוּךְ אַתָּה יי, עַל הָאָרֶץ וְעַל הַמָּזוֹן.

Ka-ka-tuv v'akhal-ta / v'sa-vata u-vei-rakhta / et Adonai Elo-he-kha / al ha-aretz ha-tova asher natan lakh / Ba-rukh ata Adonai al ha-aretz v'al ha-mazon.

The Torah says: "*After you have eaten and are satisfied, you should bless Adonai your God for the good land God has given you*" (Deuteronomy 8:10).

Blessed are You, Adonai, for the land and for the food.

Third Blessing: For Jerusalem

רַחֵם נָא יי אֱלֹהֵינוּ עַל יִשְׂרָאֵל עַמֶּךָ וְעַל יְרוּשָׁלַיִם עִירֶךָ וְעַל צִיּוֹן מִשְׁכַּן כְּבוֹדֶךָ וְעַל מַלְכוּת בֵּית דָּוִד מְשִׁיחֶךָ וְעַל הַבַּיִת הַגָּדוֹל וְהַקָּדוֹשׁ שֶׁנִּקְרָא שִׁמְךָ עָלָיו.

אֱלֹהֵינוּ, אָבִינוּ, רְעֵנוּ זוּנֵנוּ פַּרְנְסֵנוּ וְכַלְכְּלֵנוּ וְהַרְוִיחֵנוּ, וְהַרְוַח לָנוּ יי אֱלֹהֵינוּ מְהֵרָה מִכָּל צָרוֹתֵינוּ. וְנָא אַל תַּצְרִיכֵנוּ, יי אֱלֹהֵינוּ, לֹא לִידֵי מַתְּנַת בָּשָׂר וָדָם וְלֹא לִידֵי הַלְוָאָתָם, כִּי אִם לְיָדְךָ הַמְּלֵאָה, הַפְּתוּחָה, הַקְּדוֹשָׁה וְהָרְחָבָה, שֶׁלֹּא נֵבוֹשׁ וְלֹא נִכָּלֵם לְעוֹלָם וָעֶד.

[On Shabbat add]:
רְצֵה וְהַחֲלִיצֵנוּ יי אֱלֹהֵינוּ בְּמִצְוֹתֶיךָ וּבְמִצְוַת יוֹם הַשְּׁבִיעִי, הַשַּׁבָּת הַגָּדוֹל וְהַקָּדוֹשׁ הַזֶּה, כִּי יוֹם זֶה גָּדוֹל וְקָדוֹשׁ הוּא לְפָנֶיךָ, לִשְׁבָּת בּוֹ וְלָנוּחַ בּוֹ בְּאַהֲבָה כְּמִצְוַת רְצוֹנֶךָ. וּבִרְצוֹנְךָ הָנִיחַ לָנוּ, יי אֱלֹהֵינוּ, שֶׁלֹּא תְהֵא צָרָה וְיָגוֹן וַאֲנָחָה בְּיוֹם מְנוּחָתֵנוּ. וְהַרְאֵנוּ יי אֱלֹהֵינוּ בְּנֶחָמַת צִיּוֹן עִירֶךָ וּבְבִנְיַן יְרוּשָׁלַיִם עִיר קָדְשֶׁךָ, כִּי אַתָּה הוּא בַּעַל הַיְשׁוּעוֹת וּבַעַל הַנֶּחָמוֹת.

[On Pesach add:]
אֱלֹהֵינוּ וֵאלֹהֵי אֲבוֹתֵינוּ, יַעֲלֶה וְיָבֹא וְיַגִּיעַ וְיֵרָאֶה וְיֵרָצֶה וְיִשָּׁמַע וְיִפָּקֵד וְיִזָּכֵר זִכְרוֹנֵנוּ וּפִקְדוֹנֵנוּ, וְזִכְרוֹן אֲבוֹתֵינוּ, וְזִכְרוֹן מָשִׁיחַ בֶּן דָּוִד עַבְדֶּךָ, וְזִכְרוֹן יְרוּשָׁלַיִם עִיר קָדְשֶׁךָ, וְזִכְרוֹן כָּל עַמְּךָ בֵּית יִשְׂרָאֵל, לְפָנֶיךָ, לִפְלֵיטָה, לְטוֹבָה, לְחֵן וּלְחֶסֶד וּלְרַחֲמִים, לְחַיִּים וּלְשָׁלוֹם בְּיוֹם חַג הַמַּצּוֹת הַזֶּה, זָכְרֵנוּ יי אֱלֹהֵינוּ בּוֹ לְטוֹבָה, וּפָקְדֵנוּ בוֹ לִבְרָכָה, וְהוֹשִׁיעֵנוּ בוֹ לְחַיִּים טוֹבִים. וּבִדְבַר יְשׁוּעָה וְרַחֲמִים חוּס וְחָנֵּנוּ וְרַחֵם עָלֵינוּ וְהוֹשִׁיעֵנוּ, כִּי אֵלֶיךָ עֵינֵינוּ, כִּי אֵל מֶלֶךְ חַנּוּן וְרַחוּם אָתָּה.

וּבְנֵה יְרוּשָׁלַיִם עִיר הַקֹּדֶשׁ בִּמְהֵרָה בְיָמֵינוּ. בָּרוּךְ אַתָּה יי, בּוֹנֶה בְרַחֲמָיו יְרוּשָׁלַיִם. אָמֵן.

U-v'nei Yeru-sha-layeem eer ha-kodesh beem-hei-ra b'ya-meinu / Ba-rukh ata Adonai, Bo-neh v'ra-kha-mav / Yeru-sha-layeem, Amen.

Rebuild Jerusalem the sacred city quickly, in our era.
Blessed are You, Adonai, who rebuilds Jerusalem in mercy. **Amen.**

108

Fourth Blessing: For Goodness and Hope

בָּרוּךְ אַתָּה יי אֱלֹהֵינוּ מֶלֶךְ הָעוֹלָם, הָאֵל, אָבִינוּ, מַלְכֵּנוּ, אַדִּירֵנוּ,
בּוֹרְאֵנוּ, גּוֹאֲלֵנוּ, יוֹצְרֵנוּ, קְדוֹשֵׁנוּ, קְדוֹשׁ יַעֲקֹב, רוֹעֵנוּ רוֹעֵה
יִשְׂרָאֵל, הַמֶּלֶךְ הַטּוֹב וְהַמֵּטִיב לַכֹּל, שֶׁבְּכָל יוֹם וָיוֹם הוּא הֵטִיב,
הוּא מֵטִיב, הוּא יֵיטִיב לָנוּ. הוּא גְמָלָנוּ הוּא גוֹמְלֵנוּ הוּא יִגְמְלֵנוּ
לָעַד, לְחֵן וּלְחֶסֶד וּלְרַחֲמִים וּלְרֶוַח, הַצָּלָה וְהַצְלָחָה, בְּרָכָה
וִישׁוּעָה, נֶחָמָה, פַּרְנָסָה וְכַלְכָּלָה וְרַחֲמִים וְחַיִּים וְשָׁלוֹם וְכָל טוֹב,
וּמִכָּל טוֹב לְעוֹלָם אַל יְחַסְּרֵנוּ.

הָרַחֲמָן הוּא יִמְלֹךְ עָלֵינוּ לְעוֹלָם וָעֶד.

הָרַחֲמָן הוּא יִתְבָּרַךְ בַּשָּׁמַיִם וּבָאָרֶץ.

הָרַחֲמָן הוּא יִשְׁתַּבַּח לְדוֹר דּוֹרִים, וְיִתְפָּאַר בָּנוּ לָעַד וּלְנֵצַח נְצָחִים, וְיִתְהַדַּר
בָּנוּ לָעַד וּלְעוֹלְמֵי עוֹלָמִים.

הָרַחֲמָן הוּא יְפַרְנְסֵנוּ בְּכָבוֹד.

הָרַחֲמָן הוּא יִשְׁבֹּר עֻלֵּנוּ מֵעַל צַוָּארֵנוּ, וְהוּא יוֹלִיכֵנוּ קוֹמְמִיּוּת בְּאַרְצֵנוּ.

הָרַחֲמָן הוּא יִשְׁלַח לָנוּ בְּרָכָה מְרֻבָּה בַּבַּיִת הַזֶּה וְעַל שֻׁלְחָן זֶה שֶׁאָכַלְנוּ עָלָיו.

הָרַחֲמָן הוּא יִשְׁלַח לָנוּ אֶת אֵלִיָּהוּ הַנָּבִיא זָכוּר לַטּוֹב, וִיבַשֶּׂר לָנוּ בְּשׂוֹרוֹת
טוֹבוֹת יְשׁוּעוֹת וְנֶחָמוֹת.

HaRa-kha-man /
hu yee-sh'lakh lanu et
Ei-lee-ya-hu
ha-na-vee / za-khur
la-tov / vee-vaser
lanu / b'sorot to-vot /
y'shu-ot v'ne-khamot.

הָרַחֲמָן הוּא יְבָרֵךְ אֶת בַּעַל הַבַּיִת הַזֶּה וְאֶת בַּעֲלַת הַבַּיִת הַזֶּה, אוֹתָם וְאֶת
בֵּיתָם וְאֶת זַרְעָם וְאֶת כָּל אֲשֶׁר לָהֶם, אוֹתָנוּ וְאֶת כָּל אֲשֶׁר לָנוּ,
כְּמוֹ שֶׁנִּתְבָּרְכוּ אֲבוֹתֵינוּ אַבְרָהָם יִצְחָק וְיַעֲקֹב בַּכֹּל מִכֹּל כֹּל,
כֵּן יְבָרֵךְ אוֹתָנוּ כֻּלָּנוּ יַחַד בִּבְרָכָה שְׁלֵמָה, וְנֹאמַר אָמֵן.

בַּמָּרוֹם יְלַמְּדוּ עֲלֵיהֶם וְעָלֵינוּ זְכוּת שֶׁתְּהֵא לְמִשְׁמֶרֶת שָׁלוֹם. וְנִשָּׂא בְרָכָה
מֵאֵת יי, וּצְדָקָה מֵאֱלֹהֵי יִשְׁעֵנוּ, וְנִמְצָא חֵן וְשֵׂכֶל טוֹב בְּעֵינֵי אֱלֹהִים וְאָדָם.

בשבת: הָרַחֲמָן הוּא יַנְחִילֵנוּ יוֹם שֶׁכֻּלוֹ שַׁבָּת וּמְנוּחָה לְחַיֵּי הָעוֹלָמִים.

הָרַחֲמָן הוּא יַנְחִילֵנוּ יוֹם שֶׁכֻּלוֹ טוֹב.

הָרַחֲמָן הוּא יְבָרֵךְ אֶת מְדִינַת יִשְׂרָאֵל רֵאשִׁית צְמִיחַת גְּאֻלָּתֵנוּ.

הָרַחֲמָן הוּא יַשְׁכִּין שָׁלוֹם בֵּין בְּנֵי יַעֲקֹב וּבֵין בְּנֵי יִשְׁמָעֵאל.

הָרַחֲמָן הוּא יְזַכֵּנוּ לִימוֹת הַמָּשִׁיחַ וּלְחַיֵּי הָעוֹלָם הַבָּא.

MAY the Merciful One send us Elijah
the prophet to bring us good tidings
of consolation and comfort.

MAY God bless everyone gathered
here, hosts and guests, relatives and
friends, with health, financial means
and generosity.

[On Shabbat]: [MAY God give us a day
which will be an era of perfect Shabbat
rest forever.]

[On Seder]: [MAY the Merciful One let us
inherit the day of total goodness].

MAY the Merciful One bless the State
of Israel.

MAY the Merciful One grant peace
between the children of Jacob and the
children of Ishmael.

MAY the Merciful One enable us to
live in the days of the Messiah and
earn the world to come.

מִגְדּוֹל יְשׁוּעוֹת מַלְכּוֹ וְעֹשֶׂה חֶסֶד לִמְשִׁיחוֹ, לְדָוִד
וּלְזַרְעוֹ עַד עוֹלָם. עֹשֶׂה שָׁלוֹם בִּמְרוֹמָיו, הוּא יַעֲשֶׂה
שָׁלוֹם עָלֵינוּ וְעַל כָּל יִשְׂרָאֵל, וְאִמְרוּ אָמֵן.
יְראוּ אֶת יי קְדשָׁיו, כִּי אֵין מַחְסוֹר לִירֵאָיו. כְּפִירִים
רָשׁוּ וְרָעֵבוּ, וְדֹרְשֵׁי יי לֹא יַחְסְרוּ כָל טוֹב. הוֹדוּ לַיי כִּי
טוֹב, כִּי לְעוֹלָם חַסְדּוֹ. פּוֹתֵחַ אֶת יָדֶךָ וּמַשְׂבִּיעַ לְכָל
חַי רָצוֹן. בָּרוּךְ הַגֶּבֶר אֲשֶׁר יִבְטַח בַּיי, וְהָיָה יי מִבְטַחוֹ.
נַעַר הָיִיתִי, גַם זָקַנְתִּי, וְלֹא רָאִיתִי צַדִּיק נֶעֱזָב,
וְזַרְעוֹ מְבַקֶּשׁ לָחֶם.
יי עֹז לְעַמּוֹ יִתֵּן, יי יְבָרֵךְ אֶת עַמּוֹ בַשָּׁלוֹם.

Na-ar ha-yeetee gam zakan-tee / v'lo-raeeti
tzaddik ne-eh-zav / v'zaro m'vakesh la-khem.
Adonai oz l'amo yee-tein / Adonai y'vareikh /
et amo va-Shalom.

Meegdol y'shu-ot mal-ko / v'oseh khesed leem-shee-kho /
l'-David u-l'zaro ad olam.
**Oseh Shalom beem-romav / hu ya-aseh shalom /
aleinu v'al kol Yisrael v'eemru. Amen**.

"I was once young **and now I am old but I testify that I have never seen the
just forsaken nor their children in need of bread."** (Psalm 37:25)
"Adonai will give strength to our people! Adonai will bless them with
peace!**"** (Psalms 29:11)

The Third Cup   כּוֹס שְׁלִישִׁית

בָּרוּךְ אַתָּה יי אֱלֹהֵינוּ מֶלֶךְ הָעוֹלָם,
בּוֹרֵא פְּרִי הַגָּפֶן.

Blessed are You, Adonai
our God, Ruler of the Universe,
who creates the fruit of the vine.

Ba-rukh ata Adonai / Elo-heinu me-lekh ha-olam / **bo-rei pree ha-gafen**.

We conclude the Blessing over
the Meal by drinking the Third
Cup, the Cup of Blessing, while
reclining to the left.

The person who led the Blessing
over the Meal says the blessing
over the wine.

AFTER THE GUESTS DEPART

Unfortunately, many of us delude ourselves into believing that we are good at expressing gratitude when we are not. Thus, we think that thanking our hosts at the end of an evening is sufficient. But if you have ever left a social event after telling your hosts what a wonderful time you had, and then spent the ride home engaging in a critical character analysis of the very people who have just hosted you, you have practiced ingratitude, not gratitude. I know that when my wife and I entertain, we spend hours preparing the house and planning the event so that our guests can spend as pleasant an evening as possible. The thought that some of them might afterwards dissect us critically pains me. And I don't think I am being paranoid in suspecting that many of them do so; I realize how often I have acted that way myself.

Rabbi **Joseph Telushkin**, *The Book of Jewish Values*

EATING IS LIKE CROSSING THE RED SEA

Birkat HaMazon is a supremely important act. To be able to eat and drink is as extraordinary, as miraculous, as crossing the Red Sea. We do not recognize the miracle because, for the moment, we live in a world of plenty and because our memory is so short. Yet those in less fortunate lands understand that to satisfy one's hunger is a miracle of miracles...The route that bread travels from the earth where it grows to our mouth where it is eaten is very perilous. It is to cross the Red Sea...

Emmanuel Levinas, French Jewish philosopher

THE INVERSION OF GRATEFULNESS

Basic to human existence is a sense of indebtedness – of indebtedness to society, of indebtedness to God. What is emerging in our age is a strange inversion. Modern people believe that the world is indebted to them; that society is charged with duties toward them. Their standard preoccupation is: *What will I get out of life?* Suppressed is the question: *What will life, what will society get out of me?*

Rabbi **Abraham Joshua Heschel**

ELIJAH כּוֹס אֵלִיָּהוּ

POURING ELIJAH'S CUP AND OPENING THE DOOR

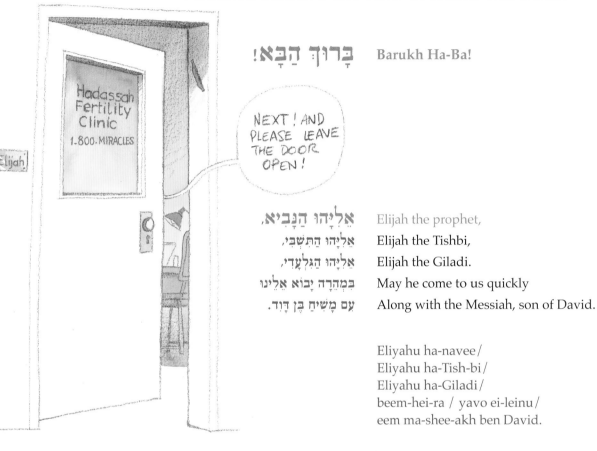

בָּרוּךְ הַבָּא!

Barukh Ha-Ba!

אֵלִיָּהוּ הַנָּבִיא,
אֵלִיָּהוּ הַתִּשְׁבִּי,
אֵלִיָּהוּ הַגִּלְעָדִי,
בִּמְהֵרָה יָבוֹא אֵלֵינוּ
עִם מָשִׁיחַ בֶּן דָּוִד.

Elijah the prophet,
Elijah the Tishbi,
Elijah the Giladi.
May he come to us quickly
Along with the Messiah, son of David.

Eliyahu ha-navee/
Eliyahu ha-Tish-bi/
Eliyahu ha-Giladi/
beem-hei-ra / yavo ei-leinu/
eem ma-shee-akh ben David.

The door is opened twice on Seder night. Once at "Ha Lakhma Anya," we opened the door to our past, slavery and poverty, and we invited the needy to join us. Now we open the door to our future, our tomorrow. So we invite Elijah, the prophet of hope and of happy endings. The question arises: What can we do to hasten redemption, to contribute to Tikkun Olam?

Pour a large cup of wine in honor of Elijah, and open the door expectantly.

Many families welcome Elijah with a prayer or a song.

FILLING THE CUP OF REDEMPTION OURSELVES

The Hassidic Rebbe Naftali Tzvi Horowitz used to go around the Seder table inviting each participant to pour from their personal cup into Elijah's cup. This symbolizes the Kabbalistic concept that Divine action will occur when there is a corresponding human action, an awakening from below that precedes it.

In some families, each participant helps to fill Elijah's cup of future redemption, while, silently or aloud, making a particular wish for a better year. May it come true with our own initiative and then with God's help.

Rabbi **Naftali Tzvi Horowitz** of Ropshitz, Poland, 18th C.

Where does Israel get the strength – the *chutzpah* – to go on believing in redemption in a world that knows mass hunger and political exile and boat people? How can Jews testify to hope and human value when they have been continuously persecuted, hated, dispelled, destroyed? Out of the memories of the Exodus! "

Rabbi **Irving Greenberg**, "The Jewish Way"

LESLIE GOLDMAN

A NOTE TO A FELLOW LEADER

On the day I came to see you, with my hands open to serve,
I found you very busy. I wanted you to know
I saw you were busy. I respected that you were busy
and waited for an opening. I sincerely wanted to meet you.
I wanted to be your friend. I wanted to work alongside you.
I was looking for a way to let you know my intent,
my needs, my passion, but found no opening.

> I understand there are ways that work for you –
> teach me your ways, or appoint someone to teach me, if you haven't the time!
> I understand, that in your life, as in mine, there are times
> we take on more than we can successfully complete –
> perhaps together we can learn how to complete more!

I want to honor you.
I respect the quiet moments you need to be alone.
I support you in taking care of yourself.
In some small way, I would like to contribute
to helping you lift your burden.

> I respect leadership. I respect those who take on what must be done,
> and develop competency to delegate and guide others.
> I, too, face the unknown. I too am a leader,
> and have purpose, though in some small humble way,
> it may be different than the task you have accepted. I am not unlike you.
> Perhaps there is something to be shared between us.

My name is Elijah. The next time I knock at your door, may it be truly open.

THE OLD MAN'S CURSE
AN IRAQI FOLKTALE

Many years ago in Baghdad, there lived a good couple who loved God, gave Tzedaka and helped the poor. All Baghdad honored the couple, and yet they had one sorrow: they had no children. Years passed, and Passover arrived. The couple sat at the Seder table, read the Haggadah, and retold the Exodus. Yet the wife was sad, as she always was at Passover. Her husband understood the reason for her grief and comforted her as he always did: "Don't worry, we'll have a child one day. God won't forget us."

While the couple were talking, there came a sudden knock at the door. At the threshold stood a ragged old man. The couple invited him to join their Seder and treated him with the greatest hospitality. However, when the old man took his leave of the pair who had hosted him so kindly, he turned to them, and instead of thanking them, said, "I pray to God that next year your Pesach table will be a wreck!" The ungrateful old man's curse astonished the couple and angered them, but out of respect, they said nothing. A month later the wife discovered that she was pregnant! And indeed, three months before the next Passover, a son was finally born to them. Their great joy cannot be described, and the old man and his curse were of course forgotten.

Next Passover, the couple sat around the Seder table and read the Haggadah with their son. The baby behaved like all babies do. He laughed and fussed and tipped over the wine. He knocked over the cups and broke the plates. But his mother and father loved their only child so much that they took pleasure even in the havoc he wreaked. This was the son they had prayed for year after year. It was only at the end of the Seder that the couple remembered the old man and his "curse." This was indeed a blessing in disguise, and the old man, they had no doubt in their hearts, was no other than Elijah himself.

שְׁפֹךְ חֲמָתְךָ

POUR OUT YOUR WRATH

Traditionally, at the
end of the Seder, we
stand before the open
door and read out a
harsh demand that our
oppressors be brought
to the bench of Divine
justice. This Haggadah
adds an unusual
prayer for righteous
Gentiles who rescued
Jews.

שְׁפֹךְ חֲמָתְךָ אֶל הַגּוֹיִם, אֲשֶׁר לֹא יְדָעוּךָ

וְעַל מַמְלָכוֹת אֲשֶׁר בְּשִׁמְךָ לֹא קָרָאוּ.

כִּי אָכַל אֶת יַעֲקֹב וְאֶת נָוֵהוּ הֵשַׁמּוּ.

שְׁפֹךְ עֲלֵיהֶם זַעֲמֶךָ וַחֲרוֹן אַפְּךָ יַשִּׂיגֵם.

תִּרְדֹּף בְּאַף וְתַשְׁמִידֵם מִתַּחַת שְׁמֵי יי.

Pour out **your fury on the nations that do not know you,**
and upon the kingdoms that do not invoke your name,
for they have devoured Jacob and destroyed his home. (Psalms 79:6-7)

Pour out **your wrath on them; may your blazing anger overtake them.** (Psalms 69:25)
Pursue them in wrath and destroy them from under the heavens of Adonai!
(Lamentations 3:66)

"Pour Out Your
Wrath," compiled
from Biblical verses,
was inserted into
the Haggadah in
the Middle Ages
in response to the
Crusades and to
the pogroms which
typically occurred
during the Easter/
Passover period.

"Pour out Your
Love," attributed to a
Haggadah manuscript
from 1521, reflects
a deep appreciation
and love for those
among the nations
who have aided and
protected the Jewish
people throughout
the generations.
Many scholars doubt
the authenticity of
this manuscript,
but descendants of
Holocaust survivors
saved by Gentiles agree
with its sentiments.

In 1943 during the Holocaust, the entire Danish Jewish community was smuggled to neutral Sweden by the Danish Christian underground movement. Israeli Memorial Stamp by A. Berg, 1973.

Pour out **your love**
on the nations who have known you
and on the kingdoms who call upon your name.
For they show kindness to the seed of Jacob
and they defend your people Israel from those
who would devour them alive.
May they live to see the Sukkah of peace spread over your chosen ones
and to participate in the joy of all your nations.

| Kiddush | Karpas | Yakhatz | Maggid | Matza | Maror | Dinner | Afikoman | Birkat | **ELIJAH** | Hallel | Songs | Next Year | 114

For One Brief Moment the Jew Stood Tall

Many Seder participants are decidedly uncomfortable with the short paragraph which asks that God's wrath be poured out on the nations that do not *"call out in God's name."* Some modern Haggadot deleted this paragraph, finding it too pregnant with vengeance and revenge. Defying the Seder's universal themes of freedom and liberation, it made their compilers uncomfortable.

I, on the other hand, love it. *Why my infatuation with this hard-hitting paragraph?*

I picture the many beleaguered Jews, particularly in Europe, for whom Passover, with its proximity to Easter, was a dangerous time. I imagine Jews who spent much of the year fearful that the non-Jewish world might violently turn on them. They knew they would have little recourse to protect themselves…

Suddenly, for one short paragraph, they opened the door of their homes – of course, most of their non-Jewish neighbors had by then retired for the night – and publicly told the world what they wished for those who had done them evil. For one brief moment they could let their desire for justice be heard publicly. They did not have to cower in fear.

And yet they did not ask God to let them pour out their own wrath. Even now when Jewish "machismo" briefly appeared, they asked God to render judgment and to punish only those who did not "call out in God's name," that is, those nations that failed to adhere to ethical standards. For one brief, shining moment, the Jew stood tall. The playing field was more than equal as the Jew turned to the Judge of all the world, the same Judge Abraham challenged in Genesis, and called upon that Judge to do justice.

And then, as suddenly as it began, it ended. The door was shut, the Jew sat down, the Seder continued, and all returned as it had been and would remain for too many years.

Deborah E. Lipstadt, Holocaust historian, and author of *History on Trial: My Day in Court with David Irving*, an account of her successful defense against a Holocaust denier who sued her for libel.

Pardon the Egyptians!

Moses demanded nothing less from the Jews, who had just left slavery for freedom, than to pardon the Egyptians! To love those who tyrannized over them for so long! Their time in Egypt itself – the abominable refuge the Jews received as slaves in a pagan land – had to be forgiven. In spite of everything, the children of Israel must not forget the air they breathed in Egypt, the water they drank there, and Egypt's ground in which they buried their dead, even though the waters of Egypt ran red with blood, the air rang with their cries and their tears watered the earth.

Moshe's words *"You shall not abhor an Egyptian, because you were a resident alien in his land"* (Deuteronomy 23:8) could have been a cruel taunt, yet they have been made wonderful by their charity and grace.

Rabbi **Eliyahu Ben Amozeg**, *Paths of Morality*, Livorno, Italy 19ᵗʰ C.

I Won't Teach Our Children to Hate

What do we do with the prayer *"Pour out your wrath"*? Is it possible to strike it out of our Haggadah? These awful words! Nowadays there are people who love us. And there are people who don't. But how can we curse even those who hate us with these horrible words?

I can't hate. And I won't teach our children to hate.

I understand the pain of the Jews, the pain and the fury that went into this prayer hundreds of years ago. The ugly face of anti-Semitism exists today, too, but not to the extent where, God forbid, we should teach our children this prayer. The foolish and the malicious can be condemned. They can be pitied. But we can't hate them – and make God part of this hatred.

Yehiel Weingarten, Kibbutz Ein Harod, 1936

DO NOT DRINK
FROM THE CUP OF
BITTERNESS

I must say to my people
who stand on the warm
threshold which leads
into the palace of justice.
In the process of gaining
our rightful place we
must not be guilty of
wrongful deeds. Let us
not seek to satisfy our
thirst for freedom by
drinking from the cup of
bitterness and hatred.

Martin Luther King

MIKHEL, THE OLD "GOY"

During the First World War, the Heschko family hid from the Cossacks at their Gentile neighbor Mikhel's, in a small Ukrainian town. **Yehuda Ya'ari** *tells the story of their Pesach Seder:*

Passover was coming. We remembered it and we didn't. When there is no matza, no wine, when there is nothing belonging to the holiday, it's better to forget. A week before the holiday, no one mentioned it. Then old Mikhel came: "Your Passover is coming," he said. "I brought you some wheat for 'matzi', some eggs, and beets for borscht... eat, friends, and remember Mikhel the old sinner."

On the eve of the Seder we laid a white cloth on the ground, because the table was small and there were no chairs in the house. We sat around the cloth until after midnight, eating and singing. Then my father told me to open the door for Elijah.

He began reading in a loud voice, "*Pour out your fury on the nations*

[literally, the "goyim" meaning nations] *that do not know you...*" and suddenly the door swung open!

Mikhel the old "*goy*" came inside wearing his best clothes. Mikhel said, "When grandfather Moshko was alive, I came to visit him every Passover, you remember, Heschko? Moshko would give me wine and matzi. I like the Jews' matzi... and Mrs. Heschko, how is the borscht?"

Father didn't finish the prayer. He went to Mikhel and embraced him. The world was at war. People were killing each other like animals, cities fell – and here stood two people, one Jewish and one Gentile, hugging each other.

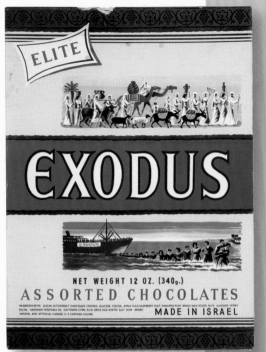

Pour Out Your Chocolates

On the fifth anniversary of the arrival of the "**S.S. Exodus 1947**" to the shores of British Mandate Israel, the Elite Chocolate Company produced a commemorative box of chocolates. The first boxes off the production line were given as gifts to the heroic crew members of that Holocaust refugee ship turned away by the British authorities. Pictured above is the box presented to John Stanley Grauel, a Methodist minister who joined the crew as a cook. He volunteered to help the illegal immigration movement after a meeting with David Ben-Gurion, later the first prime minister of Israel. After his passing, Grauel's box was donated to the US Holocaust Memorial Museum.

AN ANTIDOTE TO FANATICISM

There are good people in the world. There are evil people in the world. Evil cannot always be repelled by incantations, by demonstrations, by social analysis or by psychoanalysis. Sometimes, in the last resort, it has to be confronted by force. In my view, the ultimate evil in the world is not war itself, but aggression. Aggression is "the mother of all wars." And sometimes aggression has to be repelled by force of arms before peace can prevail.

As a very nationalistic, even chauvinistic little boy in the Jerusalem of the 1940s, I vowed never to set foot on German soil, nor ever to buy any German products. The only thing I could not boycott were German books. If you boycott the books, I told myself, you will become a little bit like '*them*'. At first, I limited myself to reading the pre-war German literature and the anti-Nazi writers. But later, in the 1960s, I began to read, in Hebrew translation, the works of the post-war generation of German writers and poets. They made me imagine myself in their place. I'll put it more bluntly: they seduced me into imagining myself in their stead, back in the dark years, and just before the dark years, and just after.

Reading these authors, and others, I could no longer go on simply hating everything German, past, present and future. I believe that imagining the other is a powerful antidote to fanaticism and hatred. I believe that books that make us imagine the other, may make us more immune to the ploys of the devil. And imagining the other – if you promise not to quote this little professional secret – is also a deep and very subtle human pleasure.

Amos Oz, Israeli novelist, upon receiving the Goethe Prize, Frankfurt, Germany, 2005

TALES OF THE RED MATZA

In the early 1970s, Saudi King Faisal told a Cairo newsman: "Two years ago when I was in Paris, police discovered the bodies of five children... Afterwards it turned out that Jews killed the children to mix their blood into their bread."

The blood libel made its debut in Norwich, England in 1144, and consists of the bizarre allegation that Jews, in their pre-Passover preparations, slaughter Christians (children preferably) to use their blood in the baking of matza. The solemn prohibition in Judaism against the consumption of blood in any form has never fazed the libelers.

There have been some 200 documented cases of blood libels!

In 1991, Nabila Shaalan, a Syrian delegate to the United Nations Human Rights Commission, recommended a "very important work that demonstrates unequivocally the historical reality of Zionist racism – namely a tome penned in 1985 by Mustafa Tlass, at the time Syrian minister of defense, entitled "The Matza of Zion," a justification of the notorious Damascus blood libel of 1840.

In Damascus the blood libel began with the disappearance of Capuchin Father Tomaso on February 5, 1840. A confession was extracted by torture from a Jewish barber. This led to pogroms against the Jewish community of Syria and the abduction of 63 Jewish children.

But Western Jewry rose to the occasion with a series of emergency measures in England, France and the United States. Many historians credit the Damascus Affair with having galvanized American Jews and created an encompassing international Jewish community for the first time.

Stuart Schoffman, *The Jerusalem Report*, 1991

Hallel הַלֵּל

P R A I S E

לֹא לָנוּ, יְיָ, לֹא לָנוּ, כִּי לְשִׁמְךָ תֵּן כָּבוֹד, עַל חַסְדְּךָ, עַל אֲמִתֶּךָ. לָמָּה יֹאמְרוּ הַגּוֹיִם: אַיֵּה נָא אֱלֹהֵיהֶם?
וֵאלֹהֵינוּ בַשָּׁמַיִם, כֹּל אֲשֶׁר חָפֵץ עָשָׂה. עֲצַבֵּיהֶם כֶּסֶף וְזָהָב, מַעֲשֵׂה יְדֵי אָדָם.
פֶּה לָהֶם וְלֹא יְדַבֵּרוּ, עֵינַיִם לָהֶם וְלֹא יִרְאוּ. אָזְנַיִם לָהֶם וְלֹא יִשְׁמָעוּ, אַף לָהֶם וְלֹא יְרִיחוּן.
יְדֵיהֶם וְלֹא יְמִישׁוּן, רַגְלֵיהֶם וְלֹא יְהַלֵּכוּ, לֹא יֶהְגּוּ בִּגְרוֹנָם. כְּמוֹהֶם יִהְיוּ עֹשֵׂיהֶם, כֹּל אֲשֶׁר בֹּטֵחַ בָּהֶם.
יִשְׂרָאֵל בְּטַח בַּיְיָ, עֶזְרָם וּמָגִנָּם הוּא. בֵּית אַהֲרֹן בִּטְחוּ בַיְיָ, עֶזְרָם וּמָגִנָּם הוּא.
יִרְאֵי יְיָ בִּטְחוּ בַיְיָ, עֶזְרָם וּמָגִנָּם הוּא.

יְיָ זְכָרָנוּ יְבָרֵךְ: יְבָרֵךְ אֶת בֵּית יִשְׂרָאֵל, יְבָרֵךְ אֶת בֵּית אַהֲרֹן, יְבָרֵךְ יִרְאֵי יְיָ, הַקְּטַנִּים עִם הַגְּדֹלִים.
יֹסֵף יְיָ עֲלֵיכֶם, עֲלֵיכֶם וְעַל בְּנֵיכֶם. בְּרוּכִים אַתֶּם לַיְיָ, עֹשֵׂה שָׁמַיִם וָאָרֶץ.
הַשָּׁמַיִם שָׁמַיִם לַיְיָ, וְהָאָרֶץ נָתַן לִבְנֵי אָדָם. לֹא הַמֵּתִים יְהַלְלוּ־יָהּ וְלֹא כָּל יֹרְדֵי דוּמָה.
וַאֲנַחְנוּ נְבָרֵךְ יָהּ מֵעַתָּה וְעַד עוֹלָם. הַלְלוּיָהּ.

אָהַבְתִּי כִּי יִשְׁמַע יְיָ אֶת קוֹלִי, תַּחֲנוּנָי. כִּי הִטָּה אָזְנוֹ לִי וּבְיָמַי אֶקְרָא.
אֲפָפוּנִי חֶבְלֵי מָוֶת וּמְצָרֵי שְׁאוֹל מְצָאוּנִי, צָרָה וְיָגוֹן אֶמְצָא. וּבְשֵׁם יְיָ אֶקְרָא: אָנָּה יְיָ מַלְּטָה נַפְשִׁי!
חַנּוּן יְיָ וְצַדִּיק, וֵאלֹהֵינוּ מְרַחֵם. שֹׁמֵר פְּתָאיִם יְיָ, דַּלּוֹתִי וְלִי יְהוֹשִׁיעַ.
שׁוּבִי נַפְשִׁי לִמְנוּחָיְכִי, כִּי יְיָ גָּמַל עָלָיְכִי. כִּי חִלַּצְתָּ נַפְשִׁי מִמָּוֶת, אֶת עֵינִי מִן דִּמְעָה, אֶת רַגְלִי מִדֶּחִי.
אֶתְהַלֵּךְ לִפְנֵי יְיָ בְּאַרְצוֹת הַחַיִּים. הֶאֱמַנְתִּי כִּי אֲדַבֵּר, אֲנִי עָנִיתִי מְאֹד. אֲנִי אָמַרְתִּי בְחָפְזִי: כָּל הָאָדָם כֹּזֵב.

מָה אָשִׁיב לַיְיָ כָּל תַּגְמוּלוֹהִי עָלָי. כּוֹס יְשׁוּעוֹת אֶשָּׂא וּבְשֵׁם יְיָ אֶקְרָא.
נְדָרַי לַיְיָ אֲשַׁלֵּם נֶגְדָה נָּא לְכָל עַמּוֹ.
יָקָר בְּעֵינֵי יְיָ הַמָּוְתָה לַחֲסִידָיו.
אָנָּה יְיָ כִּי אֲנִי עַבְדֶּךָ, אֲנִי עַבְדְּךָ בֶּן אֲמָתֶךָ, פִּתַּחְתָּ לְמוֹסֵרָי.
לְךָ אֶזְבַּח זֶבַח תּוֹדָה וּבְשֵׁם יְיָ אֶקְרָא. נְדָרַי לַיְיָ אֲשַׁלֵּם נֶגְדָה נָּא לְכָל עַמּוֹ.
בְּחַצְרוֹת בֵּית יְיָ, בְּתוֹכֵכִי יְרוּשָׁלָיִם. הַלְלוּיָהּ.
הַלְלוּ אֶת יְיָ כָּל גּוֹיִם, שַׁבְּחוּהוּ כָּל הָאֻמִּים. כִּי גָבַר עָלֵינוּ חַסְדּוֹ, וֶאֱמֶת יְיָ לְעוֹלָם. הַלְלוּיָהּ.

כִּי לְעוֹלָם חַסְדּוֹ.	הוֹדוּ לַיְיָ כִּי טוֹב
כִּי לְעוֹלָם חַסְדּוֹ.	יֹאמַר נָא יִשְׂרָאֵל
כִּי לְעוֹלָם חַסְדּוֹ.	יֹאמְרוּ נָא בֵית אַהֲרֹן
כִּי לְעוֹלָם חַסְדּוֹ.	יֹאמְרוּ נָא יִרְאֵי יְיָ

The Pesach Seder is divided into two parts by the meal itself. In fact, Hallel (Psalms 113-118) itself is split. While the first half of the Seder and of the Hallel (Psalms 113-114) is dedicated to the past, to the historical memory of the redemption from Egypt. The second half looks forward to the future and ends with the wish: "Next year in Jerusalem!" Messianic hope inspires the singing from now until the completion of the Seder.

Fill the fourth cup of wine and place it before you as you sing the Hallel.

The Psalms by King David and the Levite Band

הַלֵּל Hallel

מִן הַמֵּצַר קָרָאתִי יָּה, עָנָנִי בַמֶּרְחָב יָהּ.
יי לִי, לֹא אִירָא - מַה יַּעֲשֶׂה לִי אָדָם. יי לִי בְּעֹזְרָי וַאֲנִי אֶרְאֶה בְשֹׂנְאָי.
טוֹב לַחֲסוֹת בַּיי מִבְּטֹחַ בָּאָדָם. טוֹב לַחֲסוֹת בַּיי מִבְּטֹחַ בִּנְדִיבִים.
כָּל גּוֹיִם סְבָבוּנִי, בְּשֵׁם יי כִּי אֲמִילַם. סַבּוּנִי גַם סְבָבוּנִי, בְּשֵׁם יי כִּי אֲמִילַם.
סַבּוּנִי כִדְבֹרִים, דֹּעֲכוּ כְּאֵשׁ קוֹצִים, בְּשֵׁם יי כִּי אֲמִילַם. דָּחֹה דְחִיתַנִי לִנְפֹּל,
וַיי עֲזָרָנִי. עָזִּי וְזִמְרָת יָהּ וַיְהִי לִי לִישׁוּעָה. קוֹל רִנָּה וִישׁוּעָה בְּאָהֳלֵי צַדִּיקִים.
יְמִין יי עֹשָׂה חָיִל, יְמִין יי רוֹמֵמָה, יְמִין יי עֹשָׂה חָיִל.
לֹא אָמוּת כִּי אֶחְיֶה, וַאֲסַפֵּר מַעֲשֵׂי יָהּ. יַסֹּר יִסְּרַנִּי יָּהּ, וְלַמָּוֶת לֹא נְתָנָנִי.
פִּתְחוּ לִי שַׁעֲרֵי צֶדֶק, אָבֹא בָם, אוֹדֶה יָהּ. זֶה הַשַּׁעַר לַיי, צַדִּיקִים יָבֹאוּ בוֹ.

אוֹדְךָ כִּי עֲנִיתָנִי וַתְּהִי לִי לִישׁוּעָה. (2x)

אֶבֶן מָאֲסוּ הַבּוֹנִים הָיְתָה לְרֹאשׁ פִּנָּה. (2x)

מֵאֵת יי הָיְתָה זֹּאת הִיא נִפְלָאת בְּעֵינֵינוּ. (2x)

זֶה הַיּוֹם עָשָׂה יי נָגִילָה וְנִשְׂמְחָה בוֹ. (2x)

אָנָּא יי, הוֹשִׁיעָה נָּא.   אָנָּא יי, הוֹשִׁיעָה נָּא.

אָנָּא יי, הַצְלִיחָה נָּא.   אָנָּא יי, הַצְלִיחָה נָּא.

בָּרוּךְ הַבָּא בְּשֵׁם יי, בֵּרַכְנוּכֶם מִבֵּית יי. (2x)

אֵל יי וַיָּאֶר לָנוּ. אִסְרוּ חַג בַּעֲבֹתִים עַד קַרְנוֹת הַמִּזְבֵּחַ. (2x)

אֵלִי אַתָּה וְאוֹדֶךָּ, אֱלֹהַי - אֲרוֹמְמֶךָּ. (2x)

הוֹדוּ לַיי כִּי טוֹב, כִּי לְעוֹלָם חַסְדּוֹ. (2x)

יְהַלְלוּךָ יי אֱלֹהֵינוּ כָּל מַעֲשֶׂיךָ, וַחֲסִידֶיךָ צַדִּיקִים עוֹשֵׂי רְצוֹנֶךָ,
וְכָל עַמְּךָ בֵּית יִשְׂרָאֵל בְּרִנָּה יוֹדוּ וִיבָרְכוּ וִישַׁבְּחוּ וִיפָאֲרוּ
וִירוֹמְמוּ וְיַעֲרִיצוּ וְיַקְדִּישׁוּ וְיַמְלִיכוּ אֶת שִׁמְךָ, מַלְכֵּנוּ.
כִּי לְךָ טוֹב לְהוֹדוֹת וּלְשִׁמְךָ נָאֶה לְזַמֵּר, כִּי מֵעוֹלָם וְעַד עוֹלָם אַתָּה אֵל.

GIVE THANKS to Adonai for God is good, For God's kindness is endless.

God struck Egypt's first born,

And brought Israel out of Egypt,

With a strong hand and outstretched arm,

God split apart the Sea of Reeds,

And enabled Israel to cross through it,

God hurled Pharaoh and his army into the Sea of Reeds,

And led the people through the wilderness, to their land,

For God's kindness is endless.

הוֹדוּ לַיי כִּי טוֹב — כִּי לְעוֹלָם חַסְדּוֹ.
הוֹדוּ לֵאלֹהֵי הָאֱלֹהִים — כִּי לְעוֹלָם חַסְדּוֹ.
הוֹדוּ לַאֲדֹנֵי הָאֲדֹנִים — כִּי לְעוֹלָם חַסְדּוֹ.
לְעֹשֵׂה נִפְלָאוֹת גְּדֹלוֹת לְבַדּוֹ — כִּי לְעוֹלָם חַסְדּוֹ.
לְעֹשֵׂה הַשָּׁמַיִם בִּתְבוּנָה — כִּי לְעוֹלָם חַסְדּוֹ.
לְרֹקַע הָאָרֶץ עַל הַמָּיִם — כִּי לְעוֹלָם חַסְדּוֹ.
לְעֹשֵׂה אוֹרִים גְּדֹלִים — כִּי לְעוֹלָם חַסְדּוֹ.
אֶת הַשֶּׁמֶשׁ לְמֶמְשֶׁלֶת בַּיּוֹם — כִּי לְעוֹלָם חַסְדּוֹ.
אֶת הַיָּרֵחַ וְכוֹכָבִים לְמֶמְשְׁלוֹת בַּלַּיְלָה — כִּי לְעוֹלָם חַסְדּוֹ.
לְמַכֵּה מִצְרַיִם בִּבְכוֹרֵיהֶם — כִּי לְעוֹלָם חַסְדּוֹ.
וַיּוֹצֵא יִשְׂרָאֵל מִתּוֹכָם — כִּי לְעוֹלָם חַסְדּוֹ.
בְּיָד חֲזָקָה וּבִזְרוֹעַ נְטוּיָה — כִּי לְעוֹלָם חַסְדּוֹ.
לְגֹזֵר יַם סוּף לִגְזָרִים — כִּי לְעוֹלָם חַסְדּוֹ.
וְהֶעֱבִיר יִשְׂרָאֵל בְּתוֹכוֹ — כִּי לְעוֹלָם חַסְדּוֹ.
וְנִעֵר פַּרְעֹה וְחֵילוֹ בְיַם סוּף — כִּי לְעוֹלָם חַסְדּוֹ.
לְמוֹלִיךְ עַמּוֹ בַּמִּדְבָּר — כִּי לְעוֹלָם חַסְדּוֹ.
לְמַכֵּה מְלָכִים גְּדֹלִים — כִּי לְעוֹלָם חַסְדּוֹ.
וַיַּהֲרֹג מְלָכִים אַדִּירִים — כִּי לְעוֹלָם חַסְדּוֹ.
לְסִיחוֹן מֶלֶךְ הָאֱמֹרִי — כִּי לְעוֹלָם חַסְדּוֹ.
וּלְעוֹג מֶלֶךְ הַבָּשָׁן — כִּי לְעוֹלָם חַסְדּוֹ.
וְנָתַן אַרְצָם לְנַחֲלָה — כִּי לְעוֹלָם חַסְדּוֹ.
נַחֲלָה לְיִשְׂרָאֵל עַבְדּוֹ — כִּי לְעוֹלָם חַסְדּוֹ.
שֶׁבְּשִׁפְלֵנוּ זָכַר לָנוּ — כִּי לְעוֹלָם חַסְדּוֹ.
וַיִּפְרְקֵנוּ מִצָּרֵינוּ — כִּי לְעוֹלָם חַסְדּוֹ.
נֹתֵן לֶחֶם לְכָל בָּשָׂר — כִּי לְעוֹלָם חַסְדּוֹ.
הוֹדוּ לְאֵל הַשָּׁמָיִם — כִּי לְעוֹלָם חַסְדּוֹ.

The Blessing after the Hallel

נִשְׁמַת כָּל חַי תְּבָרֵךְ אֶת שִׁמְךָ, יְיָ אֱלֹהֵינוּ, וְרוּחַ כָּל בָּשָׂר תְּפָאֵר וּתְרוֹמֵם זִכְרְךָ, מַלְכֵּנוּ, תָּמִיד. מִן הָעוֹלָם וְעַד הָעוֹלָם אַתָּה אֵל, וּמִבַּלְעָדֶיךָ אֵין לָנוּ מֶלֶךְ גּוֹאֵל וּמוֹשִׁיעַ, פּוֹדֶה וּמַצִּיל וּמְפַרְנֵס וּמְרַחֵם בְּכָל עֵת צָרָה וְצוּקָה. אֵין לָנוּ מֶלֶךְ אֶלָּא אַתָּה. אֱלֹהֵי הָרִאשׁוֹנִים וְהָאַחֲרוֹנִים, אֱלוֹהַּ כָּל בְּרִיּוֹת, אֲדוֹן כָּל תּוֹלָדוֹת, הַמְהֻלָּל בְּרֹב הַתִּשְׁבָּחוֹת, הַמְנַהֵג עוֹלָמוֹ בְּחֶסֶד וּבְרִיּוֹתָיו בְּרַחֲמִים. וַיְיָ לֹא יָנוּם וְלֹא יִישָׁן - הַמְעוֹרֵר יְשֵׁנִים וְהַמֵּקִיץ נִרְדָּמִים, וְהַמֵּשִׂיחַ אִלְּמִים וְהַמַּתִּיר אֲסוּרִים וְהַסּוֹמֵךְ נוֹפְלִים וְהַזּוֹקֵף כְּפוּפִים. לְךָ לְבַדְּךָ אֲנַחְנוּ מוֹדִים.

וְאִלּוּ פִינוּ מָלֵא שִׁירָה כַּיָּם, וּלְשׁוֹנֵנוּ רִנָּה כַּהֲמוֹן גַּלָּיו, וְשִׂפְתוֹתֵינוּ שֶׁבַח כְּמֶרְחֲבֵי רָקִיעַ, וְעֵינֵינוּ מְאִירוֹת כַּשֶּׁמֶשׁ וְכַיָּרֵחַ, וְיָדֵינוּ פְרוּשׂוֹת כְּנִשְׁרֵי שָׁמָיִם, וְרַגְלֵינוּ קַלּוֹת כָּאַיָּלוֹת - אֵין אֲנַחְנוּ מַסְפִּיקִים לְהוֹדוֹת לְךָ, יְיָ אֱלֹהֵינוּ וֵאלֹהֵי אֲבוֹתֵינוּ, וּלְבָרֵךְ אֶת שִׁמְךָ עַל אַחַת מֵאֶלֶף אַלְפֵי אֲלָפִים וְרִבֵּי רְבָבוֹת פְּעָמִים הַטּוֹבוֹת שֶׁעָשִׂיתָ עִם אֲבוֹתֵינוּ וְעִמָּנוּ.

מִמִּצְרַיִם גְּאַלְתָּנוּ, יְיָ אֱלֹהֵינוּ, וּמִבֵּית עֲבָדִים פְּדִיתָנוּ, בְּרָעָב זַנְתָּנוּ וּבְשָׂבָע כִּלְכַּלְתָּנוּ, מֵחֶרֶב הִצַּלְתָּנוּ וּמִדֶּבֶר מִלַּטְתָּנוּ, וּמֵחֳלָיִם רָעִים וְנֶאֱמָנִים דִּלִּיתָנוּ. עַד הֵנָּה עֲזָרוּנוּ רַחֲמֶיךָ וְלֹא עֲזָבוּנוּ חֲסָדֶיךָ, וְאַל תִּטְּשֵׁנוּ, יְיָ אֱלֹהֵינוּ, לָנֶצַח. עַל כֵּן אֵבָרִים שֶׁפִּלַּגְתָּ בָּנוּ וְרוּחַ וּנְשָׁמָה שֶׁנָּפַחְתָּ בְּאַפֵּנוּ וְלָשׁוֹן אֲשֶׁר שַׂמְתָּ בְּפִינוּ, הֵן הֵם יוֹדוּ וִיבָרְכוּ וִישַׁבְּחוּ וִיפָאֲרוּ וִירוֹמְמוּ וְיַעֲרִיצוּ וְיַקְדִּישׁוּ וְיַמְלִיכוּ אֶת שִׁמְךָ מַלְכֵּנוּ. כִּי כָל פֶּה לְךָ יוֹדֶה, וְכָל לָשׁוֹן לְךָ תִשָּׁבַע, וְכָל בֶּרֶךְ לְךָ תִכְרַע, וְכָל קוֹמָה לְפָנֶיךָ תִשְׁתַּחֲוֶה, וְכָל לְבָבוֹת יִירָאוּךָ, וְכָל קֶרֶב וּכְלָיוֹת יְזַמְּרוּ לִשְׁמֶךָ, כַּדָּבָר שֶׁכָּתוּב:

"כָּל עַצְמֹתַי תֹּאמַרְנָה: יְיָ, מִי כָמוֹךָ, מַצִּיל עָנִי מֵחָזָק מִמֶּנּוּ וְעָנִי וְאֶבְיוֹן מִגֹּזְלוֹ".

מִי יִדְמֶה לָּךְ וּמִי יִשְׁוֶה לָּךְ וּמִי יַעֲרָךְ לָךְ, הָאֵל הַגָּדוֹל, הַגִּבּוֹר וְהַנּוֹרָא, אֵל עֶלְיוֹן, קֹנֵה שָׁמַיִם וָאָרֶץ. נְהַלֶּלְךָ וּנְשַׁבֵּחֲךָ וּנְפָאֶרְךָ וּנְבָרֵךְ אֶת שֵׁם קָדְשֶׁךָ, כָּאָמוּר: "לְדָוִד, בָּרְכִי נַפְשִׁי אֶת יְיָ וְכָל קְרָבַי אֶת שֵׁם קָדְשׁוֹ". הָאֵל בְּתַעֲצֻמוֹת עֻזֶּךָ, הַגָּדוֹל בִּכְבוֹד שְׁמֶךָ, הַגִּבּוֹר לָנֶצַח וְהַנּוֹרָא בְּנוֹרְאוֹתֶיךָ, הַמֶּלֶךְ הַיּוֹשֵׁב עַל כִּסֵּא רָם וְנִשָּׂא. שׁוֹכֵן עַד, מָרוֹם וְקָדוֹשׁ שְׁמוֹ. וְכָתוּב: רַנְּנוּ צַדִּיקִים בַּיְיָ, לַיְשָׁרִים נָאוָה תְהִלָּה. בְּפִי יְשָׁרִים תִּתְהַלָּל, וּבְדִבְרֵי צַדִּיקִים תִּתְבָּרַךְ, וּבִלְשׁוֹן חֲסִידִים תִּתְרוֹמָם, וּבְקֶרֶב קְדוֹשִׁים תִּתְקַדָּשׁ. וּבְמַקְהֲלוֹת רִבְבוֹת עַמְּךָ בֵּית יִשְׂרָאֵל בְּרִנָּה יִתְפָּאֵר שִׁמְךָ, מַלְכֵּנוּ, בְּכָל דּוֹר וָדוֹר, שֶׁכֵּן חוֹבַת כָּל הַיְצוּרִים לְפָנֶיךָ, יְיָ אֱלֹהֵינוּ וֵאלֹהֵי אֲבוֹתֵינוּ, לְהוֹדוֹת, לְהַלֵּל, לְשַׁבֵּחַ, לְפָאֵר, לְרוֹמֵם, לְהַדֵּר, לְבָרֵךְ, לְעַלֵּה וּלְקַלֵּס עַל כָּל דִּבְרֵי שִׁירוֹת וְתִשְׁבְּחוֹת דָּוִד בֶּן יִשַׁי עַבְדְּךָ, מְשִׁיחֶךָ.

יִשְׁתַּבַּח שִׁמְךָ לָעַד מַלְכֵּנוּ, הָאֵל הַמֶּלֶךְ הַגָּדוֹל וְהַקָּדוֹשׁ, בַּשָּׁמַיִם וּבָאָרֶץ. כִּי לְךָ נָאֶה, יְיָ אֱלֹהֵינוּ וֵאלֹהֵי אֲבוֹתֵינוּ, שִׁיר וּשְׁבָחָה, הַלֵּל וְזִמְרָה, עֹז וּמֶמְשָׁלָה, נֶצַח, גְּדֻלָּה וּגְבוּרָה, תְּהִלָּה וְתִפְאֶרֶת, קְדֻשָּׁה וּמַלְכוּת, בְּרָכוֹת וְהוֹדָאוֹת מֵעַתָּה וְעַד עוֹלָם.

בָּרוּךְ אַתָּה יְיָ, אֵל מֶלֶךְ גָּדוֹל בַּתִּשְׁבָּחוֹת, אֵל הַהוֹדָאוֹת, אֲדוֹן הַנִּפְלָאוֹת, הַבּוֹחֵר בְּשִׁירֵי זִמְרָה, מֶלֶךְ אֵל חַי הָעוֹלָמִים.

The life breath of every living thing blesses your name, God.
Without you we have no ruler and redeemer, no one to rescue us and to take pity on us in times of trouble and strife...
You release prisoners...
From Egypt You redeemed us,
from the house of bondage...
You rescue the poor from the strong, the poverty-stricken from those who rob them.

Fourth Cup כּוֹס רְבִיעִית

בָּרוּךְ אַתָּה יי אֱלֹהֵינוּ מֶלֶךְ הָעוֹלָם,

בּוֹרֵא פְּרִי הַגָּפֶן.

Blessed are You, Adonai our God,
Ruler of the Universe,
who created the **fruit of the vine**.

Ba-rukh ata Adonai / Elo-heinu me-lekh ha-olam / bo-rei **pree ha-gafen**.

בָּרוּךְ אַתָּה יי אֱלֹהֵינוּ מֶלֶךְ הָעוֹלָם, עַל הַגֶּפֶן וְעַל פְּרִי הַגֶּפֶן וְעַל תְּנוּבַת
הַשָּׂדֶה וְעַל אֶרֶץ חֶמְדָּה טוֹבָה וּרְחָבָה, שֶׁרָצִיתָ וְהִנְחַלְתָּ לַאֲבוֹתֵינוּ לֶאֱכֹל
מִפִּרְיָהּ וְלִשְׂבֹּעַ מִטּוּבָהּ. רַחֵם יי אֱלֹהֵינוּ עָלֵינוּ וְעַל יִשְׂרָאֵל עַמֶּךָ וְעַל
יְרוּשָׁלַיִם עִירֶךָ וְעַל הַר צִיּוֹן מִשְׁכַּן כְּבוֹדֶךָ וְעַל מִזְבְּחֶךָ וְעַל הֵיכָלֶךָ. וּבְנֵה
יְרוּשָׁלַיִם עִיר הַקֹּדֶשׁ בִּמְהֵרָה בְיָמֵינוּ, וְהַעֲלֵנוּ לְתוֹכָהּ וְשַׂמְּחֵנוּ בְּבִנְיָנָהּ
וּנְבָרֶכְךָ עָלֶיהָ בִּקְדֻשָּׁה וּבְטָהֳרָה. (בשבת: וּרְצֵה וְהַחֲלִיצֵנוּ בְּיוֹם הַשַּׁבָּת
הַזֶּה) וְשַׂמְּחֵנוּ בְּיוֹם חַג הַמַּצּוֹת הַזֶּה, בְּיוֹם טוֹב מִקְרָא קֹדֶשׁ הַזֶּה, כִּי אַתָּה
טוֹב וּמֵטִיב לַכֹּל וְנוֹדֶה לְּךָ יי אֱלֹהֵינוּ עַל הָאָרֶץ וְעַל פְּרִי גַפְנָהּ.
בָּרוּךְ אַתָּה יי, עַל הָאָרֶץ וְעַל פְּרִי גַפְנָהּ.

Blessing after Drinking Wine

Blessed are You, Adonai, for the vine and its
fruit, for the beautiful and spacious land You
gave us. Have mercy on us and bring us there
to eat its fruits. Grant us happiness on this
Festival of Matzot.
Blessed are You, Adonai, for the land and for
the fruit of the vine.

Ba-rukh ata Adonai / al ha-aretz v'al pree ha-gafen.

On the second night of Pesach only:

Counting the Omer סְפִירַת הָעֹמֶר

הִנְנִי מוּכָן וּמְזוּמָן לְקַיֵּם מִצְוַת עֲשֵׂה שֶׁל סְפִירַת הָעֹמֶר.

בָּרוּךְ אַתָּה יי אֱלֹהֵינוּ מֶלֶךְ הָעוֹלָם
אֲשֶׁר קִדְּשָׁנוּ בְּמִצְוֹתָיו וְצִוָּנוּ עַל
סְפִירַת הָעֹמֶר.

הַיּוֹם יוֹם אֶחָד לָעֹמֶר.

Blessed are you, Adonai our God,
Ruler of the Universe, who has
sanctified us with Divine laws and
commanded us to count **the Omer**.

Today is the first day of the Omer.

Ba-rukh ata Adonai / Elo-heinu me-lekh ha-olam / asher keed'shanu
b'meetz-vo-tav v'tzee-vanu al **s'feerat ha-omer** / Ha-yom yom ekhad la-omer.

Raise the fourth cup
of wine and recite the
blessing over it.

Recline to the left
while drinking.

On the second night
of Pesach we begin
counting the 50 days
from the Exodus to
Sinai, from Pesach,
the harvest of barley,
until Shavuot, the
harvest of wheat.
With the giving of the
Torah at Sinai, Jews
move from freedom
to responsibility.

Say the blessing and
count off the first day
of the Omer.

THE FIFTH CUP

The first four cups of wine stand for four stages of redemption promised in Exodus 6:6-7. But Rabbi Tarfon drank a fifth cup to commemorate the fifth stage of redemption: *"And I shall bring you into the land which I raised my hand and swore to give to Abraham, Isaac, and Jacob, and I give it to you as an inheritance, I am Adonai."*

(Exodus 6:8, Talmud Pesachim 118)

Rabbi Menachem M. Kasher proposes that since 1948, all Jews adopt the fifth cup:

> "It is fitting and proper that we observe this pious act, the drinking of the fifth cup, as a way to give thanks... For in our own time, we have been privileged to witness the mercies of the Holy One and our rescue through the establishment of the State of Israel, the beginning of our redemption... as God promised us: *"I shall bring you into the land."* (Exodus 6:7)

Rabbi Irving Greenberg adds:

> "Jewish tradition is not static. Adding this fifth cup is our testimony that Israel's rebirth is revelation and redemption in our own time. The fifth cup is also a statement of hope and trust that this is a lasting redemption that will not be destroyed again. Our joy and our faith in the Exodus is increased because it happened again in this generation."

THE OMER:
49 STEPS TO FREEDOM

In the Kiddush with which we began the Seder, Passover is called the "time of our freedom." But as we know, attaining inner freedom is very difficult. It is not something we can do in just one – or two – nights. The Slonimer rebbe teaches that while God took us physically out of Egypt on Pesach night, the spiritual Egypt and all of its enslaving aspects are still within us. There are still 50 spiritual aspects of enslavement within us, 50 inner steps that lead up the staircase to freedom. But God is not going to push us up those stairs, as God pushed us out of Egypt. God has already done the big work – the Exodus – from above, in a miraculous and momentous event that we, frankly, had little to do with. But it is now up to us to start our own, inner, journey towards freedom. This is what the counting of the Omer signifies.

The Kabbalists assigned a combination of God's seven attributes to each of the 49 days of the Omer: Kindness, Discipline, Compassion, Endurance, Humility, Foundation and Sovereignty, thus creating 49 different refined characteristics. On each day of the Omer we are invited to explore our personality and behavior in light of this characteristic, to refine, refresh and improve ourselves based on what we learn on each day (For example, the first night is dedicated to refining our kindness, our ability to be truly generous, not to expect a quid pro quo...).

Finally, after taking these 49 steps towards freedom, we are ready for the 50th step: receiving the Torah on Shavuot. Receiving the Torah signifies our ability to choose a path in life, a choice that only free people can make. For as the Rabbis teach us, the tablets of the covenant were inscribed with "freedom on the tablets." The Torah itself is freedom, but is granted as an achievement, not as a gift.

Concluding Songs

The Ashkenazi Haggadah concludes with a Song Book Appendix.

Two poems are sung alternatively on the first and second Seder night: The first recalls God's nighttime rescues, "In the middle of the night." At night God saved Israel with the tenth plague, helped Jacob when he was pursued by Lavan, and Mordechai when pursued by Haman.

The second poem reviews the many acts of redemption that occurred, according to tradition, on Pesach: the angels announced the birth of Isaac, the conquest of Jericho, the hanging of Haman, and so on.

For the first night:
"It Happened in the Middle of the Night"
(Exodus 12:29)

by Yannai, 5ᵗʰ C. Israel

וַיְהִי בַּחֲצִי הַלַּיְלָה

אָז רֹב נִסִּים הִפְלֵאתָ בַּלַּיְלָה,
בְּרֹאשׁ אַשְׁמוּרוֹת זֶה הַלַּיְלָה,
גֵּר צֶדֶק נִצַּחְתּוֹ כְּנֶחֱלַק לוֹ לַיְלָה,
וַיְהִי בַּחֲצִי הַלַּיְלָה.

דַּנְתָּ מֶלֶךְ גְּרָר בַּחֲלוֹם הַלַּיְלָה,
הִפְחַדְתָּ אֲרַמִּי בְּאֶמֶשׁ לַיְלָה,
וַיָּשַׂר יִשְׂרָאֵל לְמַלְאָךְ וַיּוּכַל לוֹ לַיְלָה,
וַיְהִי בַּחֲצִי הַלַּיְלָה.

זֶרַע בְּכוֹרֵי פַתְרוֹס מָחַצְתָּ בַּחֲצִי הַלַּיְלָה,
חֵילָם לֹא מָצְאוּ בְּקוּמָם בַּלַּיְלָה,
טִיסַת נְגִיד חֲרֹשֶׁת סִלִּיתָ בְכוֹכְבֵי לַיְלָה,
וַיְהִי בַּחֲצִי הַלַּיְלָה.

יָעַץ מְחָרֵף לְנוֹפֵף אִוּוּי, הוֹבַשְׁתָּ פְגָרָיו בַּלַּיְלָה,
כָּרַע בֵּל וּמַצָּבוֹ בְּאִישׁוֹן לַיְלָה,
לְאִישׁ חֲמוּדוֹת נִגְלָה רָז חֲזוֹת לַיְלָה,
וַיְהִי בַּחֲצִי הַלַּיְלָה.

מִשְׁתַּכֵּר בִּכְלֵי קֹדֶשׁ נֶהֱרַג בּוֹ בַּלַּיְלָה,
נוֹשַׁע מִבּוֹר אֲרָיוֹת פּוֹתֵר בִּעֲתוּתֵי לַיְלָה,
שִׂנְאָה נָטַר אֲגָגִי וְכָתַב סְפָרִים בַּלַּיְלָה,
וַיְהִי בַּחֲצִי הַלַּיְלָה.

עוֹרַרְתָּ נִצְחֲךָ עָלָיו בְּנֶדֶד שְׁנַת לַיְלָה,
פּוּרָה תִדְרֹךְ לְשׁוֹמֵר מַה מִּלַּיְלָה,
צָרַח כַּשּׁוֹמֵר וְשָׂח אָתָא בֹקֶר וְגַם לַיְלָה,
וַיְהִי בַּחֲצִי הַלַּיְלָה.

קָרֵב יוֹם אֲשֶׁר הוּא לֹא יוֹם וְלֹא לַיְלָה,
רָם הוֹדַע כִּי לְךָ הַיּוֹם אַף לְךָ הַלַּיְלָה,
שׁוֹמְרִים הַפְקֵד לְעִירְךָ כָּל הַיּוֹם וְכָל הַלַּיְלָה,
תָּאִיר כְּאוֹר יוֹם חֶשְׁכַת לַיְלָה,
וַיְהִי בַּחֲצִי הַלַּיְלָה.

For the second night:
"You shall say: 'It is the Passover Sacrifice.'"
(Exodus 12:27)

by Elazar HaKalir, 8ᵗʰ C. Israel

וַאֲמַרְתֶּם זֶבַח פֶּסַח

אֹמֶץ גְּבוּרוֹתֶיךָ הִפְלֵאתָ בַּפֶּסַח,
בְּרֹאשׁ כָּל מוֹעֲדוֹת נִשֵּׂאתָ פֶּסַח,
גִּלִּיתָ לְאֶזְרָחִי חֲצוֹת לֵיל פֶּסַח,
וַאֲמַרְתֶּם זֶבַח פֶּסַח.

דְּלָתָיו דָּפַקְתָּ כְּחֹם הַיּוֹם בַּפֶּסַח,
הִסְעִיד נוֹצְצִים עֻגּוֹת מַצּוֹת בַּפֶּסַח,
וְאֶל הַבָּקָר רָץ זֵכֶר לְשׁוֹר עֵרֶךְ פֶּסַח,
וַאֲמַרְתֶּם זֶבַח פֶּסַח.

זֹעֲמוּ סְדוֹמִים וְלֹהֲטוּ בָּאֵשׁ בַּפֶּסַח,
חֻלַּץ לוֹט מֵהֶם וּמַצּוֹת אָפָה בְּקֵץ פֶּסַח,
טִאטֵאתָ אַדְמַת מֹף וְנֹף בְּעָבְרְךָ בַּפֶּסַח,
וַאֲמַרְתֶּם זֶבַח פֶּסַח.

יָהּ רֹאשׁ כָּל אוֹן מָחַצְתָּ בְּלֵיל שִׁמּוּר פֶּסַח,
כַּבִּיר, עַל בֵּן בְּכוֹר פָּסַחְתָּ בְּדַם פֶּסַח,
לְבִלְתִּי תֵת מַשְׁחִית לָבֹא בִּפְתָחַי בַּפֶּסַח,
וַאֲמַרְתֶּם זֶבַח פֶּסַח.

מְסֻגֶּרֶת סֻגָּרָה בְּעִתּוֹתֵי פֶּסַח,
נִשְׁמְדָה מִדְיָן בִּצְלִיל שְׂעוֹרֵי עֹמֶר פֶּסַח,
שֹׂרְפוּ מִשְׁמַנֵּי פּוּל וְלוּד בִּיקַד יְקוֹד פֶּסַח,
וַאֲמַרְתֶּם זֶבַח פֶּסַח.

עוֹד הַיּוֹם בְּנֹב לַעֲמֹד עַד גָּעָה עוֹנַת פֶּסַח,
פַּס יַד כָּתְבָה לְקַעֲקֵעַ צוּל בַּפֶּסַח,
צָפֹה הַצָּפִית עָרֹךְ הַשֻּׁלְחָן בַּפֶּסַח,
וַאֲמַרְתֶּם זֶבַח פֶּסַח.

קָהָל כִּנְּסָה הֲדַסָּה לְשַׁלֵּשׁ צוֹם בַּפֶּסַח,
רֹאשׁ מִבֵּית רָשָׁע מָחַצְתָּ בְּעֵץ חֲמִשִּׁים בַּפֶּסַח,
שְׁתֵּי אֵלֶּה רֶגַע תָּבִיא לְעוּצִית בַּפֶּסַח,
תָּעֹז יָדְךָ תָּרוּם יְמִינְךָ כְּלֵיל הִתְקַדֵּשׁ חַג פֶּסַח,
וַאֲמַרְתֶּם זֶבַח פֶּסַח.

Adeer B'Mlukha אַדִּיר בִּמְלוּכָה

אַדִּיר בִּמְלוּכָה, בָּחוּר כַּהֲלָכָה, גְּדוּדָיו יֹאמְרוּ לוֹ:
לְךָ וּלְךָ, לְךָ כִּי לְךָ, לְךָ אַף לְךָ,
לְךָ יְיָ הַמַּמְלָכָה, כִּי לוֹ נָאֶה, כִּי לוֹ יָאֶה.

דָּגוּל בִּמְלוּכָה, הָדוּר כַּהֲלָכָה, וָתִיקָיו יֹאמְרוּ לוֹ:
לְךָ וּלְךָ, לְךָ כִּי לְךָ, לְךָ אַף לְךָ,
לְךָ יְיָ הַמַּמְלָכָה, כִּי לוֹ נָאֶה, כִּי לוֹ יָאֶה.

זַכַּאי בִּמְלוּכָה, חָסִין כַּהֲלָכָה, טַפְסְרָיו יֹאמְרוּ לוֹ:
לְךָ וּלְךָ, לְךָ כִּי לְךָ, לְךָ אַף לְךָ,
לְךָ יְיָ הַמַּמְלָכָה, כִּי לוֹ נָאֶה, כִּי לוֹ יָאֶה.

יָחִיד בִּמְלוּכָה, כַּבִּיר כַּהֲלָכָה, לִמּוּדָיו יֹאמְרוּ לוֹ:
לְךָ וּלְךָ, לְךָ כִּי לְךָ, לְךָ אַף לְךָ,
לְךָ יְיָ הַמַּמְלָכָה, כִּי לוֹ נָאֶה, כִּי לוֹ יָאֶה.

מוֹשֵׁל בִּמְלוּכָה, נוֹרָא כַּהֲלָכָה, סְבִיבָיו יֹאמְרוּ לוֹ:
לְךָ וּלְךָ, לְךָ כִּי לְךָ, לְךָ אַף לְךָ,
לְךָ יְיָ הַמַּמְלָכָה, כִּי לוֹ נָאֶה, כִּי לוֹ יָאֶה.

עָנָו בִּמְלוּכָה, פּוֹדֶה כַּהֲלָכָה, צַדִּיקָיו יֹאמְרוּ לוֹ:
לְךָ וּלְךָ, לְךָ כִּי לְךָ, לְךָ אַף לְךָ,
לְךָ יְיָ הַמַּמְלָכָה, כִּי לוֹ נָאֶה, כִּי לוֹ יָאֶה.

קָדוֹשׁ בִּמְלוּכָה, רַחוּם כַּהֲלָכָה, שִׁנְאַנָּיו יֹאמְרוּ לוֹ:
לְךָ וּלְךָ, לְךָ כִּי לְךָ, לְךָ אַף לְךָ,
לְךָ יְיָ הַמַּמְלָכָה, כִּי לוֹ נָאֶה, כִּי לוֹ יָאֶה.

תַּקִּיף בִּמְלוּכָה, תּוֹמֵךְ כַּהֲלָכָה, תְּמִימָיו יֹאמְרוּ לוֹ:
לְךָ וּלְךָ, לְךָ כִּי לְךָ, לְךָ אַף לְךָ,
לְךָ יְיָ הַמַּמְלָכָה, כִּי לוֹ נָאֶה, כִּי לוֹ יָאֶה.

It is Proper to Praise

This table song, by Jacob, a German poet, is an alphabetical acrostic praising God's many attributes. Though it has no connection to Pesach at all, it entered the Ashkenazi Haggadah after the 12th C. as a popular religious song.

The first verse typifies the style:

> "Mighty in royalty,
> Beautiful in stature,
> God's angels exclaim:
> To God alone
> Belongs the Kingdom,
> For all this is becoming
> And fitting to God!"

Refrain:

**L'kha u-l'kha, l'kha kee l'kha, l'kha af l'kha.
L'kha Adonai ha-mam-lakha.
Kee lo na-eh, kee lo ya-eh.**

Adeer Hu אַדִּיר הוּא

MIGHTY IS GOD

אַדִּיר הוּא, יִבְנֶה בֵּיתוֹ בְּקָרוֹב.
בִּמְהֵרָה, בִּמְהֵרָה, בְּיָמֵינוּ בְּקָרוֹב.
אֵל בְּנֵה, אֵל בְּנֵה, בְּנֵה בֵּיתְךָ בְּקָרוֹב.

בָּחוּר הוּא, גָּדוֹל הוּא, דָּגוּל הוּא, יִבְנֶה בֵּיתוֹ בְּקָרוֹב.
בִּמְהֵרָה, בִּמְהֵרָה, בְּיָמֵינוּ בְּקָרוֹב.
אֵל בְּנֵה, אֵל בְּנֵה, בְּנֵה בֵּיתְךָ בְּקָרוֹב.

הָדוּר הוּא, וָתִיק הוּא, זַכַּאי הוּא, יִבְנֶה בֵּיתוֹ בְּקָרוֹב.
בִּמְהֵרָה, בִּמְהֵרָה, בְּיָמֵינוּ בְּקָרוֹב.
אֵל בְּנֵה, אֵל בְּנֵה, בְּנֵה בֵּיתְךָ בְּקָרוֹב.

חָסִיד הוּא, טָהוֹר הוּא, יָחִיד הוּא, יִבְנֶה בֵּיתוֹ בְּקָרוֹב.
בִּמְהֵרָה, בִּמְהֵרָה, בְּיָמֵינוּ בְּקָרוֹב.
אֵל בְּנֵה, אֵל בְּנֵה, בְּנֵה בֵּיתְךָ בְּקָרוֹב.

כַּבִּיר הוּא, לָמוּד הוּא, מֶלֶךְ הוּא, יִבְנֶה בֵּיתוֹ בְּקָרוֹב.
בִּמְהֵרָה, בִּמְהֵרָה, בְּיָמֵינוּ בְּקָרוֹב.
אֵל בְּנֵה, אֵל בְּנֵה, בְּנֵה בֵּיתְךָ בְּקָרוֹב.

נוֹרָא הוּא, סַגִּיב הוּא, עִזּוּז הוּא, יִבְנֶה בֵּיתוֹ בְּקָרוֹב.
בִּמְהֵרָה, בִּמְהֵרָה, בְּיָמֵינוּ בְּקָרוֹב.
אֵל בְּנֵה, אֵל בְּנֵה, בְּנֵה בֵּיתְךָ בְּקָרוֹב.

פּוֹדֶה הוּא, צַדִּיק הוּא, קָדוֹשׁ הוּא, יִבְנֶה בֵּיתוֹ בְּקָרוֹב.
בִּמְהֵרָה, בִּמְהֵרָה, בְּיָמֵינוּ בְּקָרוֹב.
אֵל בְּנֵה, אֵל בְּנֵה, בְּנֵה בֵּיתְךָ בְּקָרוֹב.

רַחוּם הוּא, שַׁדַּי הוּא, תַּקִּיף הוּא, יִבְנֶה בֵּיתוֹ בְּקָרוֹב.
בִּמְהֵרָה, בִּמְהֵרָה, בְּיָמֵינוּ בְּקָרוֹב.
אֵל בְּנֵה, אֵל בְּנֵה, בְּנֵה בֵּיתְךָ בְּקָרוֹב.

The poet (15th C. Germany) recounts the Divine attributes in alphabetical order and prays for the building of the Third Temple.

Adeer hu, adeer hu

Refrain:
> Yeev-neh veito b'ka-rov,
> beem-hei-ra, beem-hei-ra,
> B'ya-mei-nu b'ka-rov, Eil b'nei,
> Eil b'nei, B'nei veit-kha b'ka-rov.

Ba-khur hu, ga-dol hu, da-gul hu,
Yeev-neh vei-to b'ka-rov . . .

Ha-dur hu, va-teek hu, za-kai hu,
Yeev-neh vei-to b'ka-rov . . .

Kha-sid hu, ta-hor hu, ya-kheed hu,
Yeev-neh vei-to b'ka-rov . . .

Ka-beer hu, la-mud hu, me-lekh hu,
Yeev-neh vei-to b'ka-rov . . .

No-ra hu, sa-geev hu, ee-zuz hu,
Yeev-neh vei-to b'ka-rov . . .

Po-deh hu, tza-deek hu, ka-dosh hu,
Yeev-neh vei-to b'ka-rov . . .

Ra-khum hu, sha-dai hu, ta-keef hu,
Yeev-neh vei-to b'ka-rov . . .

"Who knows one?" is modeled on a German folksong (15th or 16th C.). It consists of a numerical quiz.

Since the song is written in question and answer form, you may assign the answers to different participants. The whole "chorus" sings the question: "Who knows two (three, etc.)?" and the pre-assigned respondent sings the answer to their number: "I know two, two are the tablets..." every time that number comes up.

WHO PAINTS ONE?

How does one visually represent "*God who is in Heaven and on earth?*" Jews do not portray God's body literally, but they do use bodily metaphors. Michel Kichka uses Michelangelo's famous image of God stretching his hand out from "Heaven" to create Adam. It is, however, only God's "outstretched arm" we see – the Torah's chief metaphor for God's redemption of Israel from Egypt.

Can you identify the other 12 items in *Ekhad MeeYodea?*

1

Who knows one? I know one.
One is our God, who is in Heaven and on earth.

2

Who knows two? I know two.
Two are the tablets of the Covenant. One is our God, who is in heaven and on earth.

3

Three are the Fathers.

4

Four are the Mothers.

5

Five are the books of the Torah.

6

Six are the orders of Mishna.

7

Seven are the days of the Week.

8

Eight are the days before Circumcision.

9

Nine are the months of Pregnancy.

10

Ten are the Ten Commandments.

11

Eleven are the stars in Joseph's dream.

12

Twelve are the Tribes of Israel.

13

Thirteen are God's Attributes of Mercy

אֶחָד מִי יוֹדֵעַ?

אֶחָד אֲנִי יוֹדֵעַ!

אֶחָד אֱלֹהֵינוּ שֶׁבַּשָּׁמַיִם וּבָאָרֶץ.

Ekhad mee yo-dei-a?

Ekhad anee yo-dei-a.

Ekhad Elo-hei-nu she-ba-sha-ma-yeem uva-aretz.

שְׁנַיִם מִי יוֹדֵעַ?

שְׁנַיִם אֲנִי יוֹדֵעַ!

שְׁנֵי לוּחוֹת הַבְּרִית.

אֶחָד אֱלֹהֵינוּ שֶׁבַּשָּׁמַיִם וּבָאָרֶץ.

Shna-yeem mee yo-dei-a?

Shna-yeem anee yo-dei-a.

Shnei lu-khot ha-breet,

Ekhad Elo-hei-nu she-ba-sha-ma-yeem uva-aretz.

שְׁלֹשָׁה מִי יוֹדֵעַ?

שְׁלֹשָׁה אֲנִי יוֹדֵעַ!

שְׁלֹשָׁה אָבוֹת,

שְׁנֵי לוּחוֹת הַבְּרִית,

אֶחָד אֱלֹהֵינוּ שֶׁבַּשָּׁמַיִם וּבָאָרֶץ.

Shlo-sha mee yo-dei-a?

Shlo-sha anee yo-dei-a.

Shlo-sha avot,

Shnei lu-khot ha-breet,

Ekhad Elo-hei-nu she-ba-sha-ma-yeem uva-aretz.

אַרְבַּע מִי יוֹדֵעַ?

אַרְבַּע אֲנִי יוֹדֵעַ!

אַרְבַּע אִמָּהוֹת,

שְׁלֹשָׁה אָבוֹת,

שְׁנֵי לוּחוֹת הַבְּרִית,

אֶחָד אֱלֹהֵינוּ שֶׁבַּשָּׁמַיִם וּבָאָרֶץ.

Arba mee yo-dei-a?

Arba anee yo-dei-a.

Arba eema-hot,

Shlo-sha avot,

Shnei lu-khot ha-breet,

Ekhad Elo-hei-nu she-ba-sha-ma-yeem uva-aretz.

חֲמִשָּׁה מִי יוֹדֵעַ?

חֲמִשָּׁה אֲנִי יוֹדֵעַ!

חֲמִשָּׁה חֻמְשֵׁי תוֹרָה,

אַרְבַּע אִמָּהוֹת,

שְׁלֹשָׁה אָבוֹת,

שְׁנֵי לוּחוֹת הַבְּרִית,

אֶחָד אֱלֹהֵינוּ שֶׁבַּשָּׁמַיִם וּבָאָרֶץ.

Ha-mee-sha mee yo-dei-a?

Ha-mee-sha anee yo-dei-a.

Ha-mee-sha hum-shei Torah,

Arba eema-hot,

Shlo-sha avot,

Shnei lu-khot ha-breet,

Ekhad Elo-hei-nu she-ba-sha-ma-yeem uva-aretz.

שִׁשָּׁה מִי יוֹדֵעַ?

שִׁשָּׁה אֲנִי יוֹדֵעַ!

שִׁשָּׁה סִדְרֵי מִשְׁנָה,

חֲמִשָּׁה חוּמְשֵׁי תוֹרָה,

אַרְבַּע אִמָּהוֹת,

שְׁלֹשָׁה אָבוֹת,

שְׁנֵי לוּחוֹת הַבְּרִית,

אֶחָד אֱלֹהֵינוּ שֶׁבַּשָּׁמַיִם וּבָאָרֶץ.

Shee-sha mee yo-dei-a?

Shee-sha anee yo-dei-a.

Shee-sha seedrei Mishna,

Ha-meesha hum-shei Torah,

Arba eema-hot,

Shlo-sha avot,

Shnei lu-khot ha-breet,

Ekhad Elo-hei-nu she-ba-sha-ma-yeem uva-aretz.

שִׁבְעָה מִי יוֹדֵעַ?

שִׁבְעָה אֲנִי יוֹדֵעַ!

שִׁבְעָה יְמֵי שַׁבַּתָּא,

שִׁשָּׁה סִדְרֵי מִשְׁנָה,

חֲמִשָּׁה חוּמְשֵׁי תוֹרָה,

אַרְבַּע אִמָּהוֹת,

שְׁלֹשָׁה אָבוֹת,

שְׁנֵי לוּחוֹת הַבְּרִית,

אֶחָד אֱלֹהֵינוּ שֶׁבַּשָּׁמַיִם וּבָאָרֶץ.

Shee-va mee yo-dei-a?

Shee-va anee yo-dei-a.

Shee-va y'mei Shab-ta,

Shee-sha seedrei Mishna,

Ha-meesha hum-shei Torah,

Arba eema-hot,

Shlo-sha avot,

Shnei lu-khot ha-breet,

Ekhad Elo-hei-nu she-ba-sha-ma-yeem uva-aretz.

שְׁמוֹנָה מִי יוֹדֵעַ?

שְׁמוֹנָה אֲנִי יוֹדֵעַ!

שְׁמוֹנָה יְמֵי מִילָה,

שִׁבְעָה יְמֵי שַׁבַּתָּא,

שִׁשָּׁה סִדְרֵי מִשְׁנָה,

חֲמִשָּׁה חוּמְשֵׁי תוֹרָה,

אַרְבַּע אִמָּהוֹת,

שְׁלֹשָׁה אָבוֹת,

שְׁנֵי לוּחוֹת הַבְּרִית,

אֶחָד אֱלֹהֵינוּ שֶׁבַּשָּׁמַיִם וּבָאָרֶץ.

Shmona mee yo-dei-a?

Shmona anee yo-dei-a.

Shmona y'mei mee-la,

Shee-va y'mei Shab-ta,

Shee-sha seedrei Mishna,

Ha-meesha hum-shei Torah,

Arba eema-hot,

Shlo-sha avot,

Shnei lu-khot ha-breet,

Ekhad Elo-hei-nu she-ba-sha-ma-yeem uva-aretz.

תִּשְׁעָה מִי יוֹדֵעַ?
תִּשְׁעָה אֲנִי יוֹדֵעַ!
תִּשְׁעָה יַרְחֵי לֵדָה,
שְׁמוֹנָה יְמֵי מִילָה,
שִׁבְעָה יְמֵי שַׁבְּתָא,
שִׁשָּׁה סִדְרֵי מִשְׁנָה,
חֲמִשָּׁה חֻמְשֵׁי תוֹרָה,
אַרְבַּע אִמָּהוֹת,
שְׁלֹשָׁה אָבוֹת,
שְׁנֵי לוּחוֹת הַבְּרִית,
אֶחָד אֱלֹהֵינוּ שֶׁבַּשָּׁמַיִם וּבָאָרֶץ.

Tee-sha mee yo-dei-a?
Tee-sha anee yo-dei-a.
Tee-sha yar-khei lei-da,
Shmona y'mei mee-la,
Shee-va y'mei Shab-ta,
Shee-sha see-drei Mishna,
Ha-mee-sha hum-shei Torah,
Arba eema-hot,
Shlo-sha avot,
Shnei lu-khot ha-breet,
Ekhad Elo-hei-nu she-ba-sha-ma-yeem uva-aretz.

עֲשָׂרָה מִי יוֹדֵעַ?
עֲשָׂרָה אֲנִי יוֹדֵעַ!
עֲשָׂרָה דִבְּרַיָּא,
תִּשְׁעָה יַרְחֵי לֵדָה,
שְׁמוֹנָה יְמֵי מִילָה,
שִׁבְעָה יְמֵי שַׁבְּתָא,
שִׁשָּׁה סִדְרֵי מִשְׁנָה,
חֲמִשָּׁה חֻמְשֵׁי תוֹרָה,
אַרְבַּע אִמָּהוֹת,
שְׁלֹשָׁה אָבוֹת,
שְׁנֵי לוּחוֹת הַבְּרִית,
אֶחָד אֱלֹהֵינוּ שֶׁבַּשָּׁמַיִם וּבָאָרֶץ.

A-sa-ra mee yo-dei-a?
A-sa-ra anee yo-dei-a.
A-sa-ra dee-bra-ya,
Tee-sha yar-khei lei-da,
Shmona y'mei mee-la,
Shee-va y'mei Shab-ta,
Shee-sha see-drei Mishna,
Ha-mee-sha hum-shei Torah,
Arba eema-hot,
Shlo-sha avot,
Shnei lu-khot ha-breet,
Ekhad Elo-hei-nu she-ba-sha-ma-yeem uva-aretz.

אַחַד עָשָׂר מִי יוֹדֵעַ?
אַחַד עָשָׂר אֲנִי יוֹדֵעַ!
אַחַד עָשָׂר כּוֹכְבַיָּא,
עֲשָׂרָה דִבְּרַיָּא,
תִּשְׁעָה יַרְחֵי לֵדָה,
שְׁמוֹנָה יְמֵי מִילָה,
שִׁבְעָה יְמֵי שַׁבְּתָא,
שִׁשָּׁה סִדְרֵי מִשְׁנָה,
חֲמִשָּׁה חֻמְשֵׁי תוֹרָה,
אַרְבַּע אִמָּהוֹת,
שְׁלֹשָׁה אָבוֹת,
שְׁנֵי לוּחוֹת הַבְּרִית,
אֶחָד אֱלֹהֵינוּ שֶׁבַּשָּׁמַיִם וּבָאָרֶץ.

Ekhad-asar mee yo-dei-a?
Ekhad-asar anee yo-dei-a.
Ekhad-asar kokh-va-ya,
A-sa-ra dee-bra-ya,
Tee-sha yar-khei lei-da,
Shmona y'mei mee-la,
Shee-va y'mei Shab-ta,
Shee-sha see-drei Mishna,
Ha-mee-sha hum-shei Torah,
Arba eema-hot,
Shlo-sha avot,
Shnei lu-khot ha-breet,
Ekhad Elo-hei-nu she-ba-sha-ma-yeem uva-aretz.

שְׁנֵים עָשָׂר מִי יוֹדֵעַ?	Shneim-asar mee yo-dei-a?
שְׁנֵים עָשָׂר אֲנִי יוֹדֵעַ!	Shneim-asar anee yo-dei-a.
שְׁנֵים עָשָׂר שִׁבְטַיָּא,	Shneim-asar sheev-ta-ya,
אַחַד עָשָׂר כּוֹכְבַיָּא,	Ekhad-asar kokh-va-ya,
עֲשָׂרָה דִבְּרַיָּא,	A-sa-ra dee-bra-ya,
תִּשְׁעָה יַרְחֵי לֵדָה,	Tee-sha yar-khei lei-da,
שְׁמוֹנָה יְמֵי מִילָה,	Shmona y'mei mee-la,
שִׁבְעָה יְמֵי שַׁבְּתָא,	Shee-va y'mei Shab-ta,
שִׁשָּׁה סִדְרֵי מִשְׁנָה,	Shee-sha see-drei Mishna,
חֲמִשָּׁה חֻמְשֵׁי תוֹרָה,	Ha-mee-sha hum-shei Torah,
אַרְבַּע אִמָּהוֹת,	Arba eema-hot,
שְׁלֹשָׁה אָבוֹת,	Shlo-sha avot,
שְׁנֵי לוּחוֹת הַבְּרִית,	Shnei lu-khot ha-breet,
אֶחָד אֱלֹהֵינוּ שֶׁבַּשָּׁמַיִם וּבָאָרֶץ.	Ekhad Elo-hei-nu she-ba-sha-ma-yeem uva-aretz.

שְׁלֹשָׁה עָשָׂר מִי יוֹדֵעַ?	Shlo-sha-asar mee yo-dei-a?
שְׁלֹשָׁה עָשָׂר אֲנִי יוֹדֵעַ!	Shlo-sha-asar anee yo-dei-a.
שְׁלֹשָׁה עָשָׂר מִדַּיָּא,	Shlo-sha-asar mee-da-ya,
שְׁנֵים עָשָׂר שִׁבְטַיָּא,	Shneim-asar sheev-ta-ya,
אַחַד עָשָׂר כּוֹכְבַיָּא,	Ekhad-asar kokh-va-ya,
עֲשָׂרָה דִבְּרַיָּא,	A-sa-ra dee-bra-ya,
תִּשְׁעָה יַרְחֵי לֵדָה,	Tee-sha yar-khei lei-da,
שְׁמוֹנָה יְמֵי מִילָה,	Shmona y'mei mee-la,
שִׁבְעָה יְמֵי שַׁבְּתָא,	Shee-va y'mei Shab-ta,
שִׁשָּׁה סִדְרֵי מִשְׁנָה,	Shee-sha see-drei Mishna,
חֲמִשָּׁה חֻמְשֵׁי תוֹרָה,	Ha-mee-sha hum-shei Torah,
אַרְבַּע אִמָּהוֹת,	Arba eema-hot,
שְׁלֹשָׁה אָבוֹת,	Shlo-sha avot,
שְׁנֵי לוּחוֹת הַבְּרִית,	Shnei lu-khot ha-breet,
אֶחָד אֱלֹהֵינוּ שֶׁבַּשָּׁמַיִם וּבָאָרֶץ.	Ekhad Elo-hei-nu she-ba-sha-ma-yeem uva-aretz.

Khad Gadya   חַד גַּדְיָא

JUST ONE KID

Chorus:

Just one kid, just one kid
That my Abba bought for two zuzeem.
khad gadya, khad gadya.

1   Along came the cat ("meow")
and ate the kid ("maa")
that my Abba bought for two zuzeem.
khad gadya, khad gadya.

2   Along came the dog ("woof")
and bit the cat ("meow")
that ate the kid ("maa")
that my Abba bought for two zuzeem.
khad gadya, khad gadya.

3   Along came the stick ("bang")
and hit the dog ("woof") . . .

4   Along came the fire ("sizzle")
and burned the stick ("bang") . . .

5   Along came the water ("gurgle")
and quenched the fire ("sizzle") . . .

6   Along came the ox ("slurp")
and drank the water ("gurgle") . . .

Final Verse:

9   Then came the Holy One
and destroyed the angel of death
that slew the slaughterer
that killed the ox ("slurp")
that drank the water ("gurgle")
that quenched the fire ("sizzle, crackle")
that burned the stick ("bang")
that beat the dog ("woof")
that bit the cat ("meow")
that ate the kid ("maa")
that my Abba bought for two zuzeem.
khad gadya, khad gadya.

Goats For Sale in Meah Shearim, Jerusalem

Written in Aramaic
and modeled on
German folksongs,
this ballad
– which has no
overt connection to
Pesach – entered the
Ashkenazi Haggadah
(15th C.).
Hard-pressed Jewish
commentators have
discovered a moral
lesson between
the lines: **measure
for measure,
an oppressor
will always be
swallowed by
a greater oppressor
until God redeems
the world from
death.**

Pre-assign each
stanza to volunteers
who must produce
an appropriate sound
or gesture. Everyone
sings the verses,
while the
pre-assigned
participant adds a
sound and/or visual
effect each time.

חַד גַּדְיָא, חַד גַּדְיָא   Khad gad-ya, Khad gad-ya

דְּזַבֵּן אַבָּא בִּתְרֵי זוּזֵי, חַד גַּדְיָא, חַד גַּדְיָא.   D'za-been abba bee-trei zu-zei   Khad gad-ya (2x)

וְאָתָא שׁוּנְרָא וְאָכְלָה לְגַדְיָא,   V'ata shun-ra v'akh-la l'gad-ya

דְּזַבֵּן אַבָּא בִּתְרֵי זוּזֵי, חַד גַּדְיָא, חַד גַּדְיָא.   D'za-been abba bee-trei zu-zei   Khad gad-ya (2x)

וְאָתָא כַלְבָּא וְנָשַׁךְ לְשׁוּנְרָא,   V'ata khal-ba v'na-sha-kh l'shun-ra

דְּאָכְלָה לְגַדְיָא,   D'akh-la l'gad-ya

דְּזַבֵּן אַבָּא בִּתְרֵי זוּזֵי, חַד גַּדְיָא, חַד גַּדְיָא.   D'za-been abba bee-trei zu-zei   Khad gad-ya (2x)

וְאָתָא חוּטְרָא וְהִכָּה לְכַלְבָּא,   V'ata khu-tra v'hee-ka l'khal-ba

דְּנָשַׁךְ לְשׁוּנְרָא,   D'na-shakh l'shun-ra

דְּאָכְלָה לְגַדְיָא,   D'akh-la l'gad-ya

דְּזַבֵּן אַבָּא בִּתְרֵי זוּזֵי, חַד גַּדְיָא, חַד גַּדְיָא.   D'za-been abba bee-trei zu-zei   Khad gad-ya (2x)

וְאָתָא נוּרָא וְשָׂרַף לְחוּטְרָא,
V'ata nura v'saraf l'khu-tra

דְּהִכָּה לְכַלְבָּא,
D'hee-ka l'khal-ba

דְּנָשַׁךְ לְשׁוּנְרָא,
D'na-shakh l'shun-ra

דְּאָכְלָה לְגַדְיָא,
D'akh-la l'gad-ya

דְּזַבֵּן אַבָּא בִּתְרֵי זוּזֵי, חַד גַּדְיָא, חַד גַּדְיָא.
D'za-been abba bee-trei zu-zei Khad gad-ya (2x)

וְאָתָא מַיָּא וְכָבָה לְנוּרָא,
V'ata maya v'kha-va l'nura

דְּשָׂרַף לְחוּטְרָא,
D'saraf l'khu-tra

דְּהִכָּה לְכַלְבָּא,
D'hee-ka l'khal-ba

דְּנָשַׁךְ לְשׁוּנְרָא,
D'na-shakh l'shun-ra

דְּאָכְלָה לְגַדְיָא,
D'akh-la l'gad-ya

דְּזַבֵּן אַבָּא בִּתְרֵי זוּזֵי, חַד גַּדְיָא, חַד גַּדְיָא.
D'za-been abba bee-trei zu-zeiv Khad gad-ya (2x)

וְאָתָא תוֹרָא וְשָׁתָה לְמַיָּא,
V'ata tora v'shata l'maya

דְּכָבָה לְנוּרָא,
D'khava l'nura

דְּשָׂרַף לְחוּטְרָא,
D'saraf l'khu-tra

דְּהִכָּה לְכַלְבָּא,
D'hee-ka l'khal-ba

דְּנָשַׁךְ לְשׁוּנְרָא,
D'na-shakh l'shun-ra

דְּאָכְלָה לְגַדְיָא,
D'akh-la l'gad-ya

דְּזַבֵּן אַבָּא בִּתְרֵי זוּזֵי, חַד גַּדְיָא, חַד גַּדְיָא.
D'za-been abba bee-trei zu-zei Khad gad-ya (2x)

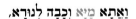

וְאָתָא הַשּׁוֹחֵט וְשָׁחַט לְתוֹרָא,
V'ata ha-sho-kheit v'sha-khat l'tora

דְּשָׁתָה לְמַיָּא,
D'shata l'maya

דְּכָבָה לְנוּרָא,
D'khava l'nura

דְּשָׂרַף לְחוּטְרָא,
D'saraf l'khu-tra

דְּהִכָּה לְכַלְבָּא,
D'hee-ka l'khal-ba

דְּנָשַׁךְ לְשׁוּנְרָא,
D'na-shakh l'shunra

דְּאָכְלָה לְגַדְיָא,
D'akh-la l'gad-ya

דְּזַבֵּן אַבָּא בִּתְרֵי זוּזֵי, חַד גַּדְיָא, חַד גַּדְיָא.
D'za-been abba bee-trei zu-zei   Khad gad-ya (2x)

וְאָתָא מַלְאַךְ הַמָּוֶת וְשָׁחַט לְשׁוֹחֵט,
V'ata ma-lakh ha-mavet v'sha-khat la-sho-kheit

דְּשָׁחַט לְתוֹרָא,
D'sha-khat l'tora

דְּשָׁתָה לְמַיָּא,
D'shata l'maya

דְּכָבָה לְנוּרָא,
D'khava l'nura

דְּשָׂרַף לְחוּטְרָא,
D'saraf l'khu-tra

דְּהִכָּה לְכַלְבָּא,
D'hee-ka l'khal-ba

דְּנָשַׁךְ לְשׁוּנְרָא,
D'na-shakh l'shunra

דְּאָכְלָה לְגַדְיָא,
D'akh-la l'gad-ya

דְּזַבֵּן אַבָּא בִּתְרֵי זוּזֵי, חַד גַּדְיָא, חַד גַּדְיָא.
D'za-been abba bee-trei zu-zei   Khad gad-ya (2x)

וְאָתָא הַקָּדוֹשׁ בָּרוּךְ הוּא וְשָׁחַט לְמַלְאַךְ הַמָּוֶת,
V'ata Ha-Ka-dosh Barukh Hu v'sha-khat l'ma-lakh ha-mavet

דְּשָׁחַט לְשׁוֹחֵט,
D'sha-khat la-sho-kheit

דְּשָׁחַט לְתוֹרָא,
D'sha-khat l'tora

דְּשָׁתָה לְמַיָּא,
D'shata l'maya

דְּכָבָה לְנוּרָא,
D'khava l'nura

דְּשָׂרַף לְחוּטְרָא,
D'saraf l'khu-tra

דְּהִכָּה לְכַלְבָּא,
D'hee-ka l'khal-ba

דְּנָשַׁךְ לְשׁוּנְרָא,
D'na-shakh l'shunra

דְּאָכְלָה לְגַדְיָא,
D'akh-la l'gad-ya

דְּזַבֵּן אַבָּא בִּתְרֵי זוּזֵי, חַד גַּדְיָא, חַד גַּדְיָא.
D'za-been abba bee-trei zu-zei   Khad gad-ya (2x)

NEXT YEAR'S SEDER

MESSIANIC JERUSALEM: IMAGINE YOUR IDEAL WORLD

Jerusalem, despite and because of its earthly conflicts, has always been the city to dream of Shalom (JeruSALEM). The following pages bring contemporary offerings of universal hope and reflections on a renewed Israel in the spirit of the prophets:

"Rejoice Jerusalem, for your messiah is coming: Victorious, triumphant; yet humble, riding upon a donkey." (Zecharia 9:9)

"And the wolf shall dwell with the lamb, and the leopard shall lie down with the kid... and a little child shall lead them... They shall not hurt nor destroy in all my holy mountain; for the earth shall be full of the knowledge of Adonai, as the waters cover the sea."

(Isaiah 11:6)

חֲסַל סִדּוּר פֶּסַח כְּהִלְכָתוֹ,

Concluded is the Pesach Seder,

כְּכָל מִשְׁפָּטוֹ וְחֻקָתוֹ.

Finished down to the last detail

כַּאֲשֶׁר זָכִינוּ לְסַדֵּר אוֹתוֹ

With all its laws and customs.

כֵּן נִזְכֶּה לַעֲשׂוֹתוֹ.

As we have been able to conduct this Seder,

So may we someday perform it in Jerusalem.

זַךְ שׁוֹכֵן מְעוֹנָה,

Pure One who dwells in the palace,

קוֹמֵם קְהַל עֲדַת מִי מָנָה.

Support your congregation countless in number.

בְּקָרוֹב נַהֵל נִטְעֵי כַנָּה

May you soon lead the offshoots of your stock,

פְּדוּיִם לְצִיּוֹן בְּרִנָּה.

Bringing the redeemed to Zion in joy.

All sing:

לְשָׁנָה הַבָּאָה בִּירוּשָׁלַיִם הַבְּנוּיָה!

Next Year in Jerusalem!

La-Shana Ha-ba-a Bee-Yeru-sha-layeem!

עוֹשֶׂה שָׁלוֹם בִּמְרוֹמָיו

God makes peace in heaven,

הוּא יַעֲשֶׂה שָׁלוֹם עָלֵינוּ

and so may God make peace over us.

וְעַל כָּל יִשְׂרָאֵל וְאִמְרוּ אָמֵן.

Amen.

Nirtza means accepted. The Pesach Seder ends with a prayer that all our efforts to perform the Seder properly may be pleasing and acceptable to God. (Written by Yosef Tov-Elem, 11th C. France).

Looking forward to next year's Seder, we sing *"Next Year in Jerusalem!"*. May we celebrate it in a more peaceful world.

Reflections on Next Year in Jerusalem on the following pages include:

On Israel p.138-139

On Hope p.140-141

On Prophetic Leaders p.142

Tomorrow's Jerusalem: Revised and Revisited by Michel Kichka

Two messianic political leaders are represented: Atop the gate entitled "The Gate of Peace," is a bearded Theodore Herzl, founder of the Zionist movement in 1896, together with Noah's dove of peace. With furrowed brow, he compares the Israeli reality below with his vision of the New Zion in his utopia, *The Jewish State*.

Atop the white donkey sits the messianic descendant of King David. The handsome biblical David was ruddy in complexion and now his seed has produced a red-haired hippy with sunglasses. A more mundane dream is expressed by the Israeli taxi driver who reads in his newspaper: "Israel has won the World Soccer Cup!"

Can you find all the traditional enemies now shaking hands? Why do three animals appear? (See verses on p. 136)

בַּשָּׁנָה הַבָּאָה	*BaShana HaBa'ah*	Next Year by Ehud Manor
בַּשָּׁנָה הַבָּאָה נֵשֵׁב עַל הַמִּרְפֶּסֶת וְנִסְפֹּר צִפֳּרִים נוֹדְדוֹת, יְלָדִים בְּחֻפְשָׁה יְשַׂחֲקוּ תּוֹפֶסֶת בֵּין הַבַּיִת לְבֵין הַשָּׂדוֹת.	Ba-sha-na ha-ba'ah ne-shev al ha-mir-peset Ve-nis-por tzi-po-rim no-de-dot Ye-la-dim be-khuf-sha ye-sakha-ku to-feset Bein ha-bayit l'vein ha-sa-dot	Next year we will sit on the porch And count the migrating birds Children on vacation will play tag Between the house and the fields
עוֹד תִּרְאֶה, עוֹד תִּרְאֶה, כַּמָּה טוֹב יִהְיֶה בַּשָּׁנָה, בַּשָּׁנָה הַבָּאָה...	Od tir'eh, od tir'eh Kama tov yi-hi-yeh Ba-sha-na ba-sha-na ha-ba'ah (2x)	You will see, you will see How good it will be Next year, Next year
עֲנָבִים אֲדֻמִּים יַבְשִׁילוּ עַד הָעֶרֶב וְיֻגְּשׁוּ צוֹנְנִים לַשֻּׁלְחָן, וְרוּחוֹת רְדוּמִים יִשְׂאוּ אֶל אֵם הַדֶּרֶךְ עִתּוֹנִים יְשָׁנִים וְעָנָן.	Ana-vim adu-mim yav-shi-lu ad ha'erev Ve-yug-shu tzo-ne-nim la-shul-khan Ve-ru-khot re-du-mim yis-u el eim ha-de-rekh I-to-nim ye-sha-nim ve'an-an	Red grapes will ripen by evening And be served cold to the table Pleasant breezes will blow on to the roads Old newspapers and clouds
עוֹד תִּרְאֶה, עוֹד תִּרְאֶה...	Od tir'eh, od tir'eh...	You will see, you will see...
בַּשָּׁנָה הַבָּאָה נִפְרֹשׂ כַּפּוֹת יָדַיִם מוּל הָאוֹר הַנִּגָּר הַלָּבָן, אֲנָפָה לְבָנָה תִּפְרֹשׂ בָּאוֹר כְּנָפַיִם, וְהַשֶּׁמֶשׁ תִּזְרַח בְּתוֹכָן.	Ba-sha-na ha-ba'ah nif-ros ka-pot ya-dayim Mul ha'or ha-ni-gar ha-la-van Anafa le-va-na tif-ros be'or k'na-fayim Ve-ha-she-mesh tiz-rach be-to-khan	Next year we will spread out our open hands Into the bright white light A white branch will spread its wings And the sun will rise in their midst
עוֹד תִּרְאֶה, עוֹד תִּרְאֶה...	Od tir'eh, od tir'eh...	You will see, you will see...

SONGS OF THE SOUL, THE NATION, HUMANITY AND THE COSMOS

There is one who sings the song of his soul, discovering in it everything – utter spiritual fulfillment.

Then there is one who sings the song of his people. Emerging from the private circle of his soul – not expansive enough, not yet tranquil – he strives for fierce heights, clinging to the entire community of Israel in tender love. Together with her, he sings her song, feels her anguish, delights in her hopes. He conceives profound insights into her past and her future, deftly probing the inwardness of her spirit with the wisdom of love.

Then there is one whose soul expands until it extends beyond the border of Israel, singing the song of humanity. In the glory of the entire human race, in the glory of the human form, his spirit spreads, aspiring to the goal of humankind, envisioning its consummation. From this spring of life, he draws all his deepest reflections, his searching, striving, and vision.

Then there is one who expands even further until he unites with all existence, with all creatures, with all worlds, singing a song with them all. Then there is one who ascends with all these songs in unison – the song of the soul, the song of the nation, the song of humanity, the song of the cosmos – resounding together, blending in harmony, circulating the sap of life, the sound of holy joy.

This full comprehensiveness rises to become the song of holiness, the song of God, the song of Israel, in its full strength and beauty, in its full authenticity and greatness. The name Yisra-el (*Yashir-El*) stands for the Song of God. It is a simple song, a twofold song, a threefold song and a fourfold song. It is the *Song of Songs* of King Solomon whose name means Shalom – peace and wholeness. It is the song of the Sovereign in whom is wholeness.

Rabbi **Abraham Isaac Kook**, Zionist mystic and first Ashkenazi Chief Rabbi of Israel

Reflections on Israel

IF YOU WILL IT, IT IS NO DREAM

No one has ever thought of looking for the Promised Land in the place where it really is – and yet it lies so near. It is here: within ourselves!

For everyone will carry over there, in himself, a piece of the Promised Land. This one, in his head, that one, in his hands, the third in his savings. The Promised Land is where we carry it!

Theodore Herzl, diaries,1895

ISRAEL: PLAYING FOR REAL STAKES

Israel has become a subject of intellectual and political and human interest for me. The place was personalized for me through individuals and their anguish and their struggle: Here was a place in which to the ordinary citizen, including my friends, everything now mattered. Because the issue was an issue of survival, life and death. Places where people were playing for real stakes interested me. All this Jewish turbulence, I wanted it to tumble through me.

Philip Roth, American novelist

ISRAEL: A MENTAL STATE

Certain oddities about Israel: Because people think so hard here; and so much, and because of the length and depth of their history, this sliver of a country sometimes seems quite large. Some dimension of mind seems to extend into space.

I sometimes think there are two Israels. The real one is territorially insignificant. The other, the mental Israel, is immense, a country inestimably important; playing a major role in the world, as broad as all history – and perhaps as deep as sleep.

Saul Bellow, *To Jerusalem and Back*

RIDING ON AN ISRAELI BUS: AN AMERICAN JEW'S VIEW OF ISRAEL

When one rides a public bus in Israel and looks at the varied faces of the Jews on board, one realizes: so this is Jewish peoplehood, this is the place in the world where all Jews come together, to live and quarrel and manage their affairs in close proximity.

This perception – often forceful – perhaps accounts for the sense of homecoming reported by many American Jewish visitors, who cannot speak Hebrew, find the landscape and the food unfamiliar, and are disturbed by the lack of civility in ordinary human interactions, yet feel somehow at home.

It is not just that sides have obviously been drawn up before they arrived, and like it or not they belong to one of them: the covenant of fate. Nor is it just the pride at collective achievement: the sight of blooming deserts, roads clogged with traffic, and immigrants who have been absorbed by the hundreds of thousands – the marks of collective Jewish action, the covenant of destiny. The point is that Jews are here, before one's eyes, not only individually but as a people. Hitler did not end the Jewish story. Life has, in this instance at least, defeated death. "*Am Yisrael Chai* "– the people of Israel lives.

That above all is the meaning of Israel for me, as it is perhaps for other American Jews. I know the reality of Israeli society, politics, and culture fairly well, but I treasure the place because its significance is mythic, larger than life, transparent to the depths of meaning. The two, myth and reality, are inextricably intertwined. I need Israel to exist – and it does, thank God. Its vitality so deeply satisfies me.

Arnold Eisen, Chancellor of the Jewish Theological Seminary, *Taking Hold of Torah*

*H*ATIKVAH: WHERE HAVE ALL OUR HOPES GONE?

Early in the fall of 2005, I visited a high school in Sha'ar HaNegev, not far from Sderot and the Gaza border, to interview some students.

I asked them two questions. "You'll be middle aged when Israel's 100 years old," I told them. "So tell me. As you imagine the future, what do you dream of, and what are you afraid of?"

These were fifteen highly intelligent, very articulate kids. But interestingly, none of them had anything terribly substantive to say about their dreams. As they sat quietly, trying to think what they could say that might not sound platitudinous, one of the guys spoke up. "Can I tell you," he asked with a slight hesitation and a cautious glance at his schoolmates, "what I'm afraid of?"

There was a moment of discomfort in the group, and a stifled giggle here and there. Sixteen-year-old guys, sitting in a group that also includes girls, aren't supposed to want to talk about what they're afraid of. But this guy wanted to speak, and within seconds, it was completely silent in the room. Everyone looked at him, and waited.

"I'm afraid," he said after a pause, "that the future will be just like this."

What does it mean to be sixteen or seventeen and to be afraid that the future will be like the present?

Rabbi **Daniel Gordis**, *If a Place can Make you Cry*

*M*ESSIANISM IS ABOUT HEALING

The notion of Messiah as an actual individual is very dangerous, something we should be on guard against.

Salvation for me is the effort that we put into understanding our deepest selves in the most honest way that we can, so that we can look not only at our own selves, but at the selves of others around us.

Messianism is about a world that's trying to be healed, redeemed; the notion of a goal toward which we are constantly navigating.

Rabbi **Chaim Potok**, author of *The Chosen*

*A*NNE FRANK: I STILL BELIEVE

That's the difficulty in these times: ideals, dreams, and cherished hopes rise within us, only to meet the horrible truth and be shattered.
It's really a wonder that I haven't dropped all my ideals, because they seem so absurd and impossible to carry out. Yet I keep them, because in spite of everything I still believe that people are really good at heart. I simply can't build up my hopes on a foundation consisting of confusion, misery, and death. I see the world gradually being turned into a wilderness. I hear the ever-approaching thunder, which will destroy us, too. I can feel the suffering of millions – and yet, if I look up into the heavens, I think it will come out all right, that this cruelty too will end, and that peace and tranquility will return again. In the meantime, I must uphold my ideals, for perhaps the time will come when I shall be able to carry them out.

Diary of **Anne Frank**, Amsterdam, 1944

Reflections on Hope

TO REACH 'NEXT YEAR IN JERUSALEM,' I NEED THE YEAR THAT HAS PASSED

The present! – how can we limit our lives in Israel to 'the present' alone?
And if there is nothing beyond 'now', then why live in such a difficult country?

"I believe in the past, the present, and the future," said Yitzhak Tabenkin, the great kibbutz educator: "Every time I hesitate on a major question, I ask the advice of two people: my grandfather – for his opinion, and my grandson – how will the decision affect his future?"
It's important to me that in answering any question, I consider both previous generations and possible effects on the future ones; not merely my own immediate future, but the farthest foreseeable unfolding of events.
I'm afraid of two things: of those who ask only how things have always been done and put only historical eggs in their basket. And I'm afraid of people who consider any future harm that may result from their decision unimportant, whose only questions are "Will I get something out of this? Will I achieve immediate gratification?"

Zvi Zameret, Israeli educator, Yad Ben Zvi Institute

THE END? IT'S ONLY THE BEGINNING

Exodus is charged with tension: between the miserable, 'childlike' state of the children of Israel, a people physically and spiritually enslaved, and the exalted role God has chosen for them, heedless of the pace of their spiritual and moral development. Perhaps this is the truly demanding journey made by the children of Israel: from clan to nation, from slavery to freedom.

Here in my study in Jerusalem, in Israel, in "the promised land" to which the Jews have returned time and again from exile, I think about my ancestors, the children of Israel, during those first days after the maelstrom that uprooted them from Egypt. They are in the desert, and the desert is empty. They are being led, like an immense herd, to an unknown destination. What can they cling to? They escaped bondage in Egypt, but also abandoned their daily routine, their habits and customs, a familiar place and the social interactions and hierarchies that had become fixed over the course of generations. Suddenly everything is new and strange. Nothing can be taken for granted.

What had appeared to be the end of the road, now appears to be its beginning.

Stunned, they stride onward, as if in a void. They follow their leader and he tells them they are at long last free men, but perhaps free is the last thing they feel or want to be. Every day brings new experiences, new religious regulations and laws, and strange food – enough for one day – that falls from the skies. If they have any spirit left they will realize that a miracle has befallen them, that they are privileged to have been given the chance to reinvent themselves, to be redeemed. If they dare, they can fashion a new identity for themselves. But to do so they must fight the ponderous gravity of habit, of anxiety and doubt, of inner bondage.

David Grossman, Israeli novelist and peace activist

Marchers crossing the bridge at Selma, Alabama, March 21, 1965, include (from left to right beginning under the "S" of Pettus Bridge): Ralph Abernathy, Martin Luther King, Ralph Bunche and Abraham Joshua Heschel. This crossing was a triumph, for two weeks earlier civil rights marchers had been turned back by tear gas, clubs and horses by the state troopers. Soon thereafter the 1965 Voting Rights Act was passed. Photograph by Robie Ray.

LIFE AS A WORK OF ART

Inspired by the prophets about whom he wrote his first book, Rabbi Abraham Joshua Heschel was always an activist, whether in struggling to liberate Soviet Jews, in opposing the Vietnam War, or in joining the Civil Rights Movement. After the Selma march he said: "I felt my legs were praying." Religion without indignation at political evils was impossible. Heschel reflected: "I felt that Jewish religious institutions have missed a great opportunity to interpret the civil rights movement in terms of Judaism, in terms of the prophetic traditions."

In spring 1968 Dr. King had accepted an invitation to join Heschel for Seder. However King was assassinated a few days before Pesach and Heschel spoke at his funeral instead.

In a "Meet the Press" TV interview in 1972, which turned out to be his last public statement before his death, Heschel was asked: "What would you tell young people?" This was his answer:

"Remember that there is meaning beyond absurdity, that every little deed counts, that every word has power – and that we can, everyone, do our share to redeem the world in spite of all the absurdities, frustrations and disappointments.

Remember that life is a celebration and above all remember that the meaning of life is to build a life as if it were a work of art."

I HAVE A DREAM TODAY!

We can never be satisfied as long as our bodies, heavy with the fatigue of travel, cannot gain lodging in the motels of the highways and the hotels of the cities.

We can never be satisfied as long as a Negro in Mississippi cannot vote and a Negro in New York believes he has nothing for which to vote.

No, no, we are not satisfied, and we will not be satisfied until justice rolls down like waters and righteousness like a mighty stream.

I have a dream today. I have a dream that one day every valley shall be exalted, every hill and mountain shall be made low, the rough places will be made plain, and the crooked places will be made straight, and the glory of the Lord shall be revealed, and all flesh shall see it together.

With this faith we will be able to hew out of the mountain of despair a stone of hope.

With this faith we will be able to transform the jangling discords of our nation into a beautiful symphony of brotherhood.

With this faith we will be able to work together, to pray together, to struggle together, to go to jail together, to stand up for freedom together, knowing that we will be free one day.

Let freedom ring from every hill and every molehill of Mississippi.

From every mountainside, let freedom ring. (Leviticus 25:10)

When we let freedom ring, we will be able to speed up that day when all of God's children, black men and white men, Jews and Gentiles, Protestants and Catholics, will be able to join hands and sing in the words of the old Negro spiritual, "Free at last! Free at last! Thank God Almighty, we are free at last!"

Martin Luther King, Jr., the Lincoln Memorial, Washington D.C., 1963, 100th Anniversary of Lincoln's Emancipation Proclamation

Way Down in Egypt Land

By Stephen Hazan Arnoff

Adapted from the story by Ya'ir Lipshitz

Our story does not begin in the castle of the king (but it will get there). And it does not begin with great heroes and heroines (but it will get there). It actually begins with slaves who were the children of slaves: the Children of Israel.

The Children of Israel were not always slaves. There was a time when things were much, much better for them. The Children of Israel – you might have heard them called the Israelites or the Hebrews or, in today's lingo, the Jews – had once lived pretty nice lives alongside the Egyptians. In fact, many years before, Joseph (who was one of the Children of Israel too) had saved the land of Egypt from a terrible famine. During this time his brothers and their families followed him down to Egypt from their homeland in Israel. These were the ancestors of the Children of Israel. Generations passed and the families grew and grew…

Things started to change when a new king, Pharaoh, whose real name was Ramses II, rose to power.

In the King's House

"Look at them," Pharaoh grumbled to his slaves. "Those families are getting huge! It's dangerous…It's very dangerous…They could…they could rebel! They could rise up against us! You'll see – they will betray us yet. We have to do something!" He screamed and stamped his feet and turned to his advisors, hollering, "Do something!"

None of Pharaoh's helpers said a word, so he clenched his teeth and tried to think of a solution on his own. "I know," he smiled to himself smugly. "We'll trick them. It's perfect! We can turn them into slaves…They'll work from morning until night and from night until morning and from morning until night and…and… from all of that hard work they won't have the energy left to even think about rebelling! And with a life like that," he continued, rubbing his hands together, "working and suffering all the time, they won't want to bring children into the world at all." Pharaoh laughed. "And then, slowly but surely, the families of the Hebrews will get smaller and smaller until they just disappear!" He was overjoyed by the idea. "Excellent!" he said, chuckling to himself.

And so it was. The Children of Israel – the Hebrews that is – began to work like crazy night and day. They made bricks from hay and water and dirt and dried them in the hot sun. Then they used the bricks to build houses and cities for the Egyptians. Day after day, night after night, this work left the Hebrews exhausted. They began to groan and moan and begged for help from God. And this was the way it was for a long time. Pharaoh punished them harshly and the Hebrews suffered. But despite all of their troubles, they still didn't stop having children.

"The work isn't enough. There are still too many of them," Pharaoh muttered. "Pretty soon there will be so many Hebrews that we won't be able to control them at all! We have

She would put the baby in a small basket and set the basket into the waters of the Nile. "This way at least there is a chance that someone will find him and have mercy on him and save him."

And that is just what she did. She took a small basket and waterproofed it with tar and put the baby inside. She wiped away his tears and wiped away her own tears and gave him a kiss on the forehead, gently placing the basket on the banks of the Nile. Then she left, her heart full of sorrow and worry.

As the mother walked away, the baby's older sister Miriam hid in the reeds at a distance. She wanted to do whatever she could to protect her little brother and see what would happen to him.

Soon a finely dressed young woman accompanied by several servants came to bathe in the Nile. Miriam recognized her immediately. It was none other than the princess, the daughter of Pharaoh. (Yes, yes, the same evil Pharaoh we talked about before.)

"No!" Miriam gasped to herself. "The princess? If she finds my little brother she will do what her father asked for and throw him into the Nile!" Miriam prayed that Pharaoh's daughter would not look into the basket, but as she crouched in the reeds she could see that the Egyptian princess was sending one of her servants to bring it to her.

"It's a baby!" Miriam heard Pharaoh's daughter say. "He's crying, the poor thing. What are you doing here in this basket by the side of the river?"

Thinking for a moment, Pharaoh's daughter understood what must have happened. The baby had to be a Hebrew that his mother had tried to save. Though she couldn't exactly remember what her father had said about Hebrew babies, as

she looked upon the face of the child, she said, "Well, whatever father thinks about those Hebrews, what could he possibly fear from a little baby as sweet as this one?" The baby smiled at her and she smiled back and the decision was made: Pharaoh's daughter would take this baby to be her own.

As Pharaoh's daughter said to her servants, "Let's take him with us!" Miriam was already running so fast that she almost knocked the princess into the mud of the Nile. "Excuse me! Excuse me! Your Majesty…" Miriam bowed, catching her breath." Perhaps I can be of assistance to the princess? Would the princess like me to find a woman to help take care of her new baby?" Miriam stood up straight but didn't look the princess in the eye.

Pharaoh's daughter looked upon the Hebrew girl with surprise. She thought: "Imagine, a total stranger – and a Hebrew no less – popping up like that in the middle of the princess' private bath!" But she was also very happy about the offer. Pharaoh's daughter didn't know very much about babies and she would certainly appreciate some help. So Miriam quickly arranged for her own mother – the baby's mother! – to serve as the baby's nanny in Pharaoh's palace. The real mother, of course, was thrilled. Her prayers had been answered and her child had been saved! The princess was quite pleased by how much the baby loved them both. Then the princess decided to call the baby "Moshe," meaning, "I took him out of the water."

Back to the House of the King

The Hebrew baby, whose name was Moshe, grew up in Pharaoh's palace and was raised as an Egyptian prince. That meant excellent food, fine clothes, beautiful toys, servants taking care of his

to find another solution!" Pharaoh glared at his advisors, who were afraid to look him in the eyes. Then he screamed, "Bring me the Hebrew midwives!" Pharaoh's helpers ran to fetch Shifrah and Puah, the leaders of the Hebrew midwives, right away. "Hello there," said Pharaoh with a smile.

"Greetings Your Majesty" said Shifra and Puah, bowing before him.

"I have a small favor to ask of you," Pharaoh said.

"We will do whatever Pharaoh our Master wishes," said the midwives.

"Well, it's not such a big deal really," Pharaoh said casually. "I just want you to make sure that from this day forward you kill all of the male Hebrew children that you deliver." Pharaoh smile widened. "That is all. Thank you."

(Now you may be asking yourselves why Pharaoh wanted to kill the males and not the females. That's an excellent question. It seems that Pharaoh was only afraid of the boys because he didn't think the girls could do a thing to bother him...Well, more on that later).

The midwives were shocked by Pharaoh's request. Their task was to bring life into the world. How could they ever follow his command to destroy it? They took their chances and just kept delivering Hebrew babies and hoped for the best.

"What?!" Pharaoh burned with rage when he heard that Shifra and Puah had disobeyed him.

"Pardon us, Master," said the two midwives as they bowed before the king once more. "It was not because of us. You see," continued the clever midwives, "these Hebrew women are not at all like the Egyptian women that gave birth properly in their homes with the help of a midwife. No, no, no! These Hebrew women give birth like animals in the woods without any help at all. We don't have time to get to the mothers in labor before the babies are born. How can we possibly fulfill our Master's wishes?"

"Is that it?" Pharaoh ranted, sputtering and spattering and his face turning red like a beet. "Well then, from this day forward every male Hebrew infant will be thrown into the Nile River! All of them! All of them! All of them!"

Shifra and Puah were horrified, but they couldn't speak a word against the enraged Pharaoh's decree. And so it was. The call went forth throughout the land that all male Hebrew babies would be killed. The fear of the Hebrews was great and so was their sorrow. Who could save them now?

In the House of the Slaves

Meanwhile, in a small house amongst the other dwellings of the slaves, a Hebrew slave had just given birth to a son. She gazed upon her newborn baby and tears filled her eyes.

"How can I kill my own child?" she whispered to herself as she wept. After much thinking and waiting, she decided that she was ready to risk her own life to save her baby. For three whole months she hid him in her house. But the bigger the child grew, the clearer it was that at some point the Egyptians would catch her and kill both of them. She was going to need to find a solution…and fast!

The Hebrew mother would lie awake worrying night after night, and then late one evening an idea came into her head:

burning and burning. The orange flame did not die out but neither was the bush burned up.

"That's very strange," Moshe said to himself. "The bush stays in one piece but it's totally covered with fire. I have to go closer to see what is happening." Moshe went closer and then he heard a voice from within the burning bush. The voice was calling him!

"Moshe! Moshe!" said the voice.

"Here I am…" whispered Moshe, continuing to come closer to the bush.

Then the voice said "I am the God of your fathers and your mothers, Abraham and Sarah, Isaac and Rebecca, and Jacob and Rachel and Leah…"

"God? Abraham and Sarah, who?" Moshe said to himself, but deep down he realized somehow that he had heard those words before. It reminded him of a lullaby his mother had sung as she told him stories of the Hebrews.

Now Moshe was scared. He covered his face, terrified to look at the fire again. He heard the voice say: "Moshe! I was there when you saw the Hebrews being beaten outside of the palace. I heard them crying. I saw my children tortured in Egypt for all those years. But now is the time for Me to save them. The time has come to take them out of Egypt and to return them to the land of their ancestors, the Land of Milk and Honey… to Israel. You will be my messenger, Moshe. You must go now to Pharaoh and tell him: 'Let My People Go!' Let me teach you the song you must teach my people":

When Israel was in Egypt's land,
"Let My people go" (Exodus 5:1).
Oppressed so hard they could not stand,
"Let My people go."

Go down, Moses,
way down in Egypt's land,
Tell old Pharaoh:
"Let My people go."

Thus said Adonai, bold Moses said,
"Let My people go."
If not, I'll smite your first-born dead,
"Let My people go."
Go down, Moses…

No more shall they in bondage toil,
"Let My people go."
Let them come out with Egypt's spoil,
"Let My people go."
Go down, Moses…

every need, and carriages with the fastest horses in the land at his disposal. Years passed. Moshe matured into a young man. His "nanny" whispered stories to him about the lives of ancestors called the Children of Israel who had come to Egypt years before from the Land of Milk and Honey only to become slaves. Moshe the Egyptian prince found the stories interesting, but he did not really think of himself as a part of the story of the Children of Israel.

Then one day, Moshe was taking a stroll outside of the castle. Feeling a little bored, he decided to walk towards an area of the royal grounds where he had never been before. He came upon the great fields where the Hebrew slaves were working under the hot sun with little water or shade. He saw how they carried giant bricks on their backs and barely had the strength to stand beneath their burden. He saw how the Egyptian task masters yelled at the slaves, cursing them and threatening them and leaving those who were too weak to work to wither away and die in the dirt. All of this

took Moshe by surprise. He had had no idea about the suffering of the Hebrew slaves. And the more he watched, the sicker and angrier he felt. Now he understood why he had heard those stories about the Children of Israel for all of those years. These were the Hebrews, his brothers and sisters, and they were suffering. Harsh words began to echo in his head "How can I live in a castle with all of its luxury, while the lives of my brothers and sisters are so awful?"

When Moshe saw an Egyptian man hit one of the Hebrew slaves, he snapped. He looked from side to side to be sure that

no one was watching and then he began hitting the Egyptian fiercely. He beat him until he was dead and then he buried him deep in the sand. Moshe ran away, terrified of being caught. When he arrived at the castle, he hoped against hope that the secret of his violent crime was buried along with the Egyptian.

But Moshe had no such luck. The story of what he had done traveled by word of mouth – first among the Hebrews and soon after among the Egyptians as well. Now Moshe knew that the moment Pharaoh heard about what Moshe had done, Pharaoh would have him executed. So away Moshe ran, away from Egypt, without even saying goodbye either to Pharaoh's daughter, the princess that had saved his life and raised him as her own son, or to the nanny who had told him so many stories about the Hebrews and their God.

Moshe arrived in the land of Midian where he met Yitro and worked with him as a shepherd, even marrying one of his daughters, Tzipporah. Life now seemed calm. Moshe was now a shepherd, not a prince. He loved taking care of the sheep. Moshe had almost forgotten his days as a prince and his origins as the son of Hebrew slaves who had placed him in the Nile River in a basket made of papyrus.

In the Desert

One day while working as a shepherd, Moshe came upon a faraway mountain, Mount Sinai. He sat on one of the rocks and watched sleepily as the sheep grazed in the field. Suddenly something strange caught his eye. He saw a small green bush

a God: Yehuda Amichai, *Patuach Sagur Patuach* (ibid.), p. 58 #4. **Photograph**: Aliza Orbach, *Olim*, 1991, (HH).

Idolatry: **I am Free of Idols**: Cynthia Ozick, in Joshua Haberman (editor), *The God I Believe In* (ibid.), p. 167. Revised by and courtesy of author. **Jewish by Choice**: Amos Oz, *All the Hopes: Thoughts on Israeli Identity*, 1998, p. 56. Courtesy of author (HH). **I Break, Therefore I am a Jew**: Ari Elon, *Doresh Shalom*: Parshat Hashavua, Bina Institute. Courtesy of author. **Freedom Begins with Imagination**: Philip Roth quote, courtesy of Words & Images, the Jerusalem literary project (ibid.): Videotaped Interview series with the great Jewish writers of our time, in conjunction with Ben Gurion University of the Negev and in cooperation with the National and University Library, Jerusalem. Words & Images: beylev@zahav.net.il. **A Frightened Person**: R. Joseph B. Soloveitchik, *Festival of Freedom* (ibid.), p. 51.

Barukh Shomer: **Next Year**: Yaakov Shneor, *Memories of my Father's House*, Be'erot Yitzhak, 1994, p. 58a. **Wherever a Jew is Persecuted**: Amos Oz, *Under this Blazing Light*, Sifriyat Poalim, 1979, p. 80. Courtesy of author (HH). **The Generation**: Arnold Eisen, *Taking Hold of Torah: Jewish Commitment and Community in America*, 1999, p. 41. Courtesy of author.

Vhi Sheamda: **Wall of Persecutions**: Based on Elijah Bar Navi (editor), *The Atlas of Jewish History*, 1993; Compiled for HH with the assistance of Mel Glatzer.

Arami: **Hamasa L'Eretz Yisrael**: By permission of ACUM. **Photograph**: Aliza Orbach, *Olim*, 1991. By permission of artist (HH). **Goy Gadol**: R. Joseph B. Soloveitchik, *Festival of Freedom*, ibid., p. 131-133. **When the Going gets Tough**: Tikvah Frymer Kensky, "Sanctifying Torah", in Irene Fine (editor), *The Shabbat Series: Excellence in Education for Jewish Women*, San Diego Women's Institute for Continuing Jewish Education, 1997. **No More Jewish Children**: Abraham Suzkever, cited in David Roskies, *Against the Apocalypse*, Harvard University Press, 1984, p. 234-235. Courtesy of author. **Sextuplets**: Aviva Zornberg Gottlieb, *The Particulars of Rapture* (ibid.), p. 18-19, 22. **Oppression and Resistance**: Toni Morrison, *Beloved*, Vintage, Random House, 1987, p. 27-28. By permission of the publisher. **Batya**: Julius Lester, "Here Am I"- A Personal Midrash on Pharaoh's Daughter, *New Traditions: Response Magazine* (Spring 1984). Courtesy of author (HH). **Rushing River of Days**: Meg Riley in E. Roberts and E. Amidon (editors), *Prayers for a Thousand Years*. Courtesy of author. **Human Role in Redemption**: R. Joseph B. Soloveitchik, *Festival of Freedom*, (ibid.), p. 152-153.

Ten Plagues: **The Ten Fears**: Shai Zarchi, written for HH. **Frogs Song**: Shirley Cohen, *Passover Music Box*, 1951, Kinor Records.

Dayenu: **Let My People Go**: Dan Reisinger. Courtesy of artist (HH).

Pesach Matza uMarror: **The Shared Meal**: R. Joseph B. Soloveitchik, *Festival of Freedom*, ibid., p. 23-24. **Matzoh**: Marge Piercy, *The Art of Blessing the Day*, Alfred Knopf,

Random House, 1999, p.164. By permission of the publisher. **Matza Star of David**: Yitzchak Yoresh, *Variations on the Israeli Flag*, Israel Museum Exhibit and catalogue. By permission of the artist (HH). **Ethiopian Girl Photo**: Yosi Roth, 1985, by permission of Israeli Government Press Office (HH).

In Every Generation: **Every Moment**: R. Nachman of Bratzlav, *Likutei Ezot HeHadash*. **Wandering, Time Traveling, Jew**: Israeli President Ezer Weizman, address to the German Bundestag and Bundesrat, 1996, written by Meir Shalev. **Stamp**: M. Prague, "Let My People Go," 1972. Courtesy of the Israel Philatelic Service (HH).

Hallelujah: **What is the Continuity of My Life**: Yehuda Amichai, *Patuach Sagur Patuach* (ibid.), p. 127 #3. **Go Tell it on the Mountain**: Martin Luther King, Jr., Speech, Memphis, 1968. **Exodus**: David Sharir, "Exodus," 1972. By permission of artist.

Second Cup: **Miriam's Cup**: Lori Lefkowitz, written for HH. **Who is that Girl**: Avirama Golan, "One Woman - Lonely and Strong," *Haaretz*, 12 April 2006. By permission of author and Haaretz. **Tambourine**: Betsy Teutsch, Miriam's Tambourine. Courtesy of artist (HH).

Matza, Maror, Haroset: **Blessing for Hametz**: Adapted from account given by Shani Harel, as well as Yosef Feuchtwanger, "Yoman HaShavua," *Makor Rishon*, April 10, 1998. **Soviet Matza Advertisement**: reprinted in David Geffen, *The American Heritage Haggadah*. **Haroset Recipe**: Granules of brick recipe, *Sephardic Haggadah of Pesach*, London, 1913.

Tzafun: **In Search of the Lost Face**: Yehuda Amichai, *Patuach Sagur Patuach* (ibid.), p. 29 #5. **Broken unto You**: Leonard Cohen, "All My Life," *Stranger Music*, Vintage, Random House, 1993, p. 333. By permission of publisher.

Birkat HaMazon: **Our Mouths will Fill**: R. Naamah Kelman, *I am Jewish*, Jewish Lights, p. 234-235. Revised by and courtesy of author. **After the Guests Depart**: R. Joseph Telushkin, *The Book of Jewish Values*, 2000, p. 307. Courtesy of author. **The Inversion of Gratefulness**: R. Abraham Joshua Heschel, *The Insecurity of Freedom*, p. 44. **Eating is Like Crossing the Red Sea**: Emmanuel Levinas, adapted from *Nine Talmudic Readings*.

Elijah: **Jewish Chutzpah**: R. Irving Greenberg, *The Jewish Way: Living the Holidays*, Touchstone, p. 37. Courtesy of author. **Elijah's Curse**: told by Avraham Barazani, blind storyteller from Iraq, Israel Folktale Archive. **A Note to a Fellow Leader**: Leslie Goldman, e-mail circulated.

Shfoch Hamatcha: **Shfoch Ahavtcha**: Naftali Ben Menahem, "*Shfoch Hamatcha v'Nuschaotav*," *Mahanaim* 80 (April, 1983) cites Rav Hayim Bloch who quotes *Haggadah of Worms*, 1521, attributed to grandson of Rashi, Yehuda ben Rav Yekutiel. See also Zecharia Goren, "*Shfoch Hamatcha*" in *Mehkarei Hag* 6 (1991), p. 97. **Won't Teach Children to Hate**: Yehiel Weingarten, Kibbutz Ein Harod, 1936. **For One Brief Moment**

the Jew Stood Tall: Deborah E. Lipstadt in Nahum N. Glatzer (editor), *Schocken Haggadah*, Schocken, 1996. Courtesy of author. **Stamp**: Danish Jewish Community Rescue, by A. Berg, 1973. Courtesy of the Israel Philatelic Service (HH). **Pardon the Egyptians**: Eliyahu Ben Amozeg, *Paths of Morality*, Italy, 1892. **Mikel the Goy**: Retold by Yehuda Yaari, in Meir Eyali, *Hagim uZmanin*, 1949, p. 255. **Antidote to Fascism**: Amos Oz, "Aggression is the Mother of All Wars - Goethe Prize Speech", *Kulturjournal* 3 (2005), Goethe-Institut. **Tales of the Red Matza**: Stuart Schoffman, "Tales of Red Matza," *The Jerusalem Report*, April 4, 1991. Courtesy of author and publisher (HH). **Exodus Elite Box**: courtesy of the USHMM Holocaust Museum collection (HH).

Hallel and Fourth Cup: **Fifth Cup**: R. Menachem M. Kasher, *Israel Passover Haggadah*, p. 335 adapted from R. Irving Greenberg, *The Jewish Way*, ibid. p. 56.

Nirtzah: **Next Year**: Ehud Manor. By permission of ACUM. **Songs of the Soul**: R. Abraham Isaac Kook, *Orot HaKodesh* 2:444-445, adapted from translation by Daniel Matt, *The Essential Kabbalah*, p.154 and Rachel Cowan, *Beginning Anew*, page 278. **A Mental State**: Saul Bellow, *To Jerusalem and Back*. **Playing for Real Stakes**: Phillip Roth, Courtesy of Words & Images (ibid). **Riding on an Israeli Bus**: Arnold Eisen, *Taking Hold of Torah* (ibid.), p. 39. **Healing**: R. Chaim Potok in Joshua Haberman, *The God I Believe In*, (ibid.), p 219. **Where Have All Our Hopes Gone**: R. Daniel Gordis, e-mail communication. Courtesy of author of *If a Place can Make you Cry*. **I Still Believe**: Anne Frank, *Diary of Anne Frank*, Amsterdam, 1944. **To Reach Next Year**: Zvi Zameret, "I Need Next Year," *Amudim* - Journal of the Religious Kibbutzim 663 (June 2002), courtesy of author (HH). **What Would You Tell Young People**: R. Abraham Joshua Heschel, TV interview "Meet the Press", cited in Dov Peretz Elkins, *Moments of Transcendence: Inspirational Readings for Yom Kippur*, Aronson, 1994. **I Have a Dream**: Martin Luther King, Jr., "I have a Dream" delivered on the steps at the Lincoln Memorial in Washington D.C. on August 28, 1963. **Stunned They Stride On**: David Grossman, "Introduction", *The Second Book of Moses called Exodus*, translation by Marsha Weinstein, pages vii-viii- ix, Grove Press, 1999. Courtesy of author.

Back Cover: Arthur Miller quote courtesy of Words & Images, the Jerusalem literary project (ibid.).

The Israeli stamps were provided courtesy of the collection of Opa Sallie Zion from Eibergen, the Netherlands.

Answers to *Ma Nishtana* in Multiple Languages (p. 27)
Hebrew Braille, Hindu, Thai, Punjabi, Greek, Spanish, Russian, Turkish, Dutch, Arabic, Chinese, Japanese, Egyptian hieroglyphics.

Answers to Pesach Math Riddles (p. 81)
A. $2 \times 40 \times (40 - 2) = 3040$
B. $(5-12) \times (10 \times 8) + (4 \times 4 \times 4) = 496$
C. $5 \times 5 + (3 \times 4) + 14 = 51$

Permissions and References

This anthology owes its richness to those who allowed us to quote their creative words. All references, permissions and copyright details are provided below. In a few cases we tried unsuccessfully to locate the authors. Our apologies, please contact us.
We thank all those who agreed to participate in this haggadah. May God grant all of you continued power to inspire humanity.

All new material copyright of Mishael Zion and Noam Zion. All original illustrations copyright of Michel Kichka.
Note that this haggadah is an expansion and translation of *Halaila Hazeh* (Israel, 2004) edited by Mishael Zion with Noam Zion, 2004, so original copyright permissions still pertain (referenced below as HH).

Bdikat Hametz: **Inspection and Introspection**: R. Moshe Alsheikh, *Peirush Alsheikh l'Haggadah*. **Prayer for Purification**: R. Yosef Hayim, *Haggadat Orakh Hayim*, p. 64.

Candle Lighting: **A Woman's Prayer**: Alice Shalvi, "Repentance, Responsibility, and Regeneration: Reflections on Isaiah," in G. Twersky Reimer and J.A. Kates: *Beginning Anew*, p. 275. Courtesy of author who revised the prayer (HH). **A Soul on the Rise**: Yaacov Isaac Halevi Horowitz, Seer of Lublin, *Pitgamim Kedoshim*, p. 113. **Blessing to Yourself**: R. Samson Raphael Hirsch, *The Nineteen Letters on Judaism*, p. 80. **Photo**: Karl Gabor, "Shabbat candles," *Denna Afton [A Different Night* Haggadah, Swedish edition]. Courtesy of photographer, of publisher Hillelforlaget, and editor Marina Burstein.

Signposts: **Four Mothers**: R. Isaiah Horowitz, *Shnei Luchot Habrit*, p. 156a; Judah Levy Loew (Maharal), *Gevurot Adonai*, p. 77d; cited in Yael Levine, *Kolech* 31 (Nissan 5761).

Karpas: **Sources for Extensive Appetizers**: *Shulkhan Arukh* O.H. 473; *Mishne Torah*, Hametz uMatza 8:2; *Bayit Hadash* on Tur O.H. 473; Rav Yaacov Weingarten in *HaSeder HaArukh*, cites rabbis eating at least an olive's size of Karpas (Beit Halevi, Hazon Ish); Daniel Goldschmidt's Haggadah brings Geniza fragments of the earliest haggadot that describe extensive dipping of various foods. **Seder for Dreamers**: Natan Sharansky, *Jerusalem Post*, April 16, 2003. Courtesy of author and Jerusalem Post (HH).

Yahatz: **What if Tomorrow**: Bina Talitman, *Reliving Exodus*, p. 38 (HH). **Being Poor**: Janet Rosenberg, *Being Poor is...*, 1973. Courtesy of author. **Ha(l)ves and Have Nots**: Adapted from mass e-mail circulated on the internet. See also: www.snopes.com/science/stats/populate.htm.

Maggid: **In Haste from Russia**: Yigal Asnis in Moti Friedman (editor), *Alei Tzameret Haggadah*, Jewish Agency, 1995. Courtesy of editor (HH). **Turtle's Memory**: Archie Carr, *So excellent a Fishe: A Natural History of Sea Turtles*, 1965. **Maggid**: Marge Piercy, *The Art of Blessing the Day*, Alfred Knopf, Random House, 1999, p.158. By permission of the publisher. **No Future without a Past**: David Hartman, "Memory and Values," in N. Zion, *A Different Night: Leader's Guide*, p. 75. Courtesy of author. **You cannot Navigate**: Chaim Potok in Joshua Haberman (editor), *The God I Believe In*, Free Press, p. 220.

Ha Lakhma: **Service with a Smile**: Avot D'Rabbi Natan, version A, XIII, 29a. **Needy but not Poor**: Rabbi Joseph B. Soloveitchik, *Festival of Freedom: Essays on Pesah and the Haggadah*, edited by Joel B. Wolowelsky and Reuven Ziegler, p. 45-46. Courtesy of Toras Harav Foundation ©2006. **Opening**

Doors: Levover Story quoted in Janet Marder, *New Emmanuel Minyan* (1994), adapted from L. Blue and J. Magonet, *The Blue Guide to the Here and the Hereafter*, p. 168. **Illustration**: Noam Nadav, *Yahid vHevrah* (2002), Shalom Hartman Institute. Courtesy of publisher (HH). **The Jewish Mayflower**: David Ben Gurion in Yom Tov Levinsky (editor), *Sefer HaMoadim: Pesach*, p. 256 (HH). **Synagogue**: Walter Seaton, courtesy of author. **Passover**: Primo Levi, *Collected Poems*, trans. by Ruth Feldman and Brian Swan, Faber and Faber, 1988. By permission of publisher. **Four Cups of Milk**: retold by M. Lipson, *Reliving the Exodus*, p. 34, from an Eastern European Folktale. **Martin Luther King, Jr.**: "Speech at Staff Retreat, Penn Center, Frogmore, South Carolina," unpublished ms., November 14, 1966, p.9. **Stamp**: A. Calderon, *An End to Famine*, 1963. Courtesy of the Israel Philatelic Service (HH).

Ma Nishtana: **Stupidity of Having an Answer**: Milan Kundera, from an interview by Philip Roth, *NY Times Book Review*, Nov. 30, 1980. Reprinted in *The Book of Laughter and Forgetting*, 1981, p. 237. **Questions are a Paradox**: Steve Greenberg, *Wrestling with God and Men: Homosexuality in the Jewish Tradition*, 2004, p. 135. Courtesy of author. **Uncle Eli's Haggadah**: Eliezer Segal, *Uncle Eli's Special-for-Kids Most Fun Ever Under-the-Table Passover Haggadah*, www.acs.ucalgary.ca/~elsegal/Uncle_Eli/Eli.html. Courtesy of author. **Torah Speaks the Language of People**: Murray Spiegel and Rickey Stein, from their manuscript of the four questions in 300 languages. Courtesy of authors. **Seder Night Reflections**: Yehuda Amichai, *Patuach Sagur Patuach*, Schocken Publishing, 1998, p. 15 #21. Translated by Steve Sager. By permission of publisher and translator.

Avadim: **The Fire of Concern**: A.J. Muste, American labor organizer for IWW, anti-nuclear Christian pacifist cited in Arthur Waskow (editor), *The Freedom Seder*, 1969. By permission of editor. **Illustration**: Leon Baxter, *The Young Moses*, MacDonald Co, London. **The Depth of Degradation**: Harriet Jacobs, *Life of a Slave Girl*, 1861. 1987 reprint p. 28, 77, 37, xv, 44, 52. **We were Politicians**: The Non Partisan Politician's Haggadah (*Haggadah Blti Mifalagtit*), 1947, Tel Aviv. **We were Zionist Pioneers**: Yitzchak Tabenkin, cited in *Mimayanot Hehag: Pesach*, Interkibbutz Archive of Holidays, 1985, p.23. **We were Hippies**: Arthur Waskow, *The Freedom Haggadah*, Micah Press, 1969, p. 19, 42-43, from National Jewish Organizing Project. By permission of author. See original *Freedom Seder* on-line, The Shalom Center at www.shalomctr.org/node/899. **The Red Haggadah**, 1927, cited by A.A. Gershuni, *Yahdut B'Soviet Russia*, 1961. **Bibliodrama**: Peter Pitzele, *Scripture Windows*, 1997. Appeared originally in Noam Zion, *A Different Night: Leader's*

Guide, p. 27. Courtesy of author. **The Hieroglyph Times** by Yair Lipshitz and Deborah Morse.

Five Rabbis: **Songs of Freedom**: Pini Nahmani story cited by Tamar Golan, *Maariv*, April 18, 1989 (HH). **The Last Ethiopian Seder**: Micha Odenheimer, 1991, by permission of author (HH). **The Hunger Strike Seder**: Golda Meir story cited in *Maariv*, April 10, 1960 (HH). **The Matzah of Hope**: Courtesy of R. Leah Kroll, Milken Community High School of Stephen S. Wise Temple, Los Angeles.

Four Children: **Too Quick to Categorize**: Robert Coles, *The Call of Service*. **Questions from the Future**: Aviva Zornberg Gottlieb, *The Particulars of Rapture*, Double Day Press, Random House, 2001, p. 180 ff. By permission of author and publisher. **The Four Children**: Danny Siegel, *The Meadow beyond the Meadow*, Town House Press, 1991. By permission of author. **The Wise Child's Real Question**: Aviva Zornberg Gottlieb (ibid.) **The Four Marx Brothers**: Richard Codor, 1981. By permission of artist (HH). **The Soviet Commissar**: Mark Podwal, *The Let My People Go Haggadah*. By permission of the artist, c/o Georges Borchardt, 1972 (HH). **Asking the Unaskable Questions**: Steven Greenberg, *Wrestling with God and Men* (ibid.), p.79. **Learning to be the Simple Child**: R. Kalonymus Kalman Shapira, *Eish Kodesh: Sacred Fire: Faith in the Warsaw Ghetto*, Seventh Day of Passover, April 18th, 1941. Courtesy of translator, Debbie Miller. **No Big Sophistication**: R. Nahman of Bratzlav, *Likutei Etzot*, "Tmimut" 4-5. **The Animated Four Sons**: Rony Oren, *Animated Haggadah*, courtesy of Pamela and Jonathan Lubell, Scopus Films/Lambda Publishers, 1985 (HH). **A Thunderous Silence**: Yariv Ben Aharon, *HaKibbutz*. Courtesy of author (HH). **Where Did You Go**: Joseph Lukinsky and Lifsa Schachter, "Are Questions Necessary?" in *Jewish Education News* (Winter 5756), p.15. Courtesy of authors. **In Praise of the Unquestioning Personality**: Zeev Jabotinsky, "Four Children" in Yom Tov Levinsky (editor), *Sefer HaMoadim: Pesach*, p. 252. **The Four Books**: David Wander, *The Haggadah in Memory of the Holocaust* 1988, courtesy of the artist (HH). **Four Generations**: Paul Cowan, *An Orphan in History*, courtesy of R. Rachel Cowan. **Four Daughters**: R. Einat Ramon, courtesy of author (HH). **Four Children in Each of Us**: Dan Reisinger, *The Freedom Haggadah*, 1982, Rabbinical Assembly of America. Courtesy of artist and publisher (HH). **Rav Yisrael Salant**: cited in Rav Menahem HaCohen, *Haggadat HaAm*, p. 56.

You Shall Tell Your Child: **Legacy of Luggage**: R. David Hartman, "Memory and Values," in N. Zion, *A Different Night: Leader's Guide*, p. 75. Courtesy of author. **My Father was**

Acknowledgements

The Passover Seder is an evening of family, of community and of friendship. Therefore it should come as no surprise that this Haggadah is the fruit of the support and hard work of many friends; that it was engendered within a unique community of learners; and that it is a testimonial to a loving, beautiful, family.

Among the many **friends** who took an instrumental role in creating this Haggadah we would like to especially thank: Jay Leberman, David and Sally Lowenfeld, Jacob Ner David and Elie Wurtman, Phil and Juliet Wachs, for their ongoing support, encouragement and assistance. In the production of this book we wish to acknowledge our friends and professional partners: Joe Buchwald Gelles, Michel Kichka, Ehud Zion Waldoks, Deborah Morse, Yair Lipshitz, and Stephen and Basmat Hazan Arnoff, who have put an amazing effort into turning this Haggadah into a reality. Above all we thank Dvora Lipshitz, an inspiration and a great friend, who has skillfully turned a jumble of texts into a work of art.

The conception of and the scholarship for this Haggadah were nurtured within a creative **community** of learning, the **Shalom Hartman Institute in Jerusalem**. Under the leadership of Rabbis David and Donniel Hartman, who toil constantly for the welfare and future of the Jewish people and for the Hartman Institute's scholars, staff and students. The Hartman Institute has been our spiritual-intellectual home for decades. Here we can teach, learn and experience the sweet taste of Talmud Torah, constantly challenged to make it applicable to contemporary needs.

For Mishael, Yeshivat Maale Gilboa has been a second home and a most meaningful community of learners, led by Rabbis David Bigman, Yehuda Gilad and Shmuel Reiner.

Finally, this Haggadah is the product not of two individuals, but of an amazing **family**, whose energy and initiative humble and inspire us on a daily basis. First of all our octogenarian, Rabbi Moshe "Opa" Sachs who, with his beloved wife, Frances "Oma" Rachel, initiated creative Seders fifty years ago. Marcelle Zion is a spouse and a mother of unsurpassed energies and wisdom. She is the true center of this family. Elana Zion Golumbic is a spouse and daughter-in-law with that most unique combination of vision, belief and empowerment. Yedidya, Eden, Heftziba and Jonathan, Tanya and Ehud are our ready partners and sounding board in every creative endeavor.

This Haggadah is being published just as we are entering new familial roles, becoming, for the first time, **father and grandfather**. May God, and the spirit of hundreds of years of Jewish existence, grant us the wisdom to truly fulfill the mitzvah of לְסַפֵּר בִּיצִיאַת מִצְרַיִם, telling our story to the next generation.

תַּם וְנִשְׁלָם, שֶׁבַח לָאֵל בּוֹרֵא עוֹלָם.

Mishael and Noam Zion
Jerusalem, Pesach, 5767